THE FRENCH REVOLUTION

THE
FRENCH
REVOLUTION

M. J. SYDENHAM

B. T. BATSFORD LTD LONDON

FIRST PUBLISHED 1965
REPRINTED 1969

MADE AND PRINTED IN GREAT BRITAIN BY
WILLIAM CLOWES AND SONS LTD, LONDON AND BECCLES
FOR THE PUBLISHERS
B. T. BATSFORD LTD
4 FITZHARDINGE STREET, PORTMAN SQUARE, LONDON W.I

Preface

The French Revolution is nothing if not controversial. Seen in the nineteenth century both as a mighty liberal movement and as an atrocious outburst of anarchy, it has been viewed by our more sophisticated age as an early essay in totalitarianism and as an episode in the rise of the bourgeoisie. Danton, once the greatest hero of republican democracy, is now condemned as corrupt; Robespierre, long abhorred as a monster, has been restored to popularity as the truest friend of the people, and then accused of attempting to moderate the Revolution in the interest of the middle-class. The plain fact is that the Revolution is so integral a part of the modern world that it has still not passed from politics into history, and whoever ventures to write about it does so at his peril. Moreover, so much scholarship has been and is being devoted to it that hardly a line can be written without encroaching upon ground covered by several specialised studies.

This book has nevertheless been written as an attempt to show that it is possible to write a general history of a complex subject in terms which will convey to the general reader something of the atmosphere and achievement of the time, but still be sufficiently in line with recent scholarship to be useful to the student. Based upon standard secondary authorities and documents available in print, it is of necessity a personal interpretation of the Revolution: while saying something of the social and economic factors to which so much attention has recently been given, I have deliberately chosen to reassert the importance of political developments, and in doing this I have concerned myself particularly with what seem to me to be the central features of the Revolution—the emergence of the new religion of nationalism and the attempt to reconcile constitutional authority with popular control of power. Above all, however, I have tried to follow a strictly chronological sequence and to remain aware of that dark curtain which at any point in time conceals the uncertain future.

Students should appreciate that a substantial part of the present work was completed before Professor Cobban's *The Social Interpretation of the French Revolution* appeared in print, and that the whole was written before either the second volume of Professor Palmer's *Age of the Democratic Revolution* or Professor Sobul's most recent work (*La Révolution française :* I *De la Bastille à la Gironde ;* II *De la Montagne à Brumaire*) was published.

My most grateful thanks are due to all those who have helped me in the completion of this book, particularly my long-suffering family and the many students whose enthusiasm has so often served to stimulate my interest as

5

their tutor. I am also considerably indebted to Mr John Naylor for his courtesy and encouragement. Finally, I should like to express my gratitude to my good friends Mrs N. and Miss B. Rose of Wimborne for their part in preparing the typescript, as well as to Miss C. Moth of Portchester for her patient typing of the bibliography.

May 1965   M.J.S.

Contents

(handwritten annotation: top 127)

The Illustrations

The Maps

Acknowledgment

The Author and Publishers wish to thank the following for permission to reproduce the illustrations which appear in this book:
Bulloz, for fig. 4
Documentation Française, for figs. 11, 16, 17, and 20
Giraudon, for fig. 3
The Mansell Collection, for figs. 1, 13, 15 and 21
The *Radio Times* Hulton Picture Library, for figs. 2, 5-10, 12, 14, 18 and 19

'*Your Nation is now in a most important Crisis, and the great Question, shall we hereafter have a constitution or shall Will continue to be Law, employs every Mind and agitates every Heart in France.*'

Gouverneur Morris, 23rd February 1789

(in a letter to the Comte de Moustier, French Minister to the United States)

I

The King's Good Pleasure

In the early morning of 3rd March 1766 King Louis XV of France rode at speed with a party of soldiers from the Palace of Versailles to Paris. He crossed the Seine by the Pont Neuf and unexpectedly appeared in the Palais de Justice, there to confront the hastily assembled magistrates of the Parlement de Paris, the supreme law-court of the greater part of his kingdom. No formal ceremony could be held at such short notice in the Grand' Chambre of the Parlement, from the corner dais of which the kings of France were accustomed to admonish and overrule the judges. Louis spoke in his riding attire from an ordinary armchair, but he spoke to the point. Reminding the magistrates that they were his officers, charged with rendering justice to his subjects, he asserted his absolute authority as King:

> It is in my person alone that sovereign power resides. . . . It is from me alone that my courts derive their authority; and the plenitude of this authority, which they exercise only in my name, remains always in me. . . . It is to me alone that the legislative power belongs, without any dependence and without any division. . . . The whole public order emanates from me, and the rights and interests of the nation . . . are necessarily joined with mine and rest only in my hands.

So forceful a public pronouncement of the sovereign authority of the crown by a reigning monarch was without precedent in France. Indeed, its assertion by a king as habitually idle and ineffectual as Louis XV suggests that the substance of power was slipping from his grasp, for an acknowledged authority needs no formal definition. The effective force of the monarchy was in fact in decline; the king's action on this occasion, the so-called *séance de la flagellation*, had no immediate sequel. He had nevertheless accurately stated the concept of political authority with which the monarchy was identified. As Louis XIV had put it in a memoir written for the private reading of his son, 'Kings are absolute lords, having full authority over all people, secular and ecclesiastical'. Royal powers were exercised either by the king in person or by the nominated officials to whom they were delegated, and in theory every function of government was an operation of the *bon plaisir* of the king, who was at once the embodiment of the executive, the supreme giver of law, and the ultimate arbiter of justice. To say, as the

13

aristocracy later alleged, that France had a constitution before the Revolution, was to say no more than that the country had some established institutions and was ruled, under God, by a consecrated king of the legitimate descent, and not by the inconstant will of some upstart tyrant.

The effective power of the state which the king thus personified was, moreover, considerable. Despite all the complexities caused by the survival of a multiplicity of medieval institutions and jurisdictions, the great bureaucratic machine built up over the centuries by the Capetian kings had imposed an increasing measure of administrative unity upon France. The great Louis XIV, by incessant effort, had personally supervised the work of his royal councils, and he had particularly directed the small *Conseil d'état*, to which all matters of importance were referred for final decision. This central body, wielding supreme power in the king's name, had in turn directed the activities of its principal provincial agents, the intendants, of whom John Law had remarked with astonishment that thirty of them governed the whole kingdom and held the happiness and prosperity of provinces in their hands.

By the end of Louis XIV's reign this bureaucracy was becoming less dependent on the monarch. Under Louis XV the powers of the Council were increasingly arrogated by the heads of the departments of state, particularly by the Keeper of the Seals and by the Controller-General, who was responsible for finance and for most matters of internal administration. From the death of Fleury in 1743 until the appointment of Brienne in 1787 there was no effective co-ordination of the actions of these officials, either by the king or by any principal minister. The central direction of government thus became enfeebled; but the essential structure of the authoritarian bureaucracy remained intact. Each of the great officers of state stood at the head of a powerful and well-organised department, and the intendants extended their regulation of provincial life in accordance with instructions from the capital. In de Tocqueville's words, government 'already had influence in a thousand ways not only over the general conduct of affairs, but over the destiny of families and over the private life of every man'.

This remarkable concentration of authority had been developed in response to the real needs of king and people alike, for France was born in insecurity. The medieval monarchy had only very gradually extended its control over the independent fiefs of its nominal vassals. Not until 1532 was Brittany, the last of the duchies, incorporated into the kingdom. Hardly had the state begun to recover from the long agony of the Hundred Years War than it was again torn asunder by the Wars of Religion, when the great noble houses enlisted foreign intervention and contended for the crown amidst all the savagery of religious strife. To a countryside rent by apparently perpetual civil war, and constantly menaced by the encircling power of the Hapsburgs,

Divine Right monarchy had come as a progressive force, signifying order and unity, prosperity and peace. Small wonder that Bodin exalted the king as the image of God on earth, or that Bossuet wrote of Louis XIV as 'the embodiment of the public weal and the safety of the state', whom the good subject should love 'as the air he breathes, as the light of his eyes, as his life and more than his life'. Even in the eighteenth century, criticism of the crown was directed almost as much against its loss of competence as against its absolutism. By that time, the first great work of the monarchy had been accomplished: kings and cardinals had fashioned the medieval conglomeration into a dynastic state, a single territorial area with a single sovereign authority, and innumerable anonymous officials had carried uniformity of administration far enough to facilitate the identification of cultural nationality with political unity. Despite military defeats and some superficial decadence, France before the Revolution, with a population of twenty-five millions, a revenue twenty-five times that of the United States, an expanding economy and an overseas trade comparable to that of Great Britain, was clearly the greatest state in Europe as well as the centre of European civilisation.[1] She stood also upon the threshold of national consciousness.

The royal bureaucracy had, however, necessarily been created within the framework of medieval society. Some of the older institutions, particularly the Council, had developed as essential parts of the autocracy, and others, like the Estates-General, had been left behind as obsolete; but privilege, particularism and provincialism remained, preserving ancient practices, which had become abuses, and preventing the emergence of real national unity. Even Louis XIV had had to rely upon co-operation and consent in the consolidation of his power, which was in reality based upon a series of unspoken bargains, upon what has been called 'a gigantic system of bribery'. He had broken the last remnants of the military power of the nobility of the sword and attracted many of the first gentlemen of France to Versailles; but the magnates who allowed themselves to be superseded by the intendants in the administration of their estates did not do so without reward. The court was the source of both honours and emoluments, and although countless costly sinecures were created to satisfy the aspirations of the courtiers, government office and policy in the late eighteenth century became shockingly subject to the influences of intrigue and faction.

Moreover, the nobility could not be deprived of their prescriptive exemption from payment of the *taille*, the basic direct tax of the *ancien régime*, which remained the hallmark of social status. Even the two taxes which Louis XIV levied on all his subjects in an attempt to meet the costs of his wars, the *capitation* and the *dixième*, were soon so evaded that they lost almost

---

[1] The population of Great Britain is generally taken as being nine millions in 1785.

15

all significance so far as the wealthier members of the privileged classes were concerned. The Church similarly remained an exceedingly powerful body, enormously rich in endowments and influential in all administration. Although it acknowledged the king's authority in secular matters, and supported him in opposing interference from Rome and in suppressing freedom of thought, the Church sought always to govern itself, jealously guarding its own control of the contribution of the clergy to direct taxation. The 'voluntary' grants periodically made to the state by the Assembly of the Clergy have been estimated as being less than 1 per cent of the ecclesiastical revenues, and as even these were in reality largely borrowed from financiers, the Church's true contribution to the treasury amounted to little more than the interest on the loans. Nor were the privileges of total or partial tax-exemption by any means confined to, or even coincident with, the orders of the nobility and the clergy. On the one hand the poorer nobles could not avoid paying taxes other than the *taille*, and these the government tried always to increase. On the other hand, however, some whole provinces, notably Brittany and Languedoc, still retained sufficient strength to bargain with the crown about taxation, and as the eighteenth century progressed a great many towns succeeded in shaking off the financial supervision of the intendant, establishing immunities and reducing their return considerably. Moreover, all who, by residence and the possession of property in a town, were entitled to call themselves bourgeois, secured exemption from the *taille* and, in practice, from such later taxes as the *vingtième* as well.

With so great a proportion of the wealth of the country untapped, the monarchy was driven to press the more heavily upon the unprivileged in direct taxation, and to exploit indirect taxation to the uttermost. It thus became a characteristic of the old order that those least able to pay were the most burdened by taxes.

This evil, moreover, was aggravated a hundred-fold by the principal expedient developed to off-set it, that of the sale of offices. Initially this device had presented apparently endless possibilities: offices, once sold, could be reclaimed by the crown and sold again at a higher price, and their value could be increased by granting their holders exemptions from taxation or patents of nobility, or even hereditary exemptions and ennoblements. By the early eighteenth century the worst abuses of this system of exploitation were ended, for purchasers were no longer prepared to pay high prices without adequate security of tenure; but there remained a great multiplicity of offices in the royal administration and judiciary which carried the privilege of tax-exemption. Innumerable municipal offices of the same sort, at first exposed to royal confiscation unless redeemed by 'free gifts' to the government, were similarly acquired as the towns grew in independence. Widespread venality thus allowed what may broadly be called an administrative

16

middle-class to acquire social status and to practise tax-evasion upon a very considerable scale. Still more important, however, was the fact that the majority of offices could be held, bought and sold, and transmitted to an heir, as pieces of personal property. This led directly to the growth of a new aristocracy of office-holders which permeated the administration and was capable of paralysing government whenever it felt its interests to be in jeopardy.

At the head of this aristocracy of office-holders, which had increasingly intermarried and intermingled both with the old nobility and with those few whose riches had enabled them to purchase high titles, stood the wealthiest and most influential of the *noblesse de la robe*, the *parlementaires*. These magistrates were members of the parlements, the courts of appeal which had been established by the medieval monarchy in newly-acquired provinces in order to reconcile all inferior jurisdictions with the royal will. There were, at the end of the eighteenth century, thirteen of these so-called sovereign courts, the greatest being the oldest, the Parlement of Paris, which had jurisdiction over one-third of the land. All had administrative functions, deriving from their need to enforce their decisions, and all claimed—and, save in the reign of Louis XIV, maintained—what was in effect a legislative and political function as well. Since they had to enforce royal decrees, they asserted that these were invalid until they had been accepted and registered by the parlements, and that this by ancient custom involved a right of protest or remonstrance if the edict appeared inconsistent with earlier legislation or with the principles of law itself. Kings could, and often did, compel the Parlement of Paris to submit by means of a *lit de justice*: by attending the court in person, the monarch superseded its lesser judicial authority by the ultimate justice of the crown. Moreover, individual magistrates, or even the whole assembly, could if necessary be banished from the capital. Such measures as these, however, were very difficult to maintain when the magistrates had become hereditary owners of their offices and were nobles of the second or even the third generation. Irremovable themselves, they were able in the eighteenth century to resist royal pressure by refusing to administer justice, and by encouraging similar resistance by other parlements throughout the country. Further aid could be enlisted from Brittany and Languedoc, where ancient representative assemblies, or 'Estates', had not only survived, but grown in independence. Both areas had much to teach the rest of France about administration, but their assemblies were controlled by the aristocracy and were really allies of the parlements, whose aid they could themselves invoke against the local intendants.

The power of the aristocracy, judicial and clerical, was made manifest during the long reign of Louis XV. Although well-intentioned, he delayed any serious attempt to govern his kingdom until his power was almost lost

17

beyond recall. In a prolonged conflict, the parlements nominally supported the cause of Gallicanism against that of the Papacy, the Jesuits and the *dévot* group at court, but in reality they discredited religion and undermined the authority of the Church and king alike. In alliance with the clergy and with their colleagues in the provinces, the magistrates of Paris blocked every effort ministers made to reform the financial system, most notably defeating Machault's attempt in 1749–51 to introduce a general tax of one-twentieth on all personal incomes, and Bertin's attempt in 1763 to impose a tax upon all property-in-office. The *vingtième* remained only as a tax levied with increasing frequency upon the poorer nobles and commons, who could not contrive to buy exemption from it. In the provinces, too, reforms and public works were obstructed, even the intendants being haled before the courts if they became too persistent. Only in these circumstances did Louis in the closing years of his reign support his ministers in positive action: in 1771 the Keeper of the Seals, Maupeou, not only exiled the magistrates of Paris to the barren Auvergne, but also abolished their offices without compensation and began to create a completely new judicial system for the country as a whole. In 1774, while this was being done, and while Terray, the Controller-General, was beginning to effect real financial reforms, Louis died.

His legacy to his successor was a discredited crown and a fleeting moment of real opportunity, which the new sovereign swiftly cast away. The stolid young man who, at the age of twenty, became king as Louis XVI was sincerely benevolent: he was also inexperienced, easily influenced, and soon wearied by the tedious business of government. In a determined effort to ensure that his court should not be tarnished by the scandals that had disgraced his grandfather's name, he despatched Madame du Barry, the last of the royal mistresses, to a convent, and abolished the customary Accession Tax. In the same spirit he dismissed Maupeou and Terray, whose ruthlessness and realism had earned them bitter hatred, and accepted instead as minister an elderly courtier, Maurepas, who recommended Turgot as Controller-General. To Voltaire, who thought that 'no better fortune could befall France or the mind of man', it seemed as if a new age had dawned, for Turgot had already effected remarkable reforms as intendant at Limoges. He was also well-known as one of the Physiocrats, the school of thinkers who believed that as land was the source of wealth, all landowners should pay taxation and all artificial restrictions on trade should be abolished.

Louis, however, had already made the first of many errors of judgment. Never able to assess the realities of a situation, he had recalled the parlements as another mark of the new reign, and the magistrates soon recovered sufficient confidence to bring Turgot down. The reformer's introduction of internal free-trade in corn offended powerful interests, and when in 1776 he attempted to liberalise the economy further and to replace compulsory peasant labour on the roads by a general land-tax, the parlements rose up in defence of the existing order. On Maurepas's advice, Turgot was dismissed. The bishops ordered prayers of thanksgiving; but Voltaire wrote: 'It is a disaster. I see nothing before me now but death. I am struck to the heart by this blow, and shall never be consoled for having seen the beginning and the end of the golden age which Turgot was preparing for us.'

The despondency of the old *philosophe*, who was indeed to die within two years, may be taken as a measure of the harm that the judicial aristocracy had done by perpetually opposing royal government. They had, admittedly, no control over government expenditure, nor any guarantee that a temporary tax, once accepted, would not be made permanent; but it is evident that they sought not merely to maintain their privileges but also to increase their power. During the conflicts which preceded their dismissal by Louis XV, they had co-ordinated their activities and asserted the wholly unhistorical claim that the separate courts of the provinces and of Paris were in reality the component parts of a single body, which the Parlement of Rouen described as 'the one and only public, legal and necessary council of the sovereign, . . . the plenary, universal, capital, metropolitan and sovereign court of France'. Yet it was reform, and not tyranny, which they opposed, exploiting their position as an independent judiciary to impose a legislative veto upon the crown in the interests of entrenched privilege. Extravagant as Versailles was, and inadequate as were Louis XV and Louis XVI as rulers, reform was in the air in the second half of the eighteenth century, and many measures for the improvement of institutions and the relief of individuals were envisaged by the king's ministers only to be abandoned at the insistence of his magistrates. Of Turgot's proposal to abolish the *corvée*,[1] a member of the Paris parlement wrote: 'All public financial burdens should be borne by the lower orders. These are subject by virtue of their birth to the imposition of the *taille* and, without any limitations whatever, to the *corvée*. The nobles, on the contrary, are exempted by birth from the imposition of all taxation.' Implacably opposed to all freedom of thought, the parlements sanctioned the use of torture and ordered inhuman executions even after the Church itself had become averse to persecution. The *philosophes*, whom they tried in vain to silence, were their inveterate enemies, and Voltaire rejoiced—prematurely—when they were dismissed in 1771: 'Have they not often been persecuting and barbarous? . . . For myself, I think that the King is right, and since it is necessary to serve, I would rather do so under a lion of good pedigree . . . than under two hundred rats of my own kind.' The interest of a developing society in elementary reform, no less than the interest of the monarchy,

[1] I.e. the obligation of the peasant to perform labour services for the state, particularly in the making and maintenance of roads.

19

required that these 'constituent bodies' of the aristocracy should be deprived of their immunities, the prop of so much particularism.

The aristocracy's challenge to royal absolutism had nevertheless led to the formulation of an alternative theory of authority, in which arbitrary government was repudiated and the supremacy of law asserted. At the close of the reign of Louis XIV some aristocratic writers, notably Fénelon, had attacked autocracy, and a small but not insignificant group had then high hopes that the succession to the throne of the liberally-minded Duke of Bourgogne, grandson of Louis XIV and father of Louis XV, would be marked by the 'restoration' of an aristocratic constitution. The death of the Duke caused deep disappointment, and the system of Louis XIV survived to dominate the eighteenth century. By then, however, John Locke's *Treatises on Government* had laid the foundations of liberalism for France as well as for the English-speaking world. He had clearly proclaimed the ultimate sovereignty of the people; the natural rights of men to life, liberty and the possession of property; and the limitation of the authority of government to the preservation of these rights as the trustee of society at large.

Locke's influence, and an abiding hatred of arbitrary government, inspired the writings of Montesquieu, himself perhaps the most influential French writer of the century. In his greatest work, *De l'esprit des lois*, which was published at Geneva in 1748, he did not even pay Divine Right monarchy the compliment of consideration, but sought to show by a historical study of institutions that authority in every community must accord with the long-established laws and customs which together amounted to a fundamental law. Of this, the virtue of the citizens was for Montesquieu the ultimate guardian. Influenced by Locke, and still more by the practical example of England, he taught the desirability of government by consent and of the distribution of power amongst 'intermediate bodies', balanced between themselves and capable of resisting encroachment either from above or from below.

These ideas agreed well with the ancient claim of the parlements to be the interpreters of a fundamental law, and before Louis XV died he had been repeatedly told that he owed his throne to this law, of which the parlements were the guardians, and that he was bound to govern in accordance with it. In a remonstrance in 1764, for example, the Parlement of Paris asserted that the purpose of civil government was to ensure that citizens should enjoy the rights guaranteed by the laws, and that consequently 'it is the law which commands, or, precisely, the sovereign commands by the law'. Moreover, the attempt which was made to prove that the parlements were in reality only separate branches of a single body was significantly accompanied by the claim that this 'Parlement of France' was representative of the 'Nation', and that the law existed only by consent of the 'Nation'. The parlements, in fact, did much to popularise terms like 'the rights of the nation' and 'the general will', and to suggest the idea that society was something distinct from, and greater than, the State. But although it was they who first provided France with a political opposition to the monarchy, they also provided the nation with a prolonged object-lesson in intransigence and in the technique of stimulating mob-violence. If they did something to make Montesquieu's teaching popular and to advance the idea that the power of the government should be subject to the sanction of an established law, they provided no solution to the essential problem of the period, that of substituting constitutional for arbitrary power while yet increasing the social and geographical cohesion of the nation. Their arrogant attitude over half a century is sufficient indication that they could never have done more than filch sovereignty from the crown and share it amongst their own exclusive aristocracy. Their 'Nation' was no more than an oligarchy of notabilities.

In reality, as the Revolution was to show, the aristocracy were wholly dependent upon the support of their social inferiors, the Third Estate. The first two Orders, the clergy and the nobility both of the sword and the robe, together numbered little more than half a million, or but one in fifty of the population, and only some few thousand of these, who were known as *les Grands*, were really wealthy. If the lords of the Church were obviously rich, the parish priests were clearly poor. The needy nobles of the provincial countryside were frequently as impoverished as the peasantry. Although some men and women of title had inherited—or married—immense wealth, and some great titles had been acquired by purchase, most influential nobles at court owed their magnificence to success in the scramble for sinecures, or to good fortune at the gaming tables. With their estates sold or mortgaged to commoners, they lived largely on borrowed money, and even sardonically measured one another's merit by the amount of their debts. In social status alone was the aristocracy distinct, and this, as the century progressed, it strove ever more assiduously to preserve.

By contrast, the upper middle-class was much more numerous and wealthy, although it, too, formed but a small minority of perhaps half a million, in an agricultural country with a predominantly peasant population. The true bourgeois was one who, although not of noble rank, literally 'lived like a lord' on a considerable income wholly derived from landed property; but the greater merchants, particularly those engaged in France's expanding overseas trade, were wealthier, as were the merchant-manufacturers of the cloth trade, and wealthier still were the bankers, contractors and tax-farmers who financed the régime and flourished amid its anomalies. Wealth alone, however, does not altogether explain the structure of a social order which, in the towns as in the country, was founded less upon class than upon status. A great many of the lesser bourgeoisie, numbering about a million, were small tradesmen or master-craftsmen, living in respectable frugality alongside their journeymen-labourers. Many, too, were minor officials performing some function in the complicated system of judicial administration.

Bourgeois society, at once distinct from, but in close touch with, the life of the labourers in town and country—for all aspired to the possession of some small plot of land—thus ascended through immeasurable gradations of prosperity, in which almost every family and every office had its own particular position. The story of the Danton family illustrates the fact that society was then more fluid than is sometimes supposed: the grandfather, a peasant of Champagne, gave his son some education, and saw him established 'in town', in the little town of Arcis-sur-Aube, of which he eventually became *procureur*, or attorney for the district; in the third generation, Georges-Jacques Danton, son of the *procureur*, left Arcis for Paris, became a barrister entitled to plead before the central administrative courts, and as his practice grew, began to describe himself as *M. d'Anton*. In this lies an indication of one cause of bourgeois support for the aristocracy: prospering members of the middle-class, far from despising rank and privilege, aspired to possess them. Although real wealth was gradually becoming more important than rank, the older attitude remained strong, and, even in the Revolution, many rising men adopted imaginary territorial titles, becoming Brissot *de Warville*, Roland *de la Platière*, Pétion *de Villeneuve*, and so on.

Modern historians have nevertheless found it remarkable that the middle-class should have so long supported the aristocracy of France against the monarchy which was striving to initiate reforms and to break down some of the barriers of privilege, particularly as the eighteenth century is commonly called the Age of Reason, or that of Enlightenment. Educated opinion was fully aware of the need for reforms, particularly so far as the liberation of internal trade from a mass of antiquated regulations and tariffs was concerned, and a great many Frenchmen, denied any opportunity of political life, became interested in intellectual speculation and in the practical application of scientific discoveries to everyday life. People of ability and letters formed innumerable local literary and philosophical societies, and many a minor landowner developed plans for the improvement of agriculture or for the cutting of roads and canals—all too often to be frustrated by the apathy of officials or the antagonism of established interests. In Paris, the intellectual capital of Europe, cultured men and women, noble and commoner alike, met on terms of familiarity in the salons of such great ladies as Madame de Tencin, Madame Geoffrin and Madame du Deffand, and found there a 'republic of letters' many times more attractive than either the court or the moribund universities. Here they encountered, and helped to disseminate, the ideas of the *philosophes*, men above all eager to unloose 'the triple-forg'd fetters of times' and to call indiscriminately into question all hoary prejudice and every hallowed faith.

The thought of an era famed by the names of men like Montesquieu, Voltaire, Rousseau and Condorcet, is not to be neatly summarised in a sentence. Indeed, ill-advised attempts to confine it to some limited interpretation explain much of the controversy that still rages over its contemporary political significance. Its main stream, however, was marked by a tremendous faith in the potential power of human reason, which only required release from subservience to outworn shibboleths and antiquated institutions. In the late seventeenth century Fontenelle's *Discourse on the Plurality of Worlds* had for the first time popularised the teaching of Copernicus and Galileo, and revealed something of the immensity of the universe and the apparent insignificance of man—now reduced in Voltaire's phrase, to an insect creeping on a mud-heap. The effect of this revelation was, however, soon much mitigated, for Newton's discoveries seemed conclusive proof not only that all nature was subject to immutable laws, but that, as Descartes had asserted, these laws were rational and within the reach of human understanding. To some, as to Addison in England, all this enhanced appreciation of the majesty and power of the Almighty; but many saw only the vindication of scientific thought and of conclusions founded solely upon the testing of hypotheses by experiment and observation. Such men saw a magnificent vista of intellectual and material progress; they supposed that the conduct of men must be governed, as were the heavens, by fixed rules, and they believed that the discovery of these would enable enlightened governments to end most human ills. The supra-natural, if not altogether denied, became remote from reality, and all metaphysical authority was anathema.

Within three years of the appearance of Newton's *Principia*, John Locke, described by Voltaire as the 'greatest influence since Plato', struck another mighty blow at traditional beliefs. In his *Essay concerning Human Understanding* he contended that men are born possessed of active minds but without innate ideas, and so are formed solely by the reaction of their senses to impressions from the external world. This psychology implied a denial of the doctrine of Original Sin, and seemed to render superfluous most of the sanctions imposed upon humanity by the traditional authority of the Church and the state. It contributed also to that faith in the goodness of man which lies at the heart of so much of the thought of the eighteenth century, and which helped to suggest that, as prejudice and irrational institutions had corrupted man, so rational and useful institutions, intended to promote public happiness, might eventually perfect human nature itself.

This philosophy was the theme of what was probably the most influential in its period of all French books, the *Encyclopédie*. The work of many hands, including those of Turgot and Montesquieu, d'Alembert and Holbach, and both Voltaire and Rousseau, the book was banned by royal decree after the first volume appeared. Publication nevertheless continued until the seventh volume had been reached in 1758, and the Church was roused to condemnation and prohibition by an article about Geneva, which was really concerned with religious toleration. The remaining ten volumes were then completed in secret by Diderot, the man whose passionate determination had inspired the whole work. Immensely popular in France in the 1770's, the *Encyclopédie* typifies the supreme confidence of the *philosophes* that a future full of promise awaited mankind as enlightenment widened, and their rejection of irrational privileges and abuses, of cruelties and injustice, of the obsolete and the obscurantist. To philosophise was indeed, as Madame de Lambert had said in 1715, 'to shake off the yoke of authority'.

The extent to which opinion in France was influenced towards revolution by the writings of the *philosophes* has been disputed ever since 1789. The view that revolutions are made in the minds of men, the assertion that Frenchmen became intoxicated by what Burke called 'the heady wine of the *philosophes*', is recurrent in the writings of conservative historians, and it is recurrently challenged by writers of liberal or socialist outlook, who see the Revolution either as a spontaneous upsurge of the human spirit against oppression, or as the product of conflicting economic interests and of the fluctuation of price levels. Yet even those who minimise the importance of ideas are more concerned to question the existence of a connection between the teachings of the *philosophes* and the ideology of the Revolution, than to deny the destructive impact of their disdain of things extant and their optimism about things to come. Liberal-minded and humanitarian as most of them were, they undoubtedly did much to undermine the confidence of those who might have upheld the old order against excessive change, and to set a fashion of faith in man and in the efficiency of enlightened government.

The monarchy, on the other hand, proceeded as far as possible without publicity, making no attempt to win support or even to encourage confidence. Not until 1781, when the insolvency of the state was fast passing beyond control, was any sort of financial statement made to the public, and this, the *Compte-rendu* which Necker issued, was wholly fictitious, being intended only to restore the credit of the treasury. The court nevertheless preserved most of the ostentation deliberately developed by Louis XIV to impress the nobility with his power. Thus royal extravagance and the deficiencies of government were everywhere apparent, uncorrected by any appearance of their benefits. The parlements, for their part, not only published their remonstrances for sale to a politically-starved public, but also harried the crown into enunciating the principles of absolutism in its own defence, and so succeeded in identifying the monarchy with despotism and tyranny, while the aristocracy appeared as the champions of reform. Educated men in the middle-class, brought up on classical history and exposed to the scepticism of the *philosophes*, accepted this propaganda all too easily.

As Voltaire realised when he expressed his astonishment that 'the ignorant' should support such 'insolent and intractable' men as the magistrates of Paris, the Third Estate had become the victim of an illusion. Not only was the aristocracy, particularly that of the law, blocking every royal attempt to reform taxation and the administration, it was also becoming increasingly exclusive. This was not simply a matter of social status, although the established nobility were resentful of the intrusion into the royal service of jumped-up bourgeois creatures who had acquired offices and titles. Rather was it a question of employment. All the children of true noblemen, as distinct from some who were peers for life alone, inherited noble rank and title; but primogeniture was normal in the inheritance of estates. Competition for offices which were both remunerative and worthy of the dignity of a nobleman was consequently acute, for attempts by the monarchy from the time of Colbert onwards to establish a nobility founded upon commercial enterprise had been unsuccessful, and participation in business life was held equivalent to derogation of status. Thus as the middle-class pressed forward in ever-increasing numbers upon a limited number of appointments, it inevitably encountered aristocratic opposition and created a problem which an impoverished crown could not relieve.

Under Louis XV and Louis XVI, moreover, the nobility had secured a veritable stranglehold upon the royal government which should itself have curbed aristocratic influence. By the 1780's all the intendants, all the bishops, and all the royal ministers save Necker,[1] the Swiss banker who was the hero of the Third Estate, were nobles, and many, indeed, were of the second or third generation of nobility. In consequence, the aristocracy was able to control appointments to office very largely as it pleased. In 1762, for example, the Parlement of Grenoble ruled that only the descendants of its magistrates, or men in the fourth generation of nobility, might henceforth be admitted to its bench, and it made only a minor concession to the protests this rule evoked from the barristers whose advancement it prohibited. The fate of the royal attempt to create a functional nobility in the army is even more revealing. An edict of 1750 entitled non-noble officers to the tax-exemption of a noble after thirty years of service. In 1781, however, when the specified period had expired, a new ordinance required that all candidates for military commissions, other than men rising from the ranks, should show formal proof of at least four quarterings of nobility. So high, indeed, had the pretensions of the aristocracy soared by 1789 that their electoral assemblies then commonly demanded even the abolition of venality in office, as well as

[1] Necker (Jacques), b. 1732, a banker at Geneva, director of finances in France 1776–81, 1788–12th July 1789, and 15th July 1789–3rd September 1790. Retired to Coppet, d. 1804. Father of Madame de Staël.

recognition by the king of the age-old claim of the nobility that only men of high birth were entitled to advise him or exercise authority in his name.

The lives of the men who made the Revolution afford ample evidence that this situation was one of its fundamental causes. Some had been unfortunate, and a few were social misfits, but a great many were men who had found by experience that the old order interposed insuperable barriers between merit and reward, between aspiration and achievement. Sieyès,[1] as a canon at Chartres, had no hope of attaining a bishopric, nor had Carnot any prospect of ever being more than a captain of engineers. Even Napoleon had to prove his ancestry as well as his poverty before he could be admitted to the military school at Brienne. As the young Barnave wrote, 'the roads are blocked at every turn'.

The aristocracy not only provoked the Revolution in this way, it also began it. As Robespierre later wrote, 'the judiciary, the nobles, the clergy, the rich, gave the original impulse to the revolution'. The opportunity for them to try to complete their control of political power was provided by the American War of Independence, which completed the ruin of the royal finances—as well as helping to make democratic ideas fashionable among the liberals, and affording all France the strange but stimulating spectacle of its royal forces fighting to maintain a successful republican revolution. Necker, Controller-General in fact if not in name from 1776 to 1781, financed the war chiefly by loans, paying the interest from further loans. He then published his misleading *Compte-rendu*, and contrived to resign in calculated dudgeon before credit collapsed. His first effective successor, the able and confident Calonne,[2] took office in 1783, and was able for a time to stimulate credit by ostentatious extravagance; but in 1786 he realised that expedients would no longer serve, and informed Louis XVI that real financial reforms had become imperative. His subsequent efforts to effect these were sincere and soundly conceived, but his work was compromised by political ineptitude as well as by understandable public incredulity about the gravity of the situation.

[1] Sieyès (Emmanuel Joseph), b. 1748, Canon of Chartres and author of numerous pamphlets, particularly *Qu' est-ce que le tiers-état?*. Deputy for Third Estate of Paris, 1789, and for Sarthe to the Convention, 1792. The principal author of the Constitution of 1795, he became a Director and helped Napoleon to power in 1799, but after being a Consul he was relegated to comparative obscurity as a Count of the Empire and President of the Senate. Exiled in 1816, he returned to Paris in 1830 and died in 1836. Called 'the mole of the Revolution', he is perhaps best known for his reply to a question about his activities in 1791–94: '*J'ai vécu*'—'I survived.'

[2] Calonne (Charles Alexandre de), b. 1734. Became Controller-General after long experience as Intendant of Lille, and signed the Eden free-trade treaty with Britain in 1786. Disgraced and driven into exile in 1787, he later became the chief adviser to the French émigrés at Coblentz. Returned to Paris during Consulate, died there 1802.

Calonne intentionally revealed the fact that expenditure in France had long been greatly in excess of revenue, and that this evil was increasing each year. It is now estimated that in 1786 alone the deficit amounted to about 110 million livres, while the accumulated debt had reached incalculable figures. Since more than half the annual revenue went at once in interest payments, the costs of the court being only 6 per cent of expenditure, Calonne was correct in thinking that the situation was not to be saved by economy. Moreover, it is now clear that existing taxation could not have been increased, for the long eighteenth-century expansion of the economy was fast giving way to the catastrophic recession which coincided with the Revolution. The burden of direct taxation was already crippling those who paid it, and as price levels had long been rising faster than wages, further indirect taxation would only have brought falling returns as purchasing power declined. Calonne creditably rejected both inflation and a repudiation of debts in favour of fundamental reform, and renewed the attempt to tax the whole population systematically. He proposed to introduce a new tax on land, to be paid by great and small landowners alike. The assessment and allocation of this was to be determined by new provincial Estates, composed of, and elected by, landowners without distinction of social order.

The real problem, however, was not what to do, but how to do it. An able, determined and confident king could perhaps have carried the measure by a combination of appeal and authority, but Louis XVI left all to Calonne, who was compelled to seek support and self-sacrifice from the aristocracy. An ancient body known as the Assembly of Notables, which had last met in 1626, was therefore revived early in 1787, in the hope that the prelates, magnates, magistrates and officials of whom it was composed could command respect and would be willing to lend their prestige to the new proposals. The Notables, however, were mercilessly ridiculed by the cartoonists and pamphleteers of Paris, and they rejected all the fundamentals of Calonne's plan. Matters were indeed advanced by their admission of the reality of the financial crisis, and even of their own liability to taxation, but they refused to accept any responsibility for authorising new taxes. They insisted, moreover, that in any assemblies, old or new, 'the first two orders should be preserved in the ancient forms which distinguish them'. This meant that the clergy and the nobility should sit separately and apart from the commons, whom they would always be able to outvote since the decision of each order was taken as a single vote. There could be no better illustration than this of the weakness of the monarchy and the blindness of the aristocracy: unable to command, the king could only appeal to people who were not ready to make any real sacrifice of status. Calonne himself was dismissed from office and hounded into exile in England, the first of many fugitives from France.

From April 1787 until August 1788 Loménie de Brienne,[1] the Archbishop of Toulouse and Calonne's principal opponent amongst the Notables, wrestled in vain as his successor with the increasingly recalcitrant aristocracy. His attempt to persuade the Notables to accept a modification of Calonne's proposals evoked only an explicit repudiation of their competence to approve taxation, a pointed allusion to the authority of an Estates-General. Their Assembly was then dissolved, and Brienne was left with the task of compelling the Parlement of Paris to register interim taxation, to sanction further loans, and to accept the new provincial assemblies in a form much more favourable to the aristocracy. Since the Parlement would only agree to the last of these proposals, the remainder of 1787 and the beginning of 1788 was marked by a succession of violent clashes between the king and the magistrates. In these, the monarchy was once again forced to resort to arbitrary methods, and the Parlement again upheld, in the interests of the aristocracy, the sanctity of the law and the rights of the individual. On one famous occasion, when the king announced that a *lit de justice* would be held next day, Orléans called out that this was illegal, and Louis cried in reply: 'That makes no difference! It is legal because I wish it!' On another, he declared that if the parlements had their way France would become 'an aristocracy of magistrates, which would be as contrary to the rights and interests of the nation as to his own sovereign prerogative'.

The crisis came in May 1788, when the Parlement, anticipating firm measures by the Keeper of the Seals, Lamoignon, the only strong man in Brienne's ministry, published what amounted to a declaration of fundamental law. This denounced arbitrary arrest and taxation, and proclaimed the inviolability of magistrates, the sanctity of provincial customs and privileges, and the prescriptive right of the Estates-General to consent to taxation. Two days later royal forces surrounded the Palais de Justice and compelled two of the most intransigent of the *parlementaires* to surrender themselves to arrest. The Parlement was then forced to register six edicts, known as the May Edicts, which announced the creation of a new Plenary Court to register royal decrees, and of forty-seven new courts of appeal, the core of a reformed and centralised judicial system. These changes infringed seigneurial rights of justice and threatened the legal autonomy of some provinces; they did not abolish the parlements, but suspended them and deprived them of their political power as well as a great deal of their jurisdiction and income. They also violated, directly or by implication, all the

---

[1] Brienne (Étienne Charles de Loménie de), b. 1727, Archbishop of Toulouse 1763, Archbishop of Sens 1788. After being Controller-General 1787–88 he became a cardinal, but was deprived of his hat as one who took the oath prescribed by the Civil Constitution of the Clergy of 1790. Died 1794.

principles of law which the magistrates had just recapitulated. The result was a wave of disorder, known to historians as the Revolt of the Nobility, and generally regarded as the real beginning of the Revolution.

As in England in 1688, the royal government was now paralysed by general hostility. Pamphlets poured forth in favour of the parlements, and the law courts everywhere protested strongly. The peers of France, supported in the streets by agitators in the pay of the king's unscrupulous and ambitious cousin, Orléans,[1] joined in the chorus, and the Assembly of the Clergy added its remonstrance to an insultingly small 'voluntary grant' towards revenue. Paris was kept under control, but violence, undoubtedly organised by the lawyers and the lesser nobility, occurred in many provincial capitals. When attempts were made to install the new provincial assemblies and courts of appeal, their members were assaulted as renegades. In Hainault, Franche Comté, Dauphiné and Provence there was a demand for the revival of the provincial estates in their ancient form, the Estates of Dauphiné even being convoked in open defiance of an express royal prohibition. Brittany prepared almost openly for revolt: its countless petty nobles armed to resist royal forces, and committees, linked by correspondence and delegates, developed apace to organise common action. Confronted with this situation, and finding the intendants and even the army unreliable, the government could only capitulate. By August 1788 Brienne was compelled to suspend the Edicts, to agree that the Estates-General should meet on the 1st May 1789, and to resign. Necker, whom the king had to accept in his place, promptly secured the dismissal of Lamoignon and the reinstatement of the parlements, and on 23rd September 1788, the Parlement of Paris re-entered the capital in triumphant popularity.

This victory clearly meant that there would have to be fundamental changes in the government of France. The basic principles of individual freedom had been proclaimed. The clergy and the nobility had recognised that they must contribute something more to the treasury. Power, hitherto concentrated in theory in the crown, had now to be shared with some constitutional bodies and tempered by explicit consent. The French Revolution of 1788 was not, however, to end here. The nation at large, particularly the politically conscious middle-class, had been immensely stimulated by the aristocracy's successful defiance of authority, and had high hopes of wide

[1] Orléans (Louis Philippe Joseph, Duc d'), b. 1747, notable for riotous living and unscrupulous and self-interested opposition to the Court. Sent on a mission to England immediately after the events of October 1789, he returned to become a member of the Convention, adopting the name *Citizen Equality* and shocking even the Montagnards with whom he associated by voting for the death of the king. Suspected of being implicated in Dumouriez's treason in 1793, he was arrested, imprisoned at Marseilles and executed at Paris on 6th November 1793. Father of King Louis-Philippe, 1830–48.

political and social reform from the Estates-General. It was certainly in no mood to accept the domination of the aristocracy in Estates-General, parlements and provincial assemblies, which would mean the survival of a society firmly based upon the distinctions conferred by blood and title. This deep difference, signs of which had previously appeared in Brittany, now suddenly emerged as of paramount importance. On 25th September, only two days after its re-instatement, the Parlement of Paris announced its decision that the Estates-General should be constituted as at its last meeting in 1614, in three separate orders or estates, each having the same numerical strength and each possessing a single vote. This meant not only that the lay and clerical aristocracy could constantly out-vote the commons by two votes to one, but also that the caste system would remain intact. The Third Estate would stay in the condition described by Sieyès, where 'if one does not possess some privilege, one must resign oneself to enduring contempt, injury and vexations of every sort', and fundamental reforms would remain impossible.

The effects of this pronouncement were immediate and momentous. 'King, despotism and constitution are now minor questions', wrote Mallet du Pan. 'The war is between the Third Estate and the other two orders.' Being, as they believed, betrayed in the moment of victory, the leaders of the Third Estate awoke to the realisation that the aristocracy were implacably opposed to the interests they had most at heart, parity of status and equality of opportunity, and they recoiled in anger and abhorrence from their former allies. At the same time the prestige of the crown was enormously enhanced, Louis now appearing as the victim instead of the agent of reaction. Proof of his benevolence was found in an appeal he had made in the previous July for information from 'all the scholars and educated persons of his kingdom' to ensure that the Estates-General should be 'the assembly of a great family headed by a common father', with 'essential proportion and harmony in the composition of the three orders'.

The literary men of the Third Estate now wrote pamphlets in unprecedented numbers, and as the censorship had necessarily to be abandoned, these appeared freely and were avidly discussed in the salons and societies, the lodges, clubs and cafés of the whole of France.[1] In the course of a few weeks an influx of petitions and memorials marked the emergence of a nation-wide movement to secure the position of the Third Estate in the Estates-General, the demand being that its representation should be doubled, to equal that of

[1] The king's appeal to 'educated persons' should be remembered here. Arthur Young, travelling in France in these years, encountered many able and well-educated men and women, but he often expressed his astonishment at the lack of newspapers and the general ignorance of current affairs outside the greater towns.

the clergy and nobility together, and that the deputies of all three orders should sit together in a single assembly and vote as individuals to reach decisions based on real majorities. This movement was supported in Paris by a group already known as the 'patriot' party, which included Talleyrand and Mirabeau, more respectable liberal aristocrats like Condorcet, Lafayette and Sieyès, and such progressive magistrates as Adrien Duport, Le Pelletier and Hérault de Séchelles. An obscure 'Committee of Thirty', including many of these same men, subsidised pamphleteers and sent letters and agents to the provinces—and in Brittany, at least, it is now known that popular political organisation was developing rapidly by this time. The great wealth and influence of Orléans was also again employed to promote the cause and his own popularity. But even these influences do not completely explain the movement as a whole, the demand of the Third Estate for emancipation being general and at least partly spontaneous.

Although the Parlement of Paris was persuaded in December to retract its September declaration about the observance of the forms of 1614, the conservative aristocracy did not yield to the public outcry. Necker, seeking to placate the court without compromising his own popularity, called a second meeting of Notables in November, but five of its six working committees rejected the proposal for double representation for the Third Estate, and the sixth, which had the king's younger brother, the Count of Provence,[1] in the chair, only accepted it by a majority of one. The most that Necker could obtain was a ruling by the Council on the 27th December, authorising double representation for the commons but saying nothing of the manner of assembly or voting procedure. Since the one concession was pointless without the other the commons assumed that voting by order was to be abandoned and that the king was really going to effect reforms in consultation with his people; but the aristocracy, seeing that the king was uncommitted, refused to recognise more than a necessary concession to circumstances, which might perhaps provide a separate Third Estate better qualified to speak of the financial state of the country.

Throughout the months devoted to the organisation of the elections, this ambiguity prevailed, fostering conflict and hardening attitudes. On 12th December 1788, the Princes of the Blood had warned the king that 'a revolution is preparing in the principles of government. . . . Everything proclaims and proves the existence of deliberate insubordination and contempt for the laws of state.' Now, provincial estates and other assemblies

[1] Provence (Louis Stanislas Xavier, Comte de), b. 1755. Younger brother of Louis XVI, known as *Monsieur*, he emigrated on 20th June 1791 and became the leader of the *émigrés*, assuming the titles of Regent of France in 1792 and of Louis XVIII after the death of the Dauphin in 1795. Returned to France as King Louis XVIII in 1814 and 1815 and reigned until his death in 1824.

31

of the nobility issued proclamations of protest, and the *cahiers*[1] of the first two orders made it clear that they were determined to maintain all the honorific, and some at least of the financial, privileges of their position. At the same time, hunger and unemployment were aggravated by the failure of the harvest of 1788, and an exceptionally severe winter caused appalling hardship to the poor. In Brittany matters approached the point of civil war, and throughout the land the royal government began to crumble under the combined strains of political tension and economic crisis.

Thus France repudiated royal absolutism—for the king could never retreat completely once the Estates-General had been called and the demand for a constitution given expression—and thus began the process by which aristocracy and privilege were, as one, repudiated for ever. In 1788, despite some excesses of language by the wilder spirits, the commons called for no more than parity with the aristocracy. They demanded equality, not superiority, in representation, and many men of rank, including some great noblemen like La Rochefoucauld-Liancourt, were supporters of the patriot party and were for a time to be prominent among the leaders of the Revolution. But although birth alone was not to be a criterion of ostracism and persecution until the Terror was at its height in 1794, a fissure was opening in French society. The term 'aristocrat' soon implied an opponent of equality, an upholder of what Sieyès described in that most powerful and partisan of pamphlets, *Qu'est-ce que le tiers état?*, as the 'odious injustice' by which ordinary men bore the great burden of public service only to find 'all lucrative and honorary positions held by members of the privileged order', and met everywhere the interdict: 'Whatever be your services, whatever your talents, you shall go thus far and no farther. It is not fitting for you to be honoured.' As rejection of equality meant rejection of the Revolution, the name of aristocrat came to be applied to all who opposed, or were thought to oppose, any aspect of the new order of things, until eventually men and women of humble birth, minor offenders against creed or regulation, were daily executed as *aristos*. Hatred and fear of the aristocracy were to dominate men's outlook for years to come.

Sieyès, however, was much more than the prophet of social equality, important as this was. His immense influence arose because he expressed with particular force an idea fundamental to the Revolution and to the whole modern world, that of the unlimited authority of the nation. To his own question 'What is the Third Estate?' his reply was simply: 'Everything.' Asserting that the Third Estate was in reality a complete nation in its own

[1] The guiding memoranda prepared for deputies by their electoral assemblies, and for these assemblies by the general electorate, nominally as petitions calling for the redress of grievances.

1   Louis XVI

From a crayon drawing made by Joseph Ducreux three days before the king's execution

2   Sieyès

From a contemporary lithograph

right, whereas the aristocracy was but a tiny minority which of its own choice lived by a different law, he asserted also, that the representatives of the Third Estate were alone 'the true representatives of the national will . . . able to speak without error in the name of the entire nation'. They had therefore in themselves complete competence to provide France with a constitution, and they ought to have unlimited powers in doing so. Indeed, even the binding force of a constitution once established was compromised by this doctrine: the nation being extant before all things, and being the source of all things, 'it is sufficient for its will to be manifested for all positive law to vanish before it. In whatever form the nation wills, it is sufficient that it does will: all forms are good, and its will is always the supreme law.'

This belief in the sovereignty of the nation is sometimes said to derive from the earlier writings of Jean-Jacques Rousseau, the introspective genius who has well been called the first modern man. The derivation, however, can scarcely stand scrutiny. Rousseau's works, deliberately written in a style designed to appeal to a wider circle than that of the salons of the intelligentsia, were indeed revolutionary. Like the other *philosophes*, Rousseau denounced the absurdities and inequalities he saw in society, believing them to be the products of an artificial civilisation. Unlike his predecessors, he also condemned the cold and sceptical intellectualism of the Age of Reason, and voiced instead an exhilarating faith in feeling and in the convictions of conscience. Emotion was made fashionable by the success of his works, and wisdom and virtue were expected from spontaneous expression and from simple and unlettered men. His political thought, however, probably had but little influence before the Revolution, the initial editions of *The Social Contract* in 1762 and 1763 having only one successor before 1789. The book then ran through no less than thirty-two editions in the next ten years, a fact sufficient in itself to suggest that its importance was a consequence rather than a cause of the collapse of the *ancien régime*. *The Social Contract* is indeed a potent repudiation of all traditional authority, but it became important not on this account, but because Rousseau's main concern was with the problem which confronted the leaders of the Revolution, that of re-establishing authority upon a firm and legitimate footing. Both he and they found this to lie in the general consent of the community, and as the Revolution continued many of them became firmly convinced, as he was, that the real objective must be the moral regeneration of the individual by political action. Between Rousseau's teachings and the theory of national sovereignty advanced by Sieyès, however, lie differences too great to allow of much derivation. The general will, to Rousseau a moral abstraction, was to Sieyès no more than a matter of arithmetic. Moreover, since Rousseau thought not of a nation, but of a state small enough to allow every citizen to participate personally in legislation, he did not allow that any representative assembly

33

could possess any measure of sovereignty, or that government could ever be more than a trust.

The new doctrine of national sovereignty, so far as Sieyès expressed it at this time, arose less from theoretical writings than from a combination of historical circumstances. On the eve of the Revolution there was in France, as Professor Lefebvre has said, a distinct sense of national unity, the result of the work of the monarchy over several centuries. It was marked by the general demand in the *cahiers* for a single constitution, a more unified system of law and a less localised economy, as well as by the emergence of the self-styled 'patriot' or 'national' party, and it was clearly greatly stimulated by the growth of conflict between the Third Estate and the other orders. Provincialism, so strong a force in 1788, became discredited by its association with aristocracy, and the commons did not hesitate to abandon provincial Estates in favour of the Estates-General, the assembly of the nation. Sieyès, who appealed to this new sentiment even as he gave it cogent and clear expression, yet wrote principally to avert a particular danger. Like many others, he feared that an assembly of the Estates-General in its ancient form would not merely prevent all social and political progress, but would also give the older order of society a new validity—in Condorcet's[1] phrase, 'a new sanction'. To prevent this, some source of authority greater than the fundamental law and ancient custom to which the aristocracy appealed, and greater even than the Divine Right of the crown, had to be invoked, and it was to this end that Sieyès wrote. In theory, therefore, absolute monarchy, far from being replaced by an authority limited by law, was simply to be transferred from the king to the nation—or, as some said, to the people, these terms being initially interchangeable; and in practice, the struggle of the Third Estate to establish its supremacy in the Estates-General, its very effort to make France more free, necessarily increased this tendency towards authoritarianism.

[1] Condorcet (Jean Antoine Nicolas de Caritat, Marquis de), b. 1743. An illustrious mathematician and philosopher, he became a republican after the king's flight to Varennes and was elected a member of the Legislative Assembly for Paris and of the Convention for Aisne. As one associated with Brissot, he was the principal author of the constitutional proposals which the Montagnards rejected as 'federalist' in 1793, and he was denounced in July of that year for his criticisms of the Montagnard Constitution of 1793. After spending some time in hiding in Paris, he fled from the capital in March 1794 and died by his own hand on being identified at Bourg-la-Reine on 28th March.

2

The Revolution of 1789

On 24th January 1789, royal writs went out for the convocation of the first Estates-General to be held in France for almost 200 years. Louis assured his people 'from the extremities of his Kingdom and from the most obscure settlements' that their wishes would be heard, and desired them to co-operate in the election of deputies to the 'great and august assembly'. The franchise, which was extended to all beneficed clergy, all noblemen of hereditary title, and almost all male tax-payers over the age of twenty-five, was in fact remarkably liberal, and a commendable attempt was made to relate constituencies to population. This inevitably complicated the process of election, so that the Estates could not meet until 5th May, and the Paris delegation was not present until early June. Despite delays and deficiencies, however, the elections reflect the competence and the benevolence of the royal administration as well as the high hopes and seriousness of purpose of the electors.

To produce an assembly in which the Third Estate would have the agreed double representation, the constituencies, which were formed from ancient areas of jurisdiction known as *bailliages*, were required to choose four deputies each, two of whom were to be commoners. In each constituency electors were to meet separately according to their order, and to make their decision by a simple majority vote. Except in Paris the first two orders were small enough to allow their members to meet and vote directly, only the monastic orders and some cathedral clergy being required to send delegates to the electoral assemblies. In the Third Estate, however, the electorate numbered some six million people, the majority of whom were dispersed in small rural communities. The practical problem of reducing this considerable electorate to its 600 representatives was overcome by a complicated system of indirect election, based ultimately upon the principle that every 100 persons should choose someone to speak for them. The rural population was therefore grouped into units of 100 or less by households, and that of the towns by guilds and professional corporations, and the delegates chosen by these groups formed a preliminary assembly—which had often to reduce its own numbers by as much as three-quarters before proceeding further. In thinly-populated areas two stages of election sufficed, a primary assembly choosing a secondary assembly to elect the deputies; but elsewhere one, or

35

even two, initial stages were necessary before the primary assembly could be formed.

Needless to say, this procedure has incurred the censure of historians, who have seen in it both a royal attempt to swamp urban radicalism by enfranchising a loyal and conservative countryside, and an undemocratic device to silence all popular demands. It is, however, very doubtful whether the government had any political intentions at all, being simply concerned to cope as best it could with a considerable administrative problem. In fact, at a later stage in the elections seven great provincial cities—Bordeaux, Bourges, Lyons, Nîmes, Rouen, Tours and Toulouse—were recognised as electoral areas in their own right and granted sixteen deputies each; and in the last week of April particular provision was made for the relatively large city of Paris, where the franchise was drastically restricted, but where the sixty electoral districts chose forty deputies, twenty of whom were commoners. On the other hand the effect of the indirect procedure was certainly to silence the voice of the labourers and small proprietors of both town and country. Not only was voting, at all save the final stages, entirely open, but the first function of all assemblies was a deliberative one, the king's subjects being instructed 'to confer together and voice remonstrances . . . and, this done, to elect' their representatives. In the Third Estate this meant that the educated and the eloquent, the men of property and reputation, the professional men and particularly the lawyers, were chosen as local delegates after they had led the debates on the wording of the *cahiers*, and they in turn chose men of their own kind, of still greater standing, as higher delegates and eventually as deputies. The process produced an assembly which Lefebvre has described as 'made up uniquely of bourgeois'. The deputies were for the most part well-to-do townsmen, and they were very largely lawyers or men trained in the law and experienced in local and judicial administration.

The elections for all three orders were in fact strikingly successful in producing a parliament which contained many men of marked ability, and represented both the most obvious divisions and the greatest common interests of the country. In both the senior orders the men of lesser rank outweighed their superiors. Amongst the clergy the influence of the parish priests was predominant, the bishops securing only forty-six of the 300 available seats in their assembly. This result was beneficial to the Third Estate, for nearly all the parish priests were poor men who favoured reforms in both Church and state, and some of the bishops also had liberal sympathies, although the attitude of Talleyrand of Autun[1] was rather different

---

[1] Talleyrand-Périgord (Charles Maurice de), b. 1754, Bishop of Autun, 1788. After accepting the Civil Constitution of the Clergy he went to London on a diplomatic mission

from that of more sincere churchmen like Champion de Cicé, the Archbishop of Bordeaux. Some of the lesser clergy, particularly the abbé Montesquiou, were to prove staunch defenders of the rights of the Church, and some, like the abbé Maury, were able advocates of reaction, but the general sentiment of their order was best represented by the radicalism of the abbé Grégoire. On the other hand, the provincial nobility had generally voted for conservative backwoodsmen of their own kind, and only about ninety of this Estate were liberals. Amongst those of high rank and advanced views were the magistrate Adrien Duport, the brothers Charles and Alexandre de Lameth, Lally-Tollendal, the comte de Clermont-Tonnerre, the duc d'Aiguillon, the duc de la Rochefoucauld-Liancourt, the marquis de La Fayette, and Orléans himself; but in general the order chose men more like Cazalès, a royalist officer of dragoons who became an eloquent conservative. The composition of the Assembly of the Nobility held little prospect that the issues in dispute between the orders would be settled by compromise.

In the Third Estate the process of elimination by successive elections had led to the return of an unusually able body of men, whose debates were to maintain a standard well above that of many later assemblies. The majority of them were men well-known locally for their ability and integrity as well as for their enthusiasm for effective reforms. Men of the law like Lanjuinais and Le Chapelier of Rennes, the Protestant pastor Rabaut St.-Étienne from Nîmes, and Malouet, the intendant of the navy at Toulon, were typical of many of this type. Barnave,[1] the future founder of the Feuillants, and Mounier, the equal and rival of Sieyès in constitutional debate, had together played a prominent part in the revolution in Dauphiné in 1788. Sieyès himself, rejected by the clergy of his own order, accepted the seat he was offered by Paris, the delegation of which also included the illustrious jurist Target and the distinguished astronomer and philanthropist Bailly. Disreputable but dynamic, and perhaps the ablest of all politically, the comte de

---

and by remaining abroad became classed as an *émigré*. After retirement to America, he returned to France in 1796 and became Minister for Foreign Affairs 1797–July 1799 and December 1799–1807, with the title Prince of Benevento 1806. Having quarrelled with Napoleon he did much to effect the return of the Bourbons in 1814 and to re-establish the position of France in Europe at the Congress of Vienna. Died 1838.

[1] Barnave (Antoine Pierre Joseph Marie), b. 1761. A lawyer, he was at first a radical member of the Assembly, in which he sat for the Third Estate of Dauphiné; in 1791, however, as the most eloquent of the triumvirate of himself, Adrien Duport and Alexandre de Lameth, influential after the death of Mirabeau, he tried to check the Revolution. He founded the moderate Feuillant Club after the massacre of the Champ de Mars in July 1791, was arrested in 1792 and executed 30th November 1793.

Mirabeau[1] won popular support in Provence after his local nobility had refused to admit him to their assembly. Such men as these certainly acquired experience rapidly during the elections, even if local 'literary' societies had not provided it before, and boldness and conviction clearly counted for much. In March and April, 1789, the lawyer Robespierre, for example, was elected first to help draft the *cahier* of his preliminary assembly, then to represent this assembly at the general assembly of the *baillage*, and then to help draft the general *cahier ;* established as a forthright radical, he was finally chosen as one of the deputies of Arras to the National Assembly.

Moreover, although the method of election prevented any proper representation of the particular interests of the mass of the population, the peasants and the artisans, it at least ensured that the difficulties and needs of the nation were thoroughly ventilated both in the press and in innumerable assemblies. In this respect, indeed, the experiment of 1789 was all too successful, for while the great mass of the *cahiers* could not possibly be properly considered at a time of acute conflict between the orders, the consultation of the people when hardship was at its worst aroused the wildest expectations of immediate change and universal happiness. Yet if the hopes and troubles of those who worked with their hands were overshadowed as local *cahiers* were amalgamated and re-phrased by superior and more well-to-do assemblies, the interests which all classes had in common were effectively carried forward. The *cahiers* show that the Third Estate was at one with the first two orders in loyalty to the crown, in respect for the Church and in regard for the rights of property, as well as in the general determination to secure greater self-government and more political freedom. All, too, were agreed that there should be a written constitution, a declaration of civil rights, and regular meetings of an elected representative assembly to control taxation and align it more closely to real wealth. All desired to see a greater measure of decentralisation, a reform of the judicial system and of the criminal law, and a drastic reduction of internal tariffs. The deputies of the Third Estate may not have been sufficiently conscious of the peasantry's hostility to seigneurial dues, of the problems of enclosure, or of the wage-earners' resentment of the power of the guilds, but in their determination to ensure that national and local assemblies should not be dominated by an aristocratic clique, in their insistence upon full civil equality and equality of opportunity, they were justified in their confident assumption that they spoke for the nation.

A year of unparalleled political excitement had thus produced a parliament

---

[1] Mirabeau (Honoré Gabriel Riqueti, Comte de), b. 1749. Son of Victor de Riqueti, the Marquis de Mirabeau who was a disciple of the Physiocrats and called himself *The Friend of Man*. Honoré, who had long been a prolific writer, was undoubtedly both a shameless plagiarist and a man of outstanding intellectual ability. The principal member of the Third Estate for Aix-en-Provence, he died on 2nd April 1791.

THE REVOLUTION OF 1789

rich in talent, but still divided into orders which differed completely in their interpretation of their manner of procedure. In this situation, much depended upon the wisdom and initiative of the king, who could have drawn deeply upon a great reservoir of loyalty in persuading the nobility to concede, and the commons to defer, some claims. Had Louis provided the leadership for which all were looking and put forward a programme of reform based upon the principal points made in the *cahiers*, substantial progress might have been peacefully achieved. The royal government, however, proved as inept as the king himself was inadequate. Although Malouet had long since urged Necker to prepare 'a settled plan of concessions and reforms which could consolidate authority instead of destroying it', nothing had been done by the government to guide the country in the composition of its *cahiers* or in the choice of its representatives, and nothing was now done to construct a policy from the information provided by the elections.

Even the ceremonies attendant upon the opening of the Estates-General were sadly mismanaged. When the king received the deputies at Versailles on Saturday 2nd May, he was courteous and friendly; but his officers had injudiciously insisted upon the observance of antiquated ceremonials, which caused interminable delay and confusion and which placed an unfortunate emphasis upon the distinctions between the orders. The deputies of the Third Estate, clothed perforce in the sombre traditional dress of the medieval townsmen, had to wait all day before being presented to the king. The double doors of the Royal Chamber, which had been opened wide to the clergy, and half-opened to the nobility, were closed to them alone. On the following Monday, 4th May, when the deputies and their sovereign went in magnificent procession to attend High Mass at the Church of Saint Louis, the same distinctions were observed, and according to some accounts an open brawl was barely averted when the commons, who led the way into the church and naturally began to occupy the foremost seats, found that they were required to yield their places to the nobles. Although many were undoubtedly profoundly moved by the spectacle of the king's association with his people, and had the highest hopes of the future, the long sermon was only mildly radical, and Mirabeau felt that no finer opportunity was ever more completely lost than on this occasion.

The first session of the Estates next day, 5th May, revealed that there was no royal programme for reform, and even suggested that the court and the aristocracy had drawn together against the reformers. The great 'Hall of Lesser Pleasures' (*Salle des Menus Plaisirs*) was filled hours beforehand by nearly all the 1,200 deputies, dressed according to their order, and by perhaps twice as many spectators. A splendid sight was presented when Louis and Marie-Antoinette entered with all their attendant officers and ladies, but the expectant commons were profoundly disappointed by the

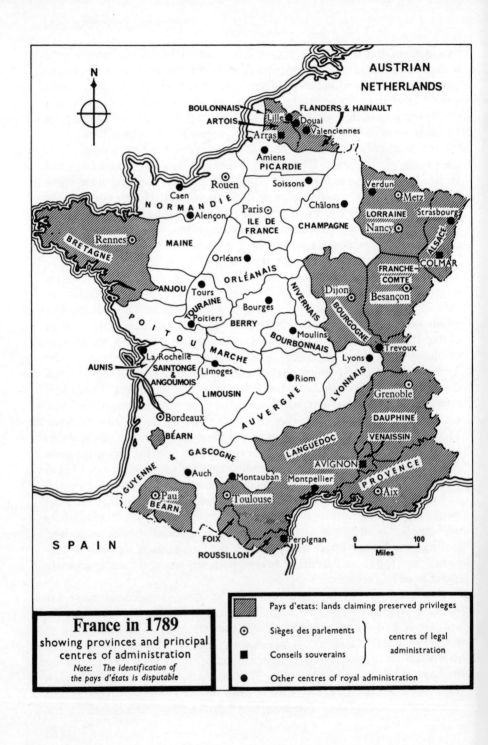

N

AUSTRIAN
NETHERLANDS

BOULONNAIS
ARTOIS
FLANDERS & HAINAULT
Lille
Douai
Valenciennes
Arras

Amiens
PICARDIE

Rouen
Caen
Soissons
Verdun

NORMANDIE
Alençon
Paris
Châlons
Metz

ILE DE
FRANCE
CHAMPAGNE
LORRAINE
Nancy
Strasbourg

Rennes
BRETAGNE
MAINE

Orléans
ORLÉANAIS
FRANCHE-
COMTÉ
ALSACE
COLMAR

ANJOU
Tours
TOURAINE
Poitiers
Bourges
BERRY
NIVERNAIS
Dijon
BOURGOGNE
Besançon

POITOU
MARCHE
Moulins
BOURBONNAIS
Trevoux

La Rochelle
SAINTONGE
&
ANGOUMOIS
Limoges
Riom
Lyons
LYONNAIS

AUNIS
LIMOUSIN
Grenoble

Bordeaux
AUVERGNE
DAUPHINÉ

BÉARN
GASCOGNE
VENAISSIN

&
LANGUEDOC
AVIGNON
PROVENCE

GUYENNE
Auch
Montauban
Montpellier
Aix

Pau
BÉARN
Toulouse

SPAIN
FOIX
Perpignan
ROUSSILLON

0   100
Miles

France in 1789
showing provinces and principal
centres of administration
Note: The identification of
the pays d'états is disputable

Pays d'etats: lands claiming preserved privileges

Sièges des parlements

Conseils souverains

} centres of legal
administration

Other centres of royal administration

sequel. Louis first spoke briefly, admonishing the Estates to be guided by wisdom and prudence and to abhor wild demands for unnecessary changes. He was succeeded first by Barentin, the Keeper of the Seals, whose speech was almost inaudible, and then by Necker, who as Controller-General had prepared a financial statement of such length that, even though a powerful reader soon took up the tale, the reading took three full hours. In all this there was nothing said of fundamental reforms, of the establishment of a constitution or of an effective redistribution of taxation. The crucial question of voting procedure was carefully avoided. So far as the attitude of the government could be comprehended at all, it seemed to be that *if* the Estates proceeded with restraint, and *if* they helped to dispose of the deficit by a willing surrender of privileges, then the orders might meet together to discuss minor reforms and matters of common interest; but in the meantime they should separate, constitute themselves formally by verifying the credentials of their members, and then initiate their own particular discussions.

The royal government's failure to do more than wait upon events led directly to a complete deadlock. The nobility, meeting on 8th May, decided to verify their credentials and on 11th May they completed their roll-call and declared their Estate constituted. The clergy confined themselves to beginning verification, to negotiations with the commons, and to some consideration of their *cahiers*. The commons, however, maintained as a matter of principle the view that even verification could only be valid if it was done by all the orders in common assembly; as they put it in a later resolution, 'the deputies of the different orders are deputies to one single assembly, the *National Assembly*'. They therefore refused to begin any verification of credentials, or even to admit that they had any corporate existence at all, and they did no more than to try to persuade the other orders to rejoin them in the Salle des Menus Plaisirs, which they occupied because the government had failed to provide any other accommodation for them. In this way they paralysed the whole parliament, for the Estates-General could clearly have no legal existence until all its orders were properly constituted.

A prolonged trial of strength ensued, in which the conflict, nominally between the orders, was in reality reflected in each of the Houses. Even such liberal nobles as La Fayette, however, felt themselves bound by the instructions of their constituents to maintain the independence of their order, or at least to refrain from jeopardising it, and the clergy, whose influence could sway the balance, were torn between their social sympathies for the commons and their natural desire to preserve the independence of the Church. The resolution of the commons, too, was severely strained by the clergy's attempts at mediation, and by belated efforts by the king to arbitrate. Several attempts were also made by deputies like Malouet and Rabaut

41

St. Étienne to secure some settlement which would preserve some rights of self-determination for each of the orders in matters affecting its particular interests. All such attempts, however, were nullified by the intransigence of the nobility, who on 26th May expressly rejected verification in common, warning the king that the monarchy itself depended on the retention of separate voting. As the weeks passed, attitudes hardened, and it became increasingly unlikely that moderation could prevail before the commons were driven by necessity and exasperation to act independently, to match intransigence with intransigence, and to assert the superiority of theoretical rights over those hallowed by time and custom.

In mid-May, Reubell had warned the other Houses that the commons might be forced to declare themselves to be the nation, and to commence their work of restoring the monarchy without the assistance of those 'presumably legally elected' by the other orders. A minority which included the Breton deputies had then supported his view. By the beginning of June this attitude was more general, and the arrival on 3rd June of the deputies of Paris, including Sieyès, seems to have turned the scale. The commons now recognised their own existence for the first time by appointing Bailly as their Dean, though not yet as their President, and on 10th June, after a final conference of committees had failed, Sieyès began to implement his announced intention of 'cutting the cable'. By his proposal, 'a last invitation' was sent to the other orders to join the commons in verifying the credentials of all who claimed to be 'Representatives of the Nation'. The doubts of more moderate deputies like Malouet being swept aside, it was agreed that an inclusive roll-call of the constituencies should begin at the next sitting, 'whether the deputies of the privileged classes be present or absent'.

On 15th June, when this roll-call was proceeding, the magnetism of resolute leadership proved its efficacy, and three curés, harbingers of clerical support, answered to their names in the list for Poitou. Encouraged by the appearance of sixteen more in the next three days, as well as by their own successful disregard of authority, the commons advanced to a still more decisive step: on 17th June Sieyès drafted a motion by which the Assembly adopted the title of the *National Assembly*, 'the only one appropriate to things as they really are'. This motion 'recognised' that as the commons represented at least 96 per cent of the nation, they alone could interpret the general will, no other assembly having any authority to impose any restraint or veto upon them, and no deputies of any order having any right to deliberate apart from them. As the name National Assembly had previously been applied only to the Estates-General as a whole, this decision was clearly an arrogation of title and authority by the commons, who indeed proceeded at once to a first act of sovereignty. To safeguard its position, the Assembly issued a declaration, formally worded as a decree, to give its sanction to existing taxation, 'despite its illegal origins', until, and only until, the Assembly itself should for any reason be dispersed.

These events mark a decisive stage in the development of the Revolution. Royal power, too long held in abeyance, was being illegally assumed by the Assembly. The royal prerogative had been infringed by the decree about taxation, and the Assembly's call to all deputies to join it 'in the great work of effecting the regeneration of France' implied that the framing of a constitution might be begun without the king's consent. Moreover, a new source of right, the general will of the people, had been invoked in justification of these measures, and although most deputies still thought with Mirabeau that the king would be the equal partner of the nation in a reformed monarchy, the conception of the nation as a superior sovereign power was implicit in the resolutions. A conflict was thus initiated which was to drive both king and commons to opposing extremes. It was also to effect a new political division in France, at first broadly corresponding to the older distinction between the aristocracy and the commons, but soon cutting across class distinctions and severing all 'patriots' from all 'enemies of the people'.

Acquiescence in the deputies' actions being equivalent to approval, which the British ambassador thought would have been 'little short of laying the crown at their feet', Louis could not but act. Indeed, the nobility, and the considerable clerical minority which had not declared in favour of sitting with the commons, were both appealing to him to intervene. A second Royal Session of the Estates was therefore announced for 22nd June, and explicit instructions were sent to Bailly that no more sittings of the commons should take place while the Salle des Menus Plaisirs was being prepared for this. This order came too late to be communicated in advance to the deputies, who arrived in the rain on 20th June to discover the doors of their meeting-place closed and guarded by royal troops. In momentary expectation of arrest, they found refuge in the indoor tennis-court nearby, and suggestions that they should seek security in Paris were rejected in favour of Mounier's proposal that they should all bind themselves to continue their work. The celebrated Tennis-Court Oath, which all present (save a single deputy) then both pronounced and signed, bound the members of the National Assembly 'never to abandon it, and to go on meeting wherever circumstances might dictate, until the constitution of the kingdom and the regeneration of the state is firmly established'. Thus, under pressure, the Assembly advanced from the first usurpation of royal authority to a first defiance of an express royal command. The deputies indeed acknowledged in the Oath that they had been summoned 'to establish the true principles of monarchy', and they ended their meeting with a cry of '*Vive le roi!*'; but their actions necessarily forced the king to turn towards the aristocracy.

An accident of circumstance—the death of the dauphin after a long illness,

and the consequent retirement of the court from Versailles to Marly—also
affected the situation, for Louis was there exposed to the combined influence
of irresponsible reactionaries like his brother, the Count of Artois,[1] and of
those who believed, like Barentin, that the monarchy should define and
enforce a policy. These contrived first to prolong discussion of Necker's
proposals for the king's speech to the Estates, and then so to pack the next
meeting of the Royal Council that essential concessions to the commons
were eliminated from the speech, and a display of force approved. The delay
alone was fatal to the plan, for the Royal Session of the Estates had in turn to
be delayed until 23rd June, and when the commons managed to meet on 22nd
June in the Church of Saint Louis—Artois having thoughtfully engaged the
Tennis Court for that day—they were joined by 149 of the clergy, including
the Archbishops of Vienne and Bordeaux, as well as by a few of the
nobility.

The Royal Session proved to be the swan song of the old order, the King
of France appearing before his Estates for the last time amid all the ancient
splendour of the royal dignity. Through Barentin, a considerable programme
of reform was at last announced, by which many abuses were either
abolished outright or were marked for modification by the Estates. Internal
freedom of trade, judicial reform, and provincial estates with double representation for the commons were promised, and parliamentary control of
taxation was to be accompanied by an annual budget. Since the king reserved
his rights of emergency taxation, and his control of the military and the
police, these proposals implied that a constitutional monarchy would be
developed under royal tutelage, and Louis always regarded this as the limit
of legitimate concession. The commons, however, could not now be satisfied
with a plan which curtailed the authority they had already begun to assert,
particularly as other provisions made it quite clear that the aristocracy was to
preserve its political and social powers unimpaired. Feudal dues and useful or
honorary rights and privileges were to be protected as property, and any
renunciation of tax-exemptions by the nobility and the clergy was to be
entirely optional. Moreover, the commons' resolutions of 17th June were
quashed, and the Estates were forbidden to meet in common to consider any
matters affecting feudal property, the prerogatives of the first two orders, or
the constitutional form of future Estates. Other subjects might be discussed

[1] Artois (Charles Philippe, Comte d'), b. 1757, youngest brother of Louis XVI, leader
of the court party before the Revolution and of the first emigration. Until the emigration
of his elder brother, Provence, he was the chief of the *émigrés*, and he remained the arch-
enemy of the revolutionaries, whose cause he did much to foster by his own intransigence
and unreliability. Returning to France as Lieutenant-General of the Kingdom in 1814,
he succeeded Louis XVIII as Charles X in 1824 and was forced to abdicate in the
Revolution of 1830. Died in exile in 1834.

in common by agreement, but even this was to be subject to royal approval and to the veto of any substantial minority.

This programme, which amounted to a royal agreement with the aristocracy for the reform of the monarchy, was presented to the Estates between an introductory and a closing speech by Louis himself, the form of proceedings being not unlike that of a *lit de justice*, and the hall being surrounded by 4,000 soldiers. Louis rebuked his audience for having achieved nothing in nearly eight weeks; he reminded them that none of their projects could have any legal force without his own explicit approval; and he warned them that if necessary he was prepared to act alone to promote the happiness of the people, of whom he was the true representative. Immediately after this re-assertion of royal autocracy, and under the almost open threat of dissolution, the Estates were ordered 'to separate at once, and to go tomorrow morning to the chambers allotted to your respective orders to resume your sessions'.

Louis then left the hall, and the majority of the nobles and a minority of the clergy obediently followed. The remainder of the deputies, however, stood fast. Mirabeau, who praised the proposals for reform, pointed to the danger of despotism and the significant presence of military force. 'Who is it', he cried, 'that gives these orders and dictates these laws? It is your own representative, it is one who should rather receive orders from us!' A dramatic scene ensued as the Marquis de Dreux-Brézé, the Master of Ceremonies, came to reiterate the royal commands. Again Mirabeau stood forward: 'If you are charged to remove us, give orders for the use of force, for we shall not leave save at the point of the bayonet.' The Marquis turned to Bailly, who was now President, only to be told that the Assembly was in debate and that 'no-one can give orders to the nation in assembly'. He withdrew, discomforted. The deputies were further encouraged by Sieyès, who asked them: 'Gentlemen, do you not feel that you are today all that you were yesterday?'; and they proceeded to re-affirm their decisions of 17th June and to proclaim their own inviolability. Meanwhile, on Louis's orders, a body of soldiers advanced to clear the hall; but their own sympathies, the hostility of the considerable crowds outside, and the intervention of a group of liberal nobles kept them from going past the doorway.

So defied, Louis yielded. With his words: 'Oh, well, devil take it, let them stay!' the first attempt to control the Revolution failed, and the superiority of parliamentary over royal authority was in fact successfully asserted. A few days later, on 27th June, the remainder of the nobility and the clergy received direct orders from the king to join the commons, and on 30th June they did so, entering the hall amid absolute silence. 'The whole business is now over', noted Arthur Young on 27th June, 'and the revolution complete.' While Europe wondered at an ending of absolutism so speedy and so peaceful, the Assembly set about its work of reconstruction: within two weeks, it had heard a first report from its Constitutional Committee, it had received from La Fayette[1] the first proposals for a Declaration of Rights, and it had adopted the title of National Constituent Assembly.

In reality, of course, this apparent concord was an illusion. Although forty-seven of the nobility, led by Clermont-Tonnerre and including Orléans, had voluntarily joined the commons before 27th June, the majority of their order had only done so under compulsion. This majority, and the minority of the clergy, 371 deputies in all, had previously approved the separation of orders commanded by the king in the Royal Session, and many of them ostentatiously disassociated themselves from the activities of the Assembly even after they had taken their places in it. Many other deputies feared that these intransigents and the reactionary party at court were only biding their time to renew the struggle, and this militated against the formation of a moderate majority group amongst the liberals. It also strengthened those who, as Arthur Young wrote on 26th June, 'lay it down for a maxim that . . . they will accept of nothing as the concession of power: they will assume and secure all to themselves, as matters of right.' Nor was the fear unfounded, for on 26th June, before the reluctant nobles had joined the Assembly, secret royal orders had been sent for the concentration at Versailles of six regiments of soldiers, and on 1st July ten more, mainly of Swiss and German mercenaries, were ordered up to the environs of Paris. When these movements became obvious, the Assembly protested, only to be told on 10th and 13th July that the king considered more troops necessary to prevent public disturbances in and around the capital, and that it was for him alone to decide what should be done. Paris and Versailles were indeed disorderly, and the royal responsibility for maintaining law and order by prerogative could indeed be invoked, but the general opinion was that Louis intended to dishonour his acceptance of the Assembly and plead that the concession had been made under duress.

The fact that Louis consistently refused to be responsible for bloodshed makes it unlikely that he intended to use the military on this occasion; but it is hard to escape the conclusion that he was doing his best to strengthen his hand before curbing the commons. On 11th July, Necker, whose name was still synonymous with reform and sound finance, was ordered into exile; his

---

[1] La Fayette (Marie Jean Paul Roch Yves Gilbert Motier, Marquis de), b. 1757, a very wealthy aristocrat noted for his liberalism. He fought in the American War of Independence, became the friend of Washington, and was known as *The Hero of Two Worlds* for his initial support for the Revolution in France. Imprisoned by the allies after his defection in 1792, he was released by Napoleon and returned to France after Brumaire. Renewing his political life after the Restoration, he was influential in securing the succession of Louis-Philippe to the throne in 1830. Died 1834.

supporters were cleared from the Council, and a new administration, headed by the baron de Breteuil, a staunch royalist, was appointed. Convinced that Louis intended to treat the Assembly as if it were a recalcitrant *parlement*, the deputies adjourned on the 12th, and then met in continuous session for the next two days, in hourly expectation of dissolution and arrest. Even at this hour, however, they confronted resurgent absolutism with the rights of the nation, re-affirming their decrees of 17th, 20th and 23rd June, proclaiming the personal responsibility of ministers for whatever might befall, and denying in advance that any power could repudiate the public debt. While they waited for the king to act, and while Louis waited for them to yield, events in Paris forced matters to a decision.

Feeling in the capital had long been running high, for the intense excitement engendered by developments at Versailles coincided with a grave economic crisis in the city. Paris, by far the largest city in France, was particularly sensitive to the soaring cost of bread, for five-sixths of its normal population of about 600,000 were either desperately poor or were people who lived precariously on very limited means. These men and their families, the shop-keepers and craftsmen, the clerks and servants, the journeymen and labourers of an un-industrialised society, suffered severely when in the spring of 1789 the labourer who earned some twenty-five sous a day had to pay fourteen and a half sous for the four-pound loaf. The problems of both earning and buying were further aggravated by the presence in the city of an increasing army of the destitute, who came in from the surrounding countryside in search of food and work and poor relief. To those who lived in the tall and close-packed apartment houses of old Paris, to the men and women of the congested courtyards and alleyways of the Cité and the Marais and the traditionally turbulent eastern Faubourgs St Antoine and St Marcel, the shortage of food seemed part of a premeditated aristocratic plot to keep the people in subservience. Hunger and anger, already apparent in the demonstrations of the previous autumn and in the Réveillon riots at the end of April, were thus combined as fear of counter-revolution, and this in a city of which Arthur Young remarked that 'nothing was so glaringly ridiculous but the mob swallowed it with undiscriminating faith'. By the beginning of July, the last month before the new harvest, tension was acute. As the American diarist, Gouverneur Morris, noted on 8th July, there was an enormous number of people in the city 'whose only Resource for Bread is in the Vigilance and Attention of Government, whose utmost exertion can but just keep pace with the Necessity'.

Responsibility for maintaining public order in Paris lay in the first instance with the Lieutenant-General of Police, who, with the inspectors and commissioners who controlled the various *quartiers* of the capital from the hated Châtelet, had some 1,500 police agents and men of the old Town

Guard at his immediate command. Ultimately, however, civil peace depended upon the loyalty and discipline of the troops garrisoned in Paris, of whom there were about 5,000. These, principally men of the French Guard, had been stationed in the city for far too long and left far too much to the care of their non-commissioned officers. Although they had opened fire upon the people of the Faubourg St Antoine at the end of April, they had become completely disaffected by July, mingling openly with the crowds in the gardens of the Palais-Royal, where Orléans encouraged any subversive oratory.[1]

Great as was the danger of disorder, the approach of powerful royal forces seemed still more menacing, for the regiments that Louis had summoned were now concentrating around the capital, and the Champ de Mars was becoming a vast military encampment. Rumour magnified the numbers of these forces and imbued their most harmless patrols with instant peril, and the news of the fall of Necker, which reached the Palais-Royal on 12th July, meant nothing less than the imminence of a new St Bartholomew's Eve.

Stirred to action by such orators as Camille Desmoulins,[2] a young and hitherto tongue-tied lawyer, the crowds bore busts of Necker and Orléans through the streets and clashed with the Royal German cavalry on the Place Louis Quinze.[3] The cavalry first cleared the square with the flat of the sabre, and then fell back on the infantry in the Champ de Mars. There, in default of orders from Versailles, the army was held inactive for the next three days. Paris was thus left wholly uncontrolled, and a fearful night followed. Some sections of the crowds systematically destroyed the customs-posts at the entrances to the city, and a more general search for arms and food rapidly degenerated into indiscriminate looting and drunken disorder. The more substantial and responsible citizens were thus confronted from the beginning of the Revolution by two dangers simultaneously: on the one hand an 'aristocratic' assault apparently impended; on the other, anarchy seemed imminent within the city. Even as the clash of bells called the people to the defence of the city against the army, local forces were being hastily formed for

---

1 This palace was that belonging to the Duke of Orléans. Its arcades and tree-lined gardens, which sheltered innumerable booths, made it a popular resort for Parisians; but it was also a notorious one, and demagogues and subversive orators flourished there, probably with the Duke's encouragement.

2 Desmoulins. (Lucie Simplice Camille Benoit), b. 1762, had become a friend of Robespierre at the Collège Louis le Grand. An enthusiastic and impulsive agitator, he was also an unusually powerful pamphleteer and journalist who did much to discredit Robespierre's opponents. Trading too far on his skill and his popularity with the revolutionaries, he was guillotined with Danton on 5th April 1794, when he was a deputy to the Convention for Paris.

3 Later the Place de la Révolution, and later again the Place de la Concorde.

3 *Mirabeau*
From an engraving by G. Fiesinger after a drawing by J. Guérin

4 (*overleaf*) The taking of the Bastille
From a contemporary water-colour

the protection of property. On 13th July the Electors of the city, who had continued to meet after their original duties were done, brushed aside the old oligarchy and appointed their own committee to cope with the crisis. This body speedily authorised each of the sixty districts of the city to form a civic guard of 200 reputable able-bodied men, who alone should carry arms. As significantly, the green cockade, which had been adopted as the symbol of resistance and had become associated with disorder, was banned, and steps were taken to make and distribute cockades in the city colours of red and blue.

The Electors, however, were themselves beleaguered in the Hôtel de Ville by an immense crowd, which filled the Place de Grève and called incessantly for arms. By 14th July these people could be fobbed off no longer. A great multitude forced its way into the Invalides and seized the 32,000 muskets and five cannon that were kept there, and then moved on to the Bastille. The crowd's purpose was partly to secure the powder this fortress contained, and partly to ensure that the people of the Faubourg St Antoine should not be caught, as they feared to be, between the guns mounted on its towers and the Royal King's Hussars, whose appearance in the streets was expected at any moment. The ancient citadel, whose 100-foot walls rose beyond an impassable moat, appeared impregnable, but the governor, Delaunay, was without stores, effective cannon, or orders from Versailles. Amicable negotiations therefore began, and during this delay two men managed to release the chains which held back the outer drawbridge. The crowd then surged forward into an exposed courtyard. A burst of musketry followed from the fortress, and the heavy casualties caused by this supposed treachery inspired a determined assault by the people and by soldiers of the French Guards. When cannon were positioned ready to fire on the main gate, Delaunay agreed to capitulate on condition that the garrison was granted safe-conduct. Despite all that such soldiers as Élie and Hulin could do to honour this promise, many murders marred the victory once the great drawbridge had been lowered. Delaunay himself was struck down and beheaded while he was being taken to the Hôtel de Ville, and De Flesselles, the former Mayor, was dragged to his death from the council chamber itself.

Sullied though it was by outrages such as these, the rising of Paris nevertheless revealed the determination of its people to defend their freedom, and that of all France. Hungry as they were, their cry had been for arms, not for bread, and the British Ambassador reported that 'the regularity and determined conduct of the populace upon the present occasion exceeds all belief'. This resolution now proved decisive. The Bastille, which had for so long towered over the faubourgs as the sign and symbol of royal power, was systematically demolished, its stones being sold as souvenirs or trodden underfoot in streets and stairways. On 15th July Louis capitulated, going in

49

person to assure the Assembly that his troops would be withdrawn from the vicinity of the capital, and on the next day he recalled Necker, dismissed Breteuil, and ordered his brother Artois, the arch-advocate of reaction, to leave the kingdom. While the royal troops began their retirement, and while Artois and his adherents began their emigration, Louis made his will and went with fifty deputies to visit Paris—to be bewildered by the warmth of his welcome from well-ordered and enthusiastic crowds. Confident that they had reconquered their king by freeing him from the influence of evil counsellors, the Parisians greeted him as 'Louis XVI, Father of the French, King of a Free People', and Louis accepted the *tricoleur*, the 'distinctive sign of the French', in which the white of the Bourbons was wedded to the red and blue of Paris. Before he left he also sanctioned the municipal revolution by recognising Bailly[1] as Mayor in the new City Council, and La Fayette as commander-in-chief of the new civic guard, the National Guard.[2]

The Assembly, freed from the immediate threat of reaction, and recognised even by the Parlement of Paris as being of sovereign authority, now sought to resume its work of regeneration and reform: but France, swept by panic, was not passively awaiting the deputies' pleasure. During July the old order disintegrated, insurrections in town and country prolonging the emergency and creating a far freer form of society. In response to the rumours of troop movements, of the fall of Necker and of the capture of the Bastille, the revolution in Paris was repeated, with infinite local variations, in the great cities of the provinces, in the smaller market towns, and even in the villages. Local forces, usually of volunteers, were everywhere armed and organised to protect the nation from the aristocracy, to safeguard food supplies, and to

[1] Bailly (Jean Sylvain), b. 1736, astronomer, writer and philanthropist, was the senior member of the delegation of the Third Estate for Paris and the first President of the National Assembly. After being Mayor 1789–91, he was executed in November 1793 on the Champ de Mars.

[2] It may be helpful for the reader to appreciate at this point that the maintenance of public order in Paris henceforth depended upon the National Guard, a force in which the bulk of the French Guard was incorporated and which was soon to become effectively a middle-class body. After the events of July, the authority of the Lieutenant-General of Police was replaced by that of a committee drawn from the sixty districts of Paris, and, when the Municipal Law of 1790 replaced these by the forty-eight sections, considerable police powers were transferred to the more conservative Directory of the Department. The events of 17th July 1791 and 20th July 1792 show clearly what this meant in practice: on the former occasion, the authorities acted together to enforce martial law against a popular movement; on the latter, the connivance of the mayor and the independence of the sections prevented the Department from checking a demonstration against the crown. After the Revolution of 10th August 1792, the Commune won from a weakened Assembly its independence of the Department, and the opening of the National Guard to all citizens effectively established real power in the sections, whence it passed during the Terror to the Committee of General Security.

maintain law and order. The tutelage of the intendants was ignored, the authority of the National Assembly acknowledged, and entrenched corporations were either swept aside by citizens' committees or subjected to their supervision. These self-appointed or co-opted bodies were then gradually made more democratic, as the Electors in Paris were replaced after 30th July by councillors formally elected by the districts of the capital. The single centralised administrative system of the old monarchy thus suddenly collapsed, and in its place there appeared a multiplicity of local authorities, dominated by the middle-class, devoted to the Revolution and even in some areas loosely linked together for its defence, but all exceedingly jealous of their newly-won independence.

Of equal, if not greater, importance was the revolt in the countryside, where more than twenty millions of Frenchmen had their homes. The risings of 1789 have been seen as the blind revolt of a repressed and starving peasantry, and as a final stride towards independence by men whose resentment of restrictions was enhanced by their growing prosperity. There is some truth in both views. In general terms, the position of the peasant had clearly improved considerably during the eighteenth century. Save in Franche Comté and Nivernais, serfdom had practically disappeared; the fearful famines of earlier times no longer decimated the population; and by 1789 some 35 per cent of the land had been acquired by peasant proprietors. On the other hand, the increase in population had led to acute land-hunger, and economic insecurity was endemic in a situation in which all but a prosperous minority of tenant-farmers were either landless labourers or held plots too small for their subsistence. In some infertile areas appalling poverty persisted, and when the long expansion of the economy gave way to a recession after 1776, distress was general. The peasantry, who lived principally by working the estates of lay and clerical landlords, either as day-labourers or as tenants entitled to only a share—usually a half—of their crops, then found that although prices fell, rents remained high and wages relatively low. The slump in textiles and domestic industry that followed the American War and the free trade treaty with England in 1786 aggravated the position, which became desperate when the harvest failed in 1788. After the exceptional severities of the winter of 1788–89 the price of bread was even higher in the country than in the towns, and unemployment and destitution were commonplace.

In 1789, moreover, this economic crisis was accompanied by great political excitement and a general sense of insecurity. The convocation of the Estates-General and the discussion of the *cahiers* had raised hopes that the 'good king' was about to do something for his people. When these remained unfulfilled, the peasantry, like the townsmen, became convinced that their disappointment, and even the shortages and the soaring prices of

51

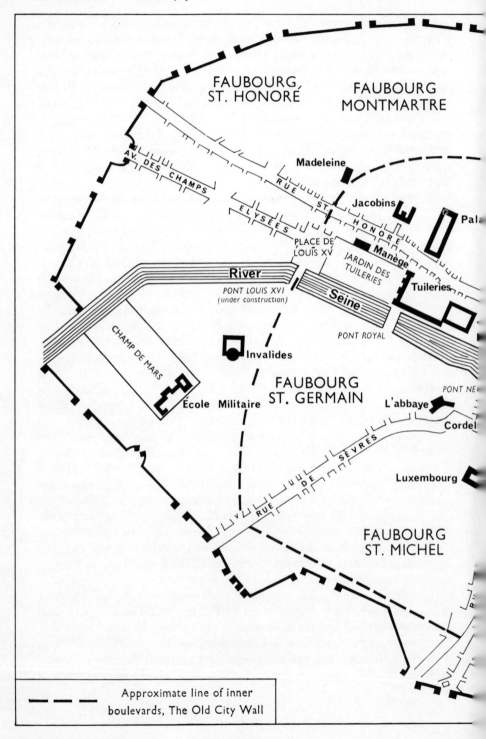

FAUBOURG ST. HONORÉ

FAUBOURG MONTMARTRE

AV. DES CHAMPS

Madeleine

RUE ST. HONORÉ

ELYSEES

Jacobins

Pal

PLACE DE LOUIS XV

Manège

JARDIN DES TUILERIES

River

Tuileries

PONT LOUIS XVI
(under construction)

Seine

PONT ROYAL

CHAMP DE MARS

Invalides

École Militaire

FAUBOURG ST. GERMAIN

L'abbaye

PONT NE

Cordel

RUE DE SÈVRES

Luxembourg

FAUBOURG ST. MICHEL

Approximate line of inner
boulevards, The Old City Wall

Paris at the time of the Revolution

FAUBOURG
DENIS

FAUBOURG
DU TEMPLE

RUE ST. DENIS

RUE ST. MARTIN

RUE DU TEMPLE

Temple

La Force

RUE DE LA ROQUETTE

Bicêtre

Châtelet

RUE ST. ANTOINE

RUE DE CHARONNE

PLACE DE GRÈVE

ais

ustice

Hôtel de
Ville

Notre Dame

PONT MARIE

Bastille

FAUBOURG
ST. ANTOINE

RUE DE MONTREUIL

Archevêché

PONT DE LA TOURNELLE

RUE DE

FAUBOURG
ST. VICTOR

Panthéon

PLACE DU
TRONE

RUE DE CHARENTON

BOURG
ACQUES

R. MOUFFETARD

Salpétriere

FAUBOURG
ST. MARCEL

the year, were due to the machinations of the aristocracy. As royal government broke down, the riots which almost invariably accompanied the movements of grain convoys became more frequent and more serious, and these in turn increased the general alarm. When the new harvest began to ripen the peasants armed themselves, often with official approval, to defend their crops and their households against 'the poor', the roving bands of vagrants who perpetually plagued rural France, their numbers now being swollen by the unemployed and the destitute. For this again the aristocracy were held responsible, it being believed that bands of brigands were being paid to terrorise the countryside and to destroy the standing corn.

Attacks upon the châteaux inevitably followed. Beginning in the spring, these were immensely stimulated in July by the crisis in the capital, by the movement of troops and by the revolutions in the towns, and as July turned to August further outbreaks accompanied the 'Great Fear', the sudden alarm that swept across France and caused almost the whole rural population to arm itself against the approach of 'brigands'. To this extent, indeed, the peasant risings were intended to anticipate the supposed plots of the aristocracy, and it may be that if Louis had not abandoned his apparent attempt to intimidate Paris, many scattered bodies of armed men might have united in a march upon the city. What happened was sufficiently decisive, for the fall of what Desmoulins called 'the 30,000 Bastilles of France' hastened the first massive emigration of the nobility in August and September.

The peasantry, however, had another objective in attacking the châteaux: the destruction of the manorial rolls which recorded the obligations every peasant proprietor and tenant had to his seigneur. Since these included onerous payments such as the *champart*, the seigneurial equivalent of the tithe which alone accounted for about an eighth of the crop, as well as antiquated restrictions upon enterprise and improvement, like the hated game laws and the monopoly in milling, they were at best a heavy additional burden upon men already bearing the weight of both royal and clerical taxation. In the years before the Revolution, however, these rights were often grossly abused and exploited. Sometimes the seigneur, himself impoverished and perhaps quite heavily taxed, tried to maintain his income and his social standing by enforcing his rights, and sometimes townsmen, or syndicates of townsmen, bought up some or all of them for a capital sum and exploited them still more ruthlessly. Against these exactions, and against the employment of skilled land-agents and experts in feudal law, the peasant had practically no redress, for whoever held the rights held also documentary evidence of them, as well as the control of the seigneurial court in which disputes were decided. Complaint in the *cahiers* having proved ineffective, the châteaux were attacked, and although violence against persons seems to have been relatively rare—perhaps because so few lords retained their rights—the manorial rolls were either destroyed separately, or went up in flames with the house that contained them. The new Municipal authorities, by no means disinterested, endeavoured to restore order, and at least one instance of savage repression occurred. The old order in the countryside, however, could never be restored.

In this way the people of France in the summer of 1789 simultaneously freed themselves from the supervision of royal bureaucracy and from the greatest burdens of the seigneurial system, and took a mighty stride towards self-government and economic independence. The deputies at Versailles could not repudiate this revolution, for it was their own: although there were concealed conflicts of interest between the middle-class and the masses, the whole of the Third Estate desired the destruction of autocracy and aristocracy. Moreover, any extensive repression of disorder could only be effected by those royal forces which the Assembly itself had most reason to fear. Yet the reports they received were exceedingly alarming: the payment of taxation was being refused, and life and property seemed everywhere in danger. In Paris itself a startling outrage occurred on 22nd July, when Berthier de Sauvigny, the intendant of the area, and his father-in-law, Fouillon de Doué, who were held to have aggravated food shortages in the capital, were torn from the hands of the municipal authorities and brutally lynched by angry crowds. Alarmed by the approach of anarchy, yet convinced of the existence of an aristocratic conspiracy, the Assembly almost recognised the reality of what was openly called 'a state of war'. Duport demanded the creation of a provisional tribunal to deal with crimes of *lèse-nation*, the new name now given to treason. Barnave alienated many more moderate men, including his colleague Mounier, by his apparent readiness to condone the murder of Berthier ('Is the blood which has run then so pure?' he asked). The necessity of regularising the situation certainly lay behind the famous session of the night of 4th August, when 'feudalism was abolished'.

This great occasion was by no means so spontaneous as used to be supposed. Apart from the obvious interest of the nobility in renouncing much that they had already lost in order to retain the rest more surely, the proceedings of the evening were prepared and initiated for a political purpose by those deputies who were members of the Breton Club, the forerunner of the future Jacobin Society. This association began even before the Estates-General was officially opened, as an informal meeting at the Café Amaury of the deputies from Brittany, who soon showed themselves such bold advocates of the cause of the Third Estate that others were attracted to their conferences. They soon became concerned with the preparation of policy: they probably contributed to the successful defiance of the king at the close of the Royal Session on 23rd June; and after the fall of the Bastille and the surrender of the king, they sought, as 'Patriots', to ensure that the victory of the Third Estate over the other orders was consolidated by a formal declaration of the rights which all men should enjoy as equals in a society stripped of privilege.

This proposal had already been considered by the Assembly's committee, and it was indeed accepted in principle early on 4th August. The Patriots, however, regarded it as a test case for the success of future legislation, and feared lest it should be frustrated by a combination of nobles and clergy and all those of the commons who felt bound to represent some particular interest. They feared, further, that if the declaration were prevented, privilege and particularism might become entrenched in an upper chamber, or at least succeed in making prohibitive majorities necessary for fundamental legislation. The members of the Club therefore resolved, as one of them wrote on 5th August, 'to use a kind of magic whereby, calling a truce to constitutional questions, we would obliterate the privileges of classes, provinces, towns and corporations'. It was arranged that the duc d'Aiguillon, a great liberal landowner, should propose that feudal dues and services should be made redeemable by purchase.

In the event, d'Aiguillon was forestalled by a younger man, the landless vicomte de Noailles, who more recklessly demanded that all personal services, as distinct from dues on peasant properties, should be abolished without compensation. This was the proposal which the Assembly first adopted. Thereafter, amid mounting excitement and in an atmosphere strangely compounded of calculation, genuine generosity and patriotic exaltation, noble deputies vied with one another in sacrificing their privileges, and the deputies of the provinces and cities of France followed the example set by the delegations of Dauphiné and Brittany in surrendering their privileges also. Only at two o'clock in the morning did the Assembly disperse, after ordering that a medal should be struck to commemorate the day and that a *Te Deum* should be sung throughout the kingdom.

In the course of the next few days these resolutions were made definitive, and the extent of what was called 'the St Bartholomew of property' became apparent. Despite the breath-taking initial announcement that 'the National Assembly abolishes the feudal régime entirely', these decrees of 5th to 11th August had something of a reactionary tendency, for it was decided to exact redemption payments for all dues not directly derived from personal servitude. In practice, however, the attempts which were made until 1793 to enforce these payments proved futile. If the peasants' enthusiasm for the new order was cooled by the discovery that while they were free, their land was not, they had nevertheless seen the greatest of their grievances—many onerous obligations, the game laws and seigneurial justice—altogether abolished. Apart from this, the decrees cleared the way for a real reorganisation of French life. All exemptions from taxation were abolished, property-in-office was suppressed (with compensation), and all employments in the public services were declared open to all without distinction of birth. As these decisions foreshadowed a reconstruction of the financial, administrative and judicial systems, so the reform of the Church was initiated by the suppression of pluralities and the abolition of the tithe, subject only to the provision of revenue for religious purposes 'by some other means'. Above all, the unification of the nation was clearly promoted by the disappearance of social privileges, as well as those of the provinces and the cities. These last were sacrificed for the sake of 'a national constitution and public liberty', and it is indeed remarkable that to this end the Assembly had assumed and exercised a degree of authority far greater than Louis XIV would have dared to contemplate even at the height of his power.

The representatives of the first two orders being sufficiently weakened by these decrees, and the worst of the popular crisis being past, the Assembly proceeded to discuss the Declaration of Rights, which was finally formulated and proclaimed on 26th August.[1] On 5th August, however, Louis XVI had written to the Archbishop of Arles: 'I will never consent to the spoliation of my clergy and of my nobility. I will not sanction decrees by which they are despoiled.' Faced first with the decrees of 5th to 11th August, and then with the Declaration of Rights, Louis adopted an inactivity as momentous, if less deliberate, than that of the Third Estate in May. His evasion forced the Assembly into premature consideration of the important constitutional question of what right the king should have to delay, or even to veto, legislation, and this caused deep divisions of opinion in the Assembly, alarming opinion in Paris for a second time.

Mounier, the hero of the Tennis-Court Oath, now appeared as the advocate of a constitutional settlement on the English model, to which all who were alarmed by radical legislation and public unrest might rally. Towards the end of August he and his supporters, who became known as the 'Englishmen' or 'Monarchicals', proposed that the constitution should establish a second chamber, and that the king should have both an absolute veto and the right of appealing to the electorate through a dissolution of the legislature. Boldly moderate though these proposals were, they were not altogether foreign to the feelings of the Assembly. The king being thought of as misled by evil advisers, the majority of deputies desired no more than, as one of them said, 'to regenerate the monarchy and reorganise the traditional régime on a sound basis'. There was also general agreement that the constitution should distribute and limit power, lest any part of government should become what Lally-Tollendal spoke of as 'a single power . . . which should end by devouring all'. Many therefore agreed with Mounier's contention that the

[1] See below, Chapter 3.

question was one of recognising realities, of accepting the monarchy as an established authority and of regulating the royal rights by agreement. His attempt to unite the aristocracy and the moderates in Versailles, as he had done in Dauphiné the year before, nevertheless failed completely. His 'Senate' was universally regarded as a new stronghold for privilege, as a thing incompatible with equality and with the supremacy of the general will. Even the Right repudiated him, foreseeing that a second chamber would represent wealth rather than rank, and being determined to compromise no further with the Revolution. The 'Senate' was therefore rejected on 10th September by 849 votes to 89, and Mounier resigned from the constitutional committee.

Still deeper differences of view developed about the veto itself, and the popular press, which now included the early numbers of Marat's[1] *L'Ami du peuple*, condemned it outright as a return to despotism. Deputies who supported it were branded as 'ignorant, corrupt and suspect'; they were hooted at from the galleries, and even threatened with violence in the streets. Agitation at the Palais-Royal reached fever pitch, and on 30th August the adventurer marquis de St-Huruge attempted to lead a march to Versailles to bring Louis to the Louvre in Paris. Despite this, Mirabeau and many others in the Assembly risked their reputations by defending the veto and showing that even an elected assembly could become corrupt and tyrannical. On the other hand, Robespierre, who had gradually become the spokesman of the extreme democrats, won his reputation in Paris by rejecting as 'a monstrosity, practically and morally inconceivable', the idea that 'one man alone' should be able to oppose the will of the nation. Theory was again still more explicitly asserted by Sieyès. In his view, the assembled representatives of the sovereign people were fully competent to create or suppress whatever they pleased, and their first care should be to secure the independence of the legislature from all outside interference: 'If the king's will is capable of equalling that of twenty-five million people . . . it would be a *lettre de cachet* against the general will.'[2]

---

[1] Marat (Jean Paul), b. 1744, was physician to the guards of the comte d'Artois before the Revolution and was bitterly resentful because the French Academy would not recognise the originality of his experiments in optics and with electricity. As the Revolution developed he came to believe that a dictatorship was necessary and adopted ever more bloodthirsty language. He was, however, genuinely concerned about the welfare of the poor and was all too often right in his denunciations of the faint-hearted and self-interested. Largely responsible for the Revolution of 2nd June 1793, he was murdered in July of that year.

[2] *Lettres de cachet*, or orders for the arrest and indefinite imprisonment of particular persons without trial by command of the king, were regarded as one of the greatest abuses of the *ancien régime*. They were in fact most commonly secured by parents for the correction of disobedient young men and women.

On 11th September, the Assembly accepted a solution proposed by Barnave, once Mounier's lieutenant and now his successful rival. By this the king was to have a suspensive veto, to last for the lifetime of two legislatures, and the right of dissolution was implicitly abandoned. This decision, probably the only possible compromise, was one full of fateful consequence. In their legitimate desire to ensure that the general will was adequately ascertained through successive elections, the Assembly had given the king a power of delay so protracted as to be for practical purposes interminable, and to place this in the hands of Louis XVI and Marie-Antoinette—'M and Mme Veto'—was almost to invite a second revolution as soon as the constitution should become operative. Of more immediate importance, the decision was the result of an understanding between Barnave and Necker by which Louis was to accept the August decrees and the Declaration of Rights if the suspensive veto were approved. Necker, however, failed in this attempt to redeem his rapidly fading reputation, for Louis remained obdurate. Thus a further major decree was added to those already awaiting the royal approval, and many deputies, feeling that they had been betrayed by the court, became sympathetic to the rising demand in Paris that Louis should be brought to the capital.

A new crisis now approached from all directions. Technically, since all the outstanding decrees were held to be constitutional in nature, and since the Assembly's constituent power was by now generally held to supersede all existing authority, the king's sanction was not essential. On 11th September even Mounier admitted: 'The Constitution needs no royal approval, for it is anterior to the monarchy.' The Assembly nevertheless tried to avoid the theoretical issue, seeking throughout September some formula by which Louis might 'promulgate', 'approve', 'publish' or 'accept' the decrees. Louis, however, evaded all approaches, and again acted as if he were preparing to fall back on military force. On 15th September 1,000 men of the Flanders Regiment were summoned to Versailles, and an attempt was made to win the support of the National Guard there. In Paris, too, poverty and hunger had again combined with political anxieties to stretch public patience to its limit. The exodus of the aristocracy had aggravated unemployment and hardship amongst all those who served and supplied them. A windless period had delayed the milling of the harvest, and the municipality's reduction of the price of bread to twelve sous for the four-pound loaf was enforced only by the presence of armed guards at the bakers' shops. All was again ascribed to an aristocratic plot, *le pacte de famine*. The presence of the king and the court in Paris seemed the solution to all these problems, and throughout September the demand for it mounted.

The occasion for a new revolutionary 'day' or *journée* was provided by a banquet given on 1st October by the officers of the Bodyguard to mark

59

the arrival of the Flanders Regiment at Versailles. Itself sufficient to arouse a hungry capital, this was accompanied by a royalist demonstration. According to angry press reports on 3rd October, the white cockade of the Bourbons and the black of Austria were flaunted as Louis and Marie-Antoinette made a tour of the tables to the strains of the royalist air 'O Richard, ô mon roi', while the national colours were trampled underfoot. Thus insulted, the Revolution seemed likely to be immolated. The district assemblies met in permanent session. Danton demanded punishments at the Cordeliers, Desmoulins exhorted the people at the Palais Royal. Early on 5th October Paris was ready and the tocsin rang. From the central markets and the Faubourg St Antoine women converged on the Hôtel de Ville, and ransacked it in search of arms. They then 'persuaded' Maillard, a lanky young man who had distinguished himself on 14th July, to lead them to beg the king and the Assembly for bread. Dragging cannon collected from the Châtelet, they set off, some 7,000 strong, to march in epic demonstration to Versailles through twelve miles and more of mud and rain.

Louis, recalled from hunting in the early afternoon, had fair warning of the advance, and ample time either to escape or to block the bridges over the Seine at Sevrès and St Cloud. Nothing was done. Soon after five o'clock the women arrived before the palace. Led by a particularly flamboyant adventuress, Théroigne de Mericourt, some of them sapped the resistance of the soldiers, while others, armed and bedraggled as they were, followed Maillard into the Assembly and joined the deputies on the benches. From the confusion, a decision emerged: Mounier, who was presiding, would lead a delegation of the women to ask the king to provision Paris 'when the decrees were accepted'—a significant indication of the deputies' readiness to make use of the masses. The interview took place, Louis being gracious and the women much moved. One, indeed, was set upon by the crowd as a suspected royalist, and was almost strangled with her own garters; but bread was promised. The crowd began to disperse, the troops were ordered to stand down. Dramatic though it was, the women's intervention had accomplished nothing. Now, however, came the news that the National Guard of Paris was also on the march. Having allowed the women to leave, La Fayette and the municipality had eventually let themselves be persuaded to 'invite' Louis to Paris, and an army of 20,000 men, including the French Guards and accompanied by further armed crowds, had left the capital at dusk. Mounier joined Marie-Antoinette and the Council in urging the king to fly, and all preparations were made. Louis, however, scorned the indignity of flight and instead at last notified the Assembly of his acceptance, 'pure and simple', of their decrees. As on 14th July, organised force had proved decisive.

Only when the National Guard had arrived and La Fayette came to the palace late at night did Louis learn that he was also expected to go to Paris.

His decision, deferred until morning, was by then made for him, for although the night passed quietly enough, ugly episodes occurred as 6th October dawned. Some of the crowd found an unguarded gate, penetrated into the palace, clashed bloodily with the queen's guards, and stabbed and slashed the bed from which she had scarcely escaped to safety. As Sergeant Hoche of the French Guards restored order in the palace, other casualties occurred in the courtyard, and when La Fayette brought the Royal Family to the balcony to calm the crowd, all stood in danger of their lives. Peace was restored, and the troops exchanged insignia, but the repeated cry '*À Paris!*' was not to be ignored. La Fayette himself announced that Louis had accepted the move as well as the Declaration of Rights, and a section of the crowd left at once for the capital, bearing as trophies of victory the severed heads of two of the Bodyguard. At mid-day the Royal Family set out, the centre of a vast procession of carts and cannon and marching men. Before them went the royal troops, disarmed amid the National Guard; beside their coach rode La Fayette; and behind came the carriages of 100 deputies, the Assembly's token of its decision to remain inseparable from the king. A mixed multitude of weary but triumphant men and women, gay and garlanded with oak and poplar, escorted all to Paris. So, after lengthy civic ceremonies, Louis came at last to the long-abandoned palace of the Tuileries.

By chance, greater prosperity returned as the court came to the capital. Although further bread riots disturbed October, the benefits of a bountiful harvest helped the authorities to control distribution, and until the spring of 1791 social peace prevailed. Orléans, to whom much villainy was ascribed, was despatched for a time to London, and many 'aristocratic' deputies—including Mounier[1] and some of the 'Monarchicals'—gave up their seats rather than accompany the Assembly to its new home in the Manège, the converted riding-school of the Tuileries. The people who crowded into the palace gardens cried '*Vive le Roi!*' as well as '*Vive la Nation!*', and for a second time the Revolution seemed to be over. As Desmoulins wrote, 'the king is in the Louvre, the National Assembly is at the Tuileries, . . . the corn-mills are grinding, the traitors are in full flight . . . the patriots have triumphed'.

The Revolution of 1789 had indeed effectively advanced the transference of power to the nation. New controversies would inevitably arise among the victors for its possession and about the purposes to which it should be applied, but its nature, and the way in which it would be exercised, particularly in

[1] Mounier (Jean Joseph), b. 1758, had led the movement in Dauphiné in 1788 and been elected for the Third Estate there in 1789. After the October Days he returned to Dauphiné and attempted to rally the moderates there to the Provincial Estates. When the National Assembly banned such assemblies, he went into exile, to return in 1801 and become a councillor of state. Died 1806.

times of crisis, had already become apparent. Twice in six months the feebleness of the king and the intransigence of the aristocracy had led the Assembly to assert its own omnicompetence as the embodiment of the general will of the sovereign people; twice had the power of Paris been deployed to counter the threat of reaction; and the revolt of the towns and the countryside had ensured that the defeat of both the royal administration and the aristocracy was nation-wide. Assembly and people alike had become familiar with the theory and the practice of national sovereignty.

3

The Regeneration of France

After the October days the National Assembly was free to apply itself to the reconstruction and regeneration of the kingdom. The Constitution nevertheless took two long years to complete, being produced piecemeal as the Assembly tried to regulate situations in accordance with the principles already proclaimed in the Declaration of Rights, the foundation deed of the Revolution.

The Declaration undoubtedly proved an embarrassment to the Assembly, and historians have not hesitated to condemn the deputies for debating it at length during the disorders of August, as well as for promulgating principles certain to conflict with any constitution that could be created. Indeed, Malouet and Mirabeau warned the Assembly at the time that it was inadvisable to inform people of their rights before they had become accustomed to constitutional government. The general faith in enlightenment, however, overcame such doubts as these. The majority of deputies were convinced that as bondage had been born of ignorance, so men's knowledge of their rights would fit them for freedom. As La Fayette put it, only a nation which could recognise liberty could learn to love it. In August, moreover, there was a real need to establish the new order upon a solid *de jure* foundation, and since historic right in France could sanction only the powers of the crown and the aristocracy, appeal had to be made to a supposedly more fundamental principle. This was found in 'the natural order of things', in rights which were deemed to be of universal validity because they were derived from the very nature of man. The assertion of the superiority of these natural rights also had a quite practical purpose: almost every article in the Declaration, however general its expression, related directly to some abuse of the *ancien régime*, as the prohibition of arrest by arbitrary order referred to administrative arrest by *lettre de cachet*. It was not for nothing that the Declaration was drafted, or that hundreds of thousands of copies of it were swiftly despatched to all parts of France. Wherever men met who professed to be patriots, it appeared as a sign of allegiance, a token of the repudiation of the past and of faith in the future.

The first words of the first article enshrined the achievement of the men of '89 in overthrowing autocracy and privilege: 'All men are born and remain free and equal in rights.' The Declaration then asserted, as natural rights, certain fundamental human freedoms and some principles essential to self-government. Arbitrary and brutal arrest, imprisonment without trial, immoderate punishments and the imposition of penalties by retrospective law were prohibited. Freedom of opinion, 'even in religion', freedom of speech and the freedom of the press were proclaimed; the right of the citizen to call officials to account, and to consent to legislation and taxation through his chosen representatives, was recognised. The sanctity of property was also asserted, for the revolutionaries were not concerned to depose property for the sake of some greater communal good, but to establish it as an attribute of freedom. Equality in rights, however, was emphatically asserted: the famous first article announced that 'social distinctions may be based only upon general utility', and other articles affirmed the equality of all citizens before the law, in liability to taxation and in admissibility to all public offices 'without other distinction than that of virtues and talents'. The Declaration of the Rights of Man and the Citizen was, and remains, an outstanding statement of the great principles of liberal democracy. It may, indeed, be criticised as encouraging an excess of individualism.

On the other hand, it also contains an authoritarian tendency, and Aulard's designation of it as 'the death certificate of the old order' has even been taken to apply not only to the autocracy of the *ancien régime* but also to the individualism characteristic of the Enlightenment. The Declaration is in fact as much concerned with society as with the individual, who is as often envisaged as a citizen as he is as a man. Many, although not all, of the rights it affirms are explicitly made relative to the interests of society, and are clearly dependent upon the operation of the law—to the summons of which the citizen is required to render instant obedience. Even the 'sacred and inalienable' right of property stands subject to the requirements of legally-constituted public necessity. Law itself is defined as being the expression of the 'general will', a phrase sometimes dismissed as a convenient catchword, and sometimes identified with a dangerously abstract moral concept. In reality, it originally meant no more than the will of the majority as expressed in an elected representative assembly. The use of the term nevertheless reflects a contradiction: the revolutionaries were determined to limit autocracy by established rights, by a constitution and by the separation of the powers of government; but they were not conditioned to think of government in terms other than those of will. In its third article, moreover, the Declaration established the foundation of the new order by affirming that 'the source of all sovereignty resides essentially in the nation'. This was no doubt intended primarily to mark the complete repudiation of the sovereignty of the crown: no longer was France to be regarded only as a piece of royal property. In effect, however, as Burke perceived, the revolutionaries were substituting for the arbitrary will of the king the no less arbitrary will of the majority, and this they were identifying with an abstraction, the nation, and making the ultimate arbiter of every right. Revolutionary liberty was thus from its inception the twin-brother of authoritarianism.

After the Assembly had moved to Paris the deputies had not only to reform the institutions of France without infringing these principles, but also to do so under the direct observation of an exceedingly suspicious city. To an English visitor, Paris even at this peaceful time seemed like a city besieged, its people roused by martial music and sent to rest to the rattle of patriot drums. The sixty electoral districts still governed the capital, so far as it was governed at all, and each guarded its independence jealously, competing with the others in patriotic ardour and vigilance. Across the river from the Manège, Danton[1] already reigned as the uncrowned king of radical opposition to all authority. Near his home the Cordeliers Club was soon to be established, sponsoring a profusion of popular political societies under its symbol, an ever-open eye. The mushroom growth of the press, moreover, had produced a multiplicity of papers and periodicals which left little unobserved. Some, like the *Moniteur*, were semi-official and restrained; some were as full of patriotic earnestness as Brissot's[2] *Patriote français*, and some were as obscene and scurrilous as the royalist *Actes des Apôtres;* but all were political.

The Assembly itself derived some benefit from its cramped accommodation in the converted riding-school, for it was now normally possible to restrict admission to the galleries to ticket-holders. On the other hand, however, it became increasingly involved in local affairs, receiving not only endless deputations demonstrative of patriotism, but also appeals such as that made to it by the Cordeliers District against the Municipality in November 1789. Speeches, too, now had to be written more for publication than for reading. Although in these circumstances the Assembly remained much more independent of its environment than did its successors, the

---

[1] Danton (George Jacques), b. 1759 at Arcis-sur-Aube. Little is known of his earlier career, but having become a solicitor's clerk in Paris in 1780 he was called to the bar in 1785 and two years later purchased position at the bar of one of the more select of the courts of appeal—the Court of the King's Councils. In 1789 he was living on the first floor of the house which stood at the corner of the Cour de Commerce and the Rue des Cordeliers on the south bank of the Seine, and as the leading member of the club which met in the disused Cordeliers convent he rapidly became prominent as a demagogue.

[2] Brissot (Jacques Pierre), b. 1754 at Chartres, the thirteenth son of a pastry-cook. Although he remained poor throughout his life, by 1789 he had acquired a considerable reputation as a reforming journalist who had visited Switzerland, Britain and America, as well as being imprisoned in the Bastille. After being a member of the new Municipal Assembly of Paris he was elected as one of the deputies of the capital to the Legislative Assembly in 1791, and as a prominent Jacobin he rapidly assumed the leadership of the left wing in that parliament. *See below, p. 88 et seq.*

removal to Paris undoubtedly ruined the hope of Sieyès that the new parliament would be as independent of the electorate as of the executive.

- A great many 'Patriot' deputies were indeed already associated in a society dedicated to the opposite purpose. The Breton Club, officially dissolved in October, was speedily re-established in Paris, first in the Place des Victoires and then in the disused Dominican monastery in the Rue St Honoré, across the road from the Manège. Commonly called, from its meeting-place, the Jacobin Club, the Society of the Friends of the Constitution soon had as its foremost function the enlightenment and the representation of public opinion. Substantial sums were spent on the distribution of patriotic propaganda throughout France, and the Society habitually had on its agenda the business that the National Assembly was to consider the next day. Moreover, it was from the beginning an exclusive body: although it followed the precedent of the Breton Club in admitting men who were not deputies, a substantial entrance fee and an annual subscription long limited membership to men of some standing. More significantly, would-be members had to have several nominations and to secure considerable, if not unanimous, support in the Club, while absence or heterodoxy brought censure and expulsion. Membership thus meant both honour and influence, and the strength of the Society steadily increased, more than 1,000 names being recorded on its roll in December 1790.

Amid these various pressures, the Assembly soon made manifest its determination that control of the Revolution should be retained by the wealthy middle-class. There was to be a constitution to end arbitrary government and to guarantee individual rights, and equality of opportunity would reinvigorate every institution, but the deputies did not propose to tolerate disorder, to see property endangered, or to act as if all men were already sufficiently enlightened and responsible to take part in matters of government. On 21st October, only two days after its arrival in Paris, the Assembly authorised local authorities to suppress public disorders by martial law. After a red flag had been displayed, public assemblies would become illegal, and might be dispersed by military force—necessarily that of the National Guard, a middle-class militia always intended as much for the maintenance of law and order as for the defence of freedom against attack from above. A week later, on 29th October, the recommendations of the Constitutional Committee regarding the electoral system were accepted. These drastically limited both the franchise and eligibility for election, a distinction being made for this purpose between 'active' and 'passive' citizens. Only 'active' citizens, those who paid the equivalent of three days' wages in annual taxation, were enfranchised, and, by a further distinction, only those paying the equivalent of ten days' wages were to be eligible for election to secondary electoral assemblies, local councils and local administrative offices. Eligibility for election to the national parliament was made conditional upon still higher qualifications, the notorious *marc d'argent* (a tax-payment equivalent to fifty-four days' labour) and the possession of some landed property.

These decrees were justified by a differentiation, first drawn by Sieyès and Barnave, between political rights and political functions. All were entitled, by this agreement, to the protection of their rights to life, liberty and property, but only some could be held competent to fulfil political duties; and the measure of responsibility and incorruptibility was property ownership. The effect of this was to reduce the electorate by about one-third, from six to four millions. If the difficulties of determining tax assessments had not proved insuperable, the effective control of elections and local government would have been left to only 50,000 men. All this caused widespread resentment amongst the politically-conscious, to whom it seemed that the Assembly, circumventing the Declaration of Rights by subtle and specious arguments, was sanctioning a new inequality and an aristocracy of wealth. It seemed obvious that the Assembly did not trust the people. 'You would relegate Christ himself to the *canaille*', wrote Desmoulins, 'the active citizens are those who took the Bastille.' Only Robespierre,[1] Buzot,[2] Pétion[3] and a few others dared to defend democracy, and so preserved their reputations for patriotic integrity.

Further, the Assembly also showed itself determined to extend the sanctity of property right, which then implied principally the right of free development, to the promotion of complete freedom of trade within the national frontiers. Free trade in corn was already established in August 1789,

[1] Robespierre (Maximilien François Marie Isadore) was born at Arras on 6th May 1758 and left an orphan at the age of seven. Educated, like Desmoulins, at the Jesuit College of Louis le Grand at Paris, he returned to Arras to become a successful lawyer who was noted for his enlightenment and sympathies for the poor. As deputy for Arras in the National Assembly and as a member of the Jacobins, he soon established himself as an uncompromising democrat.

[2] Buzot (François Nicholas Léonard), b. 1760, lawyer and deputy for the Third Estate of Évreux, to which he returned in 1791. Becoming a deputy to the Convention for the Eure in 1792, he also became an admirer of Madame Roland and one of the most active opponents of Robespierre in the Assembly. Regarded as an advocate of federalism, he was proscribed in the Revolution of 2nd June 1793, escaped to Évreux and fled from there with Pétion to the Gironde, where both were found dead near St-Émilion in 1794.

[3] Pétion de Villeneuve (Jérôme), b. 1753, lawyer and deputy for the Third Estate of Chartres, was one of those sent to bring Louis XVI back to Paris after the Flight to Varennes. Elected Mayor of Paris in November 1791, he courted popularity and avoided any assertion of authority. Thrust aside at the Revolution of 10th August, he became an opponent of Robespierre, of whom he was certainly jealous, and he fled from Paris with Guadet after the Revolution of 2nd June 1793. Going by way of Caen to St-Émilion, he was found dead with Buzot in June 1794.

and in October 1790 all internal tariff barriers were abolished. This eventually advanced both national prosperity and national unity, but it was contrary to the immediate interests of the common people of both town and country. They wanted the distribution and prices of all essential commodities to be controlled. Only the relative prosperity of 1790 and 1791 prevented serious unrest. In its economic as well as in its political decisions, the Constituent thus early identified itself with a narrow social strata, and made the security of all its work dependent upon a combination of effective government and favourable economic conditions.

The possibility of good administration, however, diminished almost daily. The Assembly could never overcome its inveterate distrust of the royal government, which it regarded at best as incompetent to effect the Revolution, and at worst as guilty of deliberate duplicity. The standing committees of the Assembly, of which there were no fewer than thirty-one, were consequently zealous in supervising ministers and in issuing their own detailed instructions for the application of general decrees. They constantly encroached upon and confused the work of government. The king himself was recognised in the constitutional decrees of 1st October 1789 as the supreme head of the executive, but in practice his powers of appointing and controlling his officers were whittled away until he was reduced to impotence, and although on several occasions he assured the Assembly of his unreserved acceptance of all that was being achieved, he could never really bring himself to put his trust in anyone who mattered.

Men, too, were lacking. Necker, once so popular, had forfeited public confidence by his failure to raise revenue or to control the court. La Fayette had power at his disposal, but he refused to accept routine responsibilities. As commander of the powerful National Guard of Paris, he controlled a carefully recruited bourgeois force, sworn to maintain the Nation, the King and the Law, and he aspired to co-ordinate and command all such forces throughout France. Nevertheless, he held himself perpetually in reserve as one dedicated to the protection of the constitution from either the king or the crowd. Louis, and still more Marie-Antoinette, regarded him as an unreliable renegade, and the radicals soon made mock of him as a figure of fun.

Mirabeau, on the other hand, could never acquire the power he so obviously desired and could have used so well. Bold, flamboyant, vigorous, and once as profligate as La Fayette was prim, he had forced the suspicious Third Estate to recognise him as its bravest champion against the other orders, and he had not hesitated to defy even the king in the interests of the nation. But although he was, as Malouet said, 'the mainspring of power in the National Assembly', he remained universally distrusted. Believing as he did that the new order could only be grounded upon the co-operation and partnership of king and commons, he courted suspicion by trying to ensure that the crown kept

5   La Fayette, as Commander of the National Guard, 1790
From an engraving by and after P. L. Debucourt

6   The Fête de la Fédération at the Champ de Mars, 14th July 1790
From an engraving by I. S. Helman after C. Monnet

7   The 'Massacre' at the Champ de Mars, 17th July 1791
From an engraving by P. G. Berthault after J. L. Prieur

sufficient strength and independence to govern effectively, and his support of the absolute veto seemed particular proof of his unreliability.

After the October days Mirabeau apparently regarded the situation of both king and country as desperate, and so proposed two courses to the court. One plan, that Louis should leave Paris and establish himself in independence in some provincial city, was to appear in an endless variety of forms in the long series of Notes which were submitted to the court in return for regular payment from the middle of 1790 onwards. The other, at first equally or even more important, was that the king should appoint a responsible ministry from the principal members of the Assembly, and that Mirabeau himself should be one of those selected. The only result of his move in this direction, however, was to end the possibility of such a solution. Neither Louis nor Marie-Antoinette would contemplate the appointment of Mirabeau. No-one, least of all La Fayette, would consider working with him. The very rumour of his plan aroused all the Assembly's devotion to the separation of powers and all its suspicions of the executive, of royal corruption and of Mirabeau himself. On 7th November 1789 a decree was passed declaring it illegal for any deputy to accept office under the crown. The problems of liaison, of political responsibility and above all of mutual trust in government, remained unsolved.

But although the foundations of the new France, in government and social unity, were to prove insufficiently secure, at the end of 1789 it seemed that the great hopes which had inspired the Revolution were at last being made into realities. Within the next eighteen months a mass of legislation was enacted, so comprehensive that such matters as army reform, religious toleration, and the laws governing marriage and inheritance were no more than minor features of it. Of more immediate importance were the decrees of 14th and 22nd December 1789, and 26th January 1790, which reformed local government, legalising the independence achieved in the revolutions of the previous July and establishing the principles of equality in nationhood which had been proclaimed in August. France was now divided into its famous eighty-three departments, the ancient provinces being disregarded as strongholds of privilege and particularism, and the *généralités* of the intendants ignored as areas of royal authority. Each department was sub-divided into districts and every town and parish was preserved as a community.[1] This

---

[1] Similar provision was made for Paris, the administration of which was technically divided between the Municipality and the Department of Paris, in the wider area of which the city was included; and the law of 21st May 1790, divided the city for administrative and electoral purposes into forty-eight sections. As elsewhere, controversy persisted between the civic authority and that of the more conservative Department; and the arrangements were resented as an attempt to destroy the independence of the original sixty districts, 'which had made the Revolution'.

The 83 Departments of France, 1790
(excluding Corsica)

THE AUSTRIAN NETHERLANDS

THE EMPIRE

SWITZERLAND

SAVOY

NICE

SPAIN

N

NORD

PAS DE CALAIS

SOMME

SEINE INFÉRIEURE

OISE

AISNE

ARDENNES

MEUSE

MOSELLE

MEURTHE

BAS-RHIN

MANCHE

CALVADOS

EURE

ORNE

SEINE ET OISE

PARIS

SEINE ET MARNE

MARNE

VOSGES

HAUT-RHIN

FINISTÈRE

CÔTES-DU-NORD

ILLE ET VILAINE

MAYENNE

SARTHE

EURE ET LOIR

AUBE

HAUTE-MARNE

MORBIHAN

LOIR-ET-CHER

LOIRET

YONNE

HAUTE-SAÔNE

LOIRE INFÉRIEURE

MAINE ET LOIRE

INDRE ET LOIRE

CÔTE D'OR

DOUBS

VENDÉE

DEUX SÈVRES

VIENNE

CHER

NIÈVRE

SAÔNE-ET-LOIRE

JURA

ALLIER

CHARENTE INFÉRIEURE

CHARENTE

HAUTE-VIENNE

CREUSE

PUY-DE-DÔME

RHÔNE ET LOIRE

AIN

CORRÈZE

DORDOGNE

CANTAL

HAUTE-LOIRE

ISÈRE

GIRONDE

LOT ET GARONNE

LOT

AVEYRON

LOZÈRE

ARDÈCHE

DRÔME

HAUTES-ALPES

LANDES

GERS

TARN

GARD

AVIGNON C. VENAISSIN

BASSES-ALPES

BASSES-PYRÉNÉES

HAUTES-PYRÉNÉES

HAUTE-GARONNE

HÉRAULT

BOUCHES-DU-RHÔNE

VAR

ARIÈGE

AUDE

PYRÉNÉES ORIENTALES

Paris became the Department
of the Seine; Rhône-et-Loire
was divided into Rhône and
Loire, as two Departments.
As a result of the first annexations,
Mont-Blanc—i.e. Savoie and Haute-Savoie—
came from Savoy; Alpes-Maritimes from Nice and
Monaco; Mont-Terrible—i.e. Territory-de-Belfort—
from the district of Porentruy; and Vaucluse from Avignon
and the Comtat-Venaissin. By 1799 there were 90 *départements* in all.

new administrative geography, while far simpler and more systematic than the old, was not imposed for the sake of symmetry, but was regarded as a restoration of the natural areas and boundaries of local life. Outside Paris, it still withstands the increasingly stringent tests of time.

In 1789, moreover, every town and village and every district of the countryside became for all practical purposes an autonomous unit, responsible not only for its communal life but also for many matters of public order and taxation which would have been better directed from a higher level. Within the limits set by the restriction of the franchise and the processes of indirect election, the public life of these innumerable local communities was intended to be highly democratic. Elaborate regulations governed elections; all officials were to be elected and subject to the supervision of elected assemblies; and assemblies and officials alike were to retire at frequent intervals. In practice this did not long endure. The complexity and frequency of elections led almost inevitably to disillusionment, and antagonisms soon developed between the departmental directories, which were generally conservative, and the more radical municipalities, which were more directly representative of the smaller property-owners. The Assembly, too, had failed to make adequate provision for financing local government, and in its distrust of the executive it had expressly forbidden the creation of any media for central co-ordination and control.

Complete confusion soon prevailed, and this provided the local political societies with endless opportunities to acquire power. Clubs, often directly descended from the 'literary' societies of the *ancien régime*, had increased enormously in numbers and in importance when the Revolution began, for all men then sought to learn the latest news from Versailles and Paris. Their members, generally respectable and fairly well-to-do townsmen of the middle or lower middle-class, now formed the active minority which voted regularly, chivvied apathetic or hostile officials about a thousand and one matters of local administration, and exploited to the hilt the jealousies and conflicts of the various authorities. The more enterprising and 'patriotic' sought greater strength in affiliation with others through some local centre, and the final reward of merit was found in direct or indirect affiliation with the Jacobin Club in Paris. A new form of centralisation thus gradually emerged from the ruins of the old, and it was one which controlled opinion as well as power. Views favoured by the Society in the Rue St Honoré were disseminated to the daughter societies throughout France, which modelled themselves upon Paris, expelled the lax and unorthodox as unpatriotic, and acted as watch-dogs of the Revolution. At the same time the Jacobins in Paris were kept informed by correspondence of revolutionary opinion in the provincial towns, and came to control the men who controlled local government.

71

The democratic experiment of 1790, however, is not a thing to be dismissed. For a short space France became a federation of democracies, in which the status of citizen was held to be an honour. The 'active' citizen was more than a tax-payer: he had also to be a man aged twenty-five or more, and one who was resident in his constituency and had publicly sworn the civic oath 'to maintain the constitution of the kingdom, to be faithful to the nation, the law and the king, and to perform with zeal and courage the civil and political duties' entrusted to him. As France paused briefly between two forms of central control, that of the monarchy and that of the modern nation, a new age seemed to dawn, in which *fraternité* seemed inseparable from *liberté*. The democracy of the day was much more a religious faith than a political expedient, and in celebrating their citizenship ordinary people experienced something of the brotherhood of man and foresaw the federation of the world. In innumerable ceremonies of confederation in 1789 and 1790 old age and youth marched together in procession, children crowned councillors with oak-leaves, ministers of rival faiths celebrated mass together, and weddings and baptisms were solemnised a second time on altars dedicated to the country. By the spring of 1790 these ingenuous festivals of fraternity and freedom had risen above regional level, and the demand for a national ceremony had become irresistible.

The *Fête de la Fédération* which was held at Paris on the first anniversary of the fall of the Bastille is not unworthy of description, for it was perhaps the greatest day of the whole Revolution. In preparation for it, all the titles and insignia of nobility were abolished, and 12,000 men were set to work to prepare an enormous arena at the Champ de Mars. When their labour proved inadequate, the people of Paris marched out each evening behind the banners of their sections, and shifted soil till sunset. Meanwhile, National Guardsmen were marching to Paris from all parts of France.[1] On the day itself, despite torrential rain and 'aristocratic' weather, a crowd approaching 400,000 strong assembled on the man-made slopes. Twelve thousand regular troops, all the Parisian National Guard, and 14,000 more from the provinces, formed up along the streets leading from the site of the Bastille and marched to the Tuileries, there to be joined by the Assembly and the Municipality.

Crossing the Seine by a bridge of boats, the procession entered the arena through a triumphal arch, and while the soldiers ranged themselves on either side of a central avenue, the deputies and the councillors from every department advanced to their places alongside the king and the court at the far end of the amphitheatre. Three hundred priests, clad in white and wearing sashes *à la nation*, then joined Talleyrand, the Bishop of Autun, in celebrating

---

[1] Sometimes singing, according to Michelet, to music which was still solemn, the hymn *ça ira*: '*Celui qui s'élève, on l'abaissera.*'

mass before the great central altar and in blessing the banners of the eighty-three departments. As the song of the choristers died away, La Fayette dismounted and went forward to swear, on behalf of the military and the citizen-militia, to be eternally faithful to the nation, the law, the king and the constitution, and 'to remain united with every Frenchman by the indissoluble ties of fraternity'. When the deputies had repeated the oath, Louis, who alone remained under cover, swore as King of the French to maintain the constitution. The queen raised the dauphin in her arms, the banners were lowered in line as cannon-fire crashed out, and all joined in a final hymn of thanksgiving. Despite the cynicism displayed by Talleyrand, the rejoicing was general and sincere: countless medals were struck to commemorate the day, and there was public dancing at night on the site of the Bastille.

A simpler ceremony, but one no less significant, took place just three months later in the Palais de Justice. The Parlements, 'buried alive' when their vacation was extended indefinitely on 3rd November 1789, had been formally suppressed on 7th September 1790; but they kept a Vacation Court in session to deal with urgent business. On 14th October the work of this court was concluded, and its officers heard their president declare: 'The sitting is raised.' All the magistrates then left the Palais, and its doors were closed to clients for the first time for almost 500 years. On the next day the Mayor, Bailly, came with La Fayette and other municipal officers to receive the keys of the building and to supervise the fixing of seals on all its courtrooms and archives. Thus the reign of the parlements ended, and the way was cleared for the inauguration of a new judicial system.

This reform was one of the principal objectives of the Revolution, and its accomplishment in the careful legislation of August 1790 is one of the most creditable and enduring achievements of the time. All existing tribunals were suppressed, and the complexity and confusion characteristic of the old judicial administration gave way to a simple and uniform system, co-ordinate with that of the reformed local government. Each constituency had its justice of the peace, each district its court of five judges, and a later decree also established a criminal court for each department. In accordance with the democratic spirit of the day, all justices and judges were to be elected and paid, venality in any form being illegal. The new courts were forbidden to recognise any privilege or priority, and they were strictly confined to judicial functions. Reform of the civil law could only be begun, but the penal code was clarified and made more humane. The work of the monarchy in abolishing torture was confirmed, and the death penalty was to be inflicted only by decapitation—an extension of an aristocratic privilege to all. Criminal procedure also ceased to be arbitrary: arrest had to be by judicial warrant; a first hearing had to take place within twenty-four hours; and trial had to be held in public and decided by a jury chosen by ballot. These were all enlightened measures, and although the use of the electoral principle may be questioned, the judges, who had to be lawyers of at least five years' standing, were in practice both well-qualified and well-chosen.

In this reform, however, the Assembly again showed that it had too much faith in the people and all too little confidence in the royal government. Some deputies certainly believed that laws could become a simple statement of the moral code, so enlightening to men that courts would be superfluous; many hoped that much litigation could give way to agreements between citizens; and almost all feared a recrudescence of the power of the crown, or of some new form of the superior courts. The judiciary was therefore made wholly independent of the king, who now lost even the prerogative of mercy and had only a formal part in the appointment of the judges. On the other hand, the Assembly did all in its power to maintain the superiority of the legislature. No Supreme Court was established to consider constitutional issues, and when the reluctant Assembly finally agreed, on 27th November 1790, to the creation of a Court of Appeal, it insisted upon receiving an annual report of its proceedings as well as particular reports of any judgement likely to affect the interpretation of the law. The trial of treason—of crime against '*la sûreté générale de l'État*'—was reserved for a further High Court, which could only be convened by the particular command of the legislative body and could only proceed on indictment from it. The power of parliament, representing the will of the people, thus remained unrestricted by the judiciary, and the creation later in the Revolution of extraordinary tribunals could not be questioned or curtailed by the established courts.

In 1791, however, optimism prevailed. On 27th January the Court of the First Arrondissement of Paris opened its session in the old Court of Requests in the Palais de Justice, its officers attired in their new dress of sombre black, relieved only by the tricolour ribbon. At the end of April 1791, the Court of Appeal was installed in the old Grand' Chambre. The new era of justice in France opened as these and other courts steadily cleared up a considerable back-log of cases, which were in general treated far more quickly and fairly than in the past.

More fatal consequences followed from the Assembly's attempt to solve the financial problems of the state by confiscating the lands of the Church. By the autumn of 1789 it had become apparent that the financial crisis was more serious than ever. Old taxes were not being paid, new ones had yet to be formulated, and while the nation was accepting great new burdens— particularly the buying-up of venal offices—Necker was reduced to day-to-day borrowings and appeals for patriotic contributions to the Treasury. At the same time the abolition of the tithe in August 1789 had committed the Assembly to making financial provision for the Church, the reform of which was in any case implicit in the Revolution. Hardly had the crisis of October

1789 passed than these issues were again brought into common focus by Talleyrand's proposal that the nation should appropriate one-third of the lands of the Church. This was developed by Mirabeau into the decree of 2nd November, a simple fiat by which all ecclesiastical property was placed 'at the disposal of the nation', subject to provision being made for the support of religion and poor relief.

The property thus acquired, estimated by Rabaut St Étienne as being one-fifth of the land of France, only needed to be made negotiable to give immediate backing to government credit. An extraordinary treasury was therefore established on 19th December to issue interest-bearing bonds to the value of 400 million livres, these being redeemable either in land or in the proceeds of its sale.[1] The public, however, were reluctant to accept these *assignats* before specific sales were arranged or before the legal position regarding existing ecclesiastical mortgages was known. The Assembly was therefore forced to press on with the reorganisation of the Church, and in April 1790 it had also to proclaim the *assignats* to be legal tender and to authorise their issue in smaller denominations. So, despite the opposition of Necker, who left the country in disgrace in October 1790, a paper currency was created. In the lifetime of the National Assembly this was beneficial and stimulating to credit and the economy, for although further issues totalling 1,500 million livres followed in September 1790 and in the May and June of 1791, these did not exceed the value of the security. Indeed, even counterfeiting and the common practice of issuing private '*billets de confiance*' akin to assignats did not cause their value to fall below 85 per cent. A tempting road to irresponsible finance and reckless policies had nonetheless been opened to future assemblies.

The appropriation of Church lands implied the prohibition of monastic vows, the pensioning-off of monks and nuns, and finally a new Civil Constitution of the Clergy, which the Assembly debated for six weeks before accepting it on 12th July 1790. The new organisation was again closely correlated to that of local government. A bishopric was allocated to each department and provision was made for a reorganisation of parishes so that there would be one for every 6,000 people. All other bishoprics and benefices, as well as a great many ecclesiastical dignities, were suppressed. Bishops and parish priests were to be elected exactly as were the departmental and district assemblies, and eligibility was made dependent upon specified terms of previous service in the priesthood in the diocese or parish. All bishops and priests were to be paid by the civil authority and were to have a pension on

---

[1] The *livre* or *franc* was a standard of value approximating to ten pence in English money at this time. For comparative purposes, it suffices to take twenty francs to the pound sterling. The *sou* was one-twentieth of the livre.

retirement, but they had also to observe strict regulations about residence. Unauthorised absence meant first a loss of salary and eventually the loss of office.

Drastic as this plan appears, it was not born of antagonism to religion. The Assembly had indeed on more than one occasion refused to recognise Catholicism as the only authorised religion of the nation, but this decision, like that which afforded toleration to men of every faith, was largely due to a reluctance to accept the existence of distinctions between equal citizens. Indifferent though they were to denominational controversy, the majority of the deputies desired to associate religion intimately with the Revolution. As the Estates-General had opened with a solemn mass, and as the night of 4th August had concluded with the call for a general *Te Deum*, so the Declaration of Rights had begun with an invocation to the Supreme Being. To men who regarded religion as eternal reason, a rational reform which would also foster men's natural desire for freedom and equality could not be irreligious.

The clergy in fact found much to attract them in their new constitution. In an age when increasing state control of the Church was commonplace in Europe, the French Church, traditionally closer to the monarchy than to Rome, was predisposed to still closer association with the temporal authority. Material advantages, too, were manifold. The lower clergy, the first allies of the Third Estate, gained by the doubling of their salaries and by the destruction of the old aristocratic monopoly of high appointments. The bishops were now freed from much of the burden of administration and estate-management that had prevented even the best of them from giving much attention to their spiritual duties, and such obvious abuses as pluralism and absenteeism would become impossible. Many priests, moreover, shared the common lay belief that the reform would restore simplicity to an over-worldly Church, and would associate the spiritual with the political regeneration of mankind.

No amount of goodwill, however, could long conceal the fact that the Assembly was reducing the Church to a department of state and requiring of its clergy, as of other officers, an oath of allegiance to the nation. Some priests were indeed able to accept the view that the organisation of the Church could be distinguished from its doctrine and controlled by the sovereign people, to whom the royal rights of appointment had reverted. To these, the clauses in the Civil Constitution which required all priests to secure 'canonical confirmation' of their appointments from an established superior, and which enjoined the bishops also to notify the Pope, seemed a sufficient guarantee of the continuity of the apostolic succession and the unity of the faith. Many others, however, regarded doctrine and discipline as inseparable and foresaw the impossibility of maintaining any spiritual unity in a Church whose priests were more responsible to a local electorate than to their own bishops.

Those who had these doubts denied the right of the state to regulate the Church before it had been consulted as a body and had expressed its own consent. No such consultation, however, was forthcoming. Some of the deputies feared that a National Council of the Church would concentrate all kinds of opposition to the Revolution, and some were convinced that the very existence of such a corporate body, bound by its nature to promote a particular interest, was incompatible with the true representation and accomplishment of the general will. Clerical criticism of the Civil Constitution could therefore only be expressed in the Assembly itself or in its Ecclesiastical Committee, and in both of these the clergy were in a minority. Those who, like Maury, challenged the rights of the state, encountered men superbly confident of the omnicompetence of a popular representative assembly. As Camus, the Jansenist lawyer who was one of the chief architects of the reform, put it: 'The Church is within the state, not the state within the Church. . . . We are a national convention. We certainly have the power to alter religion itself, but we will not do so; to abandon the Church would be a criminal act.'

In all this the clergy were left without guidance either from the monarchy or from the papacy. On the advice of the Archbishops of Aix and Bordeaux, Louis accepted the Civil Constitution on 22nd July 1790 and sought the sanction of the Holy See. Pope Pius VI had already secretly condemned the Declaration of Rights and the dissolution of the monastic orders, but now he remained silent. Influenced partly by his interests in Avignon and partly by his reluctance to precipitate a crisis, he neither condemned nor approved. In fact, of course, only men blandly indifferent to the nature and purpose of his authority could have expected him to condone a unilateral breach of the Concordat of 1516 and the complete subordination of one-third of the Catholic Church to the power of a particular state. A long delay ensued, during which some livings fell vacant, and some were filled by election, until by October the bishops had become sufficiently alarmed to publish an Exposition of Principles. Signed by all the bishops in the Assembly except Talleyrand and Gobel,[1] and subsequently approved by nearly 100 others, this implied that papal approval and proper consultation with the Church should precede the application of the Civil Constitution. The Assembly, on the other hand, felt bound to enforce its law; further decrees, accepted on 27th November and 24th December and reluctantly sanctioned by the king

---

[1] Gobel (Jean Baptiste Joseph), b. 1727, Canon of Porrentruy and Bishop of Lydda, he sat for the clergy of Belfort in 1789 and became Constitutional Bishop of Paris in 1791. Driven to renounce Christianity in 1793, he was executed with the Hébertists in 1794.

on 26th December, specifically required all holders of clerical office to take the oath of allegiance to the nation and the constitution 'and especially the decrees relative to the Civil Constitution of the Clergy'. Refusal was to entail the loss of office, and anyone who then continued his ministry would be prosecuted as a disturber of the public peace.

The clergy of France were thus forced to decide for themselves between Catholicism and the Revolution, between the sovereignty of the people and the authority of Rome, which for many of them represented the sovereignty of God. Many, indeed, were found ready to forgo all their hopes and to risk persecution for the sake of their faith. In a dramatic session of the Assembly on 2nd January 1791 two-thirds of the *curés* and every bishop present except Talleyrand and Gobel refused the oath, although there were angry and abusive crowds in the galleries and in the streets outside. A fortnight later, abuse or acclamation awaited those who made their declarations from the pulpits. The returns which were then made showed that, in all, only seven bishops and approximately half the 50,000 *curés* of France had consented to become 'constitutional' priests. This breach was soon widened by the rival authorities. The Assembly ordered new incumbents to be elected where non-jurors had sacrificed their livings, and in February 1791 Talleyrand and Gobel consecrated the first elected bishops. In March and April Pope Pius condemned all these developments: the Civil Constitution was denounced as schismatic and heretical, all elections were declared null and void, and Talleyrand and Gobel, as well as any others who failed to retract their oath within forty days, were suspended. Although many did so, the Church, which had once been fully prepared to be the partner of the state, remained irretrievably divided.

Worse still, the whole nation was gradually split asunder, the Assembly having utterly failed to appreciate the strength and sincerity of the ordinary people's attachment to their faith. Compelled in their turn to choose between one priest and another, and eventually even between civil disobedience and the risk of damnation, French men and women became as divided as their Church. There were considerable differences between regions, western France in particular remaining loyal to the orthodox clergy, but the commonest distinction was that between town and country. In general, rural areas rejected and resisted the constitutional clergy, while the towns, and more particularly the members of the Jacobin Clubs, repudiated the non-jurors as enemies of the people. On 7th May 1791, the Assembly optimistically accepted a moderate motion from Talleyrand by which full liberty of conscience was allowed to all, but in reality the situation had passed beyond legislative control. Intimidation, physical violence and administrative persecution were becoming commonplace.

The Assembly's work for the regeneration of France consequently approached completion in 1791 in circumstances wholly prejudicial to its prospects of enduring success. All the antagonisms already produced by the arbitrary introduction of revolutionary legislation were now acerbated by religious dissension. In the absence of effective government, counter-revolution seemed to have some real chance of victory. By now many of the lesser nobility, alienated by the loss of their offices, of their rights of inheritance and even of their titles, had joined the *émigrés* of 1789 and had come to believe, as they did, that France was where the lilies were, and that Artois was king while Louis was in captivity. From Turin, Artois himself had constantly intrigued to effect a military rising in France, and even in 1790 his extensive plans had brought a real threat to the security of the Revolution. The 'Languedoc plan', an attempt to exploit the bitter fighting which occurred there between the Catholics and Protestants, helped to produce a great demonstration at Jalès in August 1790, where 20,000 royalist 'national guards' swore to 'reinstate the king in his glory, the clergy in their property, the nobles in their privileges and the parlements in their ancient functions'. Another scheme, the 'Lyons plan', was exposed only a few days before 15th December 1790, the date fixed for a 'general explosion' in eastern France. After this, the *émigrés* accepted Calonne's guidance and prepared their own forces for an invasion, seeking financial and military aid from the princes of Europe, and particularly from Marie-Antoinette's brother, Leopold of Austria. Although an appeal to the emperor was rebuffed at Mantua in May, Artois moved his headquarters to Coblentz on 15th June, and Condé[1] and Mirabeau-Tonneau[2] began to assemble armies at Worms and Colmar for an invasion of France from the Rhine.

As news of these developments reached Paris the rise in public anxiety was marked by a recrudescence of patriotic disorders. On 28th February 1,000 men of the Faubourg St Antoine marched to Vincennes as to a second Bastille, supposing the *donjon* of the château to be linked to the Tuileries by some secret passage. The king's aunts, who emigrated a few days before, were barely allowed to leave Paris, and when in mid-April Louis himself tried to go to St Cloud to receive the Easter communion from non-juring priests, the royal coach was held back by hostile crowds. Suspicion of all authority was redoubled, and men began to speak of an 'Austrian committee' at court, supposedly controlling events and preparing to crush the Revolution.

[1] Condé (Louis Joseph de Bourbon, Prince de), b. 1736, had served in the Seven Years War. After emigrating in July 1789 he formed the army of the *émigrés* for the Princes and led it until 1800. Retiring to England in 1801, he returned to France at the Restoration and died in 1818.

[2] I.e. 'Barrel' Mirabeau, the orator's younger brother, a man noted for his extreme royalism, drunkenness and corpulence.

79

Economic unrest also increased the tension again, for although the price of bread remained stable at eight sous, changing conditions were creating new problems. While more and more unemployed, principally people from the declining luxury trades, had to be provided for in the municipal workshops, the first effects of inflation produced an agitation in the more prosperous trades for higher wages, and this developed rapidly into a campaign so extensive that early in June the Assembly was warned of '*une coalition générale*' among 80,000 Paris workers. Political and economic unrest alike found expression in the popular clubs which had multiplied in Paris since Dansard had founded the first of the Fraternal Societies in February 1790. Encouraged by Marat in *L'Ami du peuple* and by Bonneville in *La Bouche de fer*, as well as by the Cordeliers Club, these societies challenged authority and taught democratic and even republican ideas to 'active' and 'passive' citizens alike. By May 1791 they had their own central committee.

To this growing agitation the Municipality and the Assembly now showed increasing hostility. When Mirabeau died suddenly at the beginning of April 1791, the influence of Barnave and his associates Duport and Alexandre de Lameth[1]—together the 'Triumvirate'—increased greatly. They identified themselves with the view that, as the Constitution was almost completed and elections to the first Legislative Assembly were about to begin, the time had come to bring the Revolution to a halt. In May and June, therefore, measures were passed to consolidate middle-class control of the situation. The municipal workshops were closed down, collective petitioning was forbidden and 'passive' citizens were explicitly excluded from the National Guard. On 14th June, moreover, the famous *Loi Chapelier* forbade strikes and prohibited all associations of employers or working men. Although this law was to prove an intolerable burden to the French working class for almost 100 years, in 1791 it evoked little comment. Free individual bargaining about labour then seemed a natural corollary of the Revolution, and corporate bodies of all kinds were identified with privilege and the distortion of the general will by 'partial' interests.

[1] Duport (Adrien, 1759-98), and Lameth (Alexandre Théodore Victor, Chevalier de, 1760-1829), were associated with Barnave with the attempt to stabilise the Revolution after the death of Mirabeau and with the formation of the Feuillant Club. The former, a prominent liberal *parlementaire* and deputy for the nobility of Paris in 1789, was arrested after 10th August 1792, but escaped, probably with Danton's help, to Switzerland. The latter emigrated with La Fayette in 1792 and returned to France in 1800, holding various posts and honours under both the Empire and the Restoration. His brother, Charles Malo, Comte de Lameth, who had served with him in America and joined him as a liberal noble in 1789 and as a founder of the Feuillants, became a merchant at Hamburg after the Revolution of 1792 and lived to serve the emperor and to protest against the reactionary policy of Charles X in 1830, dying in 1832.

All this legislation was certainly supported for reasons which would now be described as social or economic, but at the time political considerations were at least equally important and the Assembly was as much, if not more, concerned about the activities of the popular societies and the exploitation of petitioning by clubs as it was about nascent trade unionism. Even Marat saw in the *Loi Chapelier* no more than an act of political discrimination against popular discussion. Disillusionment with the restrictive rule of the Assembly was no less general on this account in politically-conscious Paris. In rural France the peasantry, largely alienated by the treatment of the clergy, were also disillusioned by the Assembly's continued attempts to enforce taxation and the redemption of ancient dues, as well as by its failure to facilitate the purchase of Church lands in small plots.[1]

It was at this critical point in the Revolution that Louis elected to fly to the frontier. Despite his repeated protestations of loyalty to the Revolution, he had been considering projects for flight and for enlisting foreign aid ever since 1789. The king's real attitude is most apparent in the two documents he sent to Spain in October 1789, in which he repudiated all acts forced upon him and reaffirmed his attachment to the programme of royal reform outlined on 23rd June 1789. No serious attempt had been made to recover sufficient authority to effect this plan, for Louis had both a high sense of duty and a congenital inability to concentrate upon business or take decisions, a defect which drove his ministers to despair. He had refused, moreover, to countenance the plans of the *émigrés*, which seemed likely to lead to civil war, and he rightly suspected that Artois was more interested in the restoration of the *ancien régime* in its entirety than in the safety of the Royal Family. Mirabeau's schemes, which included increasingly desperate and irresponsible projects for discrediting the Assembly, had always insisted that the king should go into France and not towards the frontier; but these had been contemplated and cast aside, until Mirabeau died despairing of a monarchy which even he could not have saved.

By that time Louis's own secret plans were well advanced. In the autumn of 1790, when the successive resignations of his ministers had shown him something of his own impotence, the first steps had been taken: on 26th November, Breteuil was ordered to renew negotiations for foreign support, and Bouillé, the officer commanding the north-eastern frontier at Metz, was

[1] The Assembly was still trying to regulate the payment of tithe in March 1791. Although land could be bought on a twelve-year instalment plan and peasants could combine to purchase large fields for later division amongst themselves, the nationalised lands went generally to those who were already fairly well-to-do farmers. The provisions of the *Loi Chapelier* were later applied to the countryside in the Rural Code of September 1791, which also favoured freedom in agriculture—including the enclosure or free grazing of commons—at the expense of communal rights and practices.

told to prepare to receive the king. The imposition of the oath upon the clergy, which Louis only sanctioned at great cost to his conscience, certainly completed his alienation from the Revolution, and the episode on 18th April 1791, when he was prevented from going to St Cloud, as certainly confirmed him in his intention to escape. At seven o'clock in the morning of 21st June 1791 the king's valet, Lemoine, drew back the bed curtains to awaken his master, and discovered that Louis had gone.

Few episodes illustrate in so striking a manner as the king's flight the part played by fortune in the affairs of men. Between ten o'clock and midnight on 20th June the queen's devoted admirer, Count Axel de Fersen, had successfully spirited the whole Royal Family—Louis and Marie-Antoinette, their two children, the king's sister Mme Elisabeth, the governess Mme de Tourzel and two serving women—out of the Tuileries by a door which, by negligence or contrivance, La Fayette had left unguarded. At the same time the Count of Provence and his wife left the Luxembourg Palace, to arrive easily in Brussels next day. The Royal Family's chances of similar success were compromised by the queen's insistence that they should all go together, a decision which prevented the use of a fast carriage and entailed an alarming advance of detachments of troops from Metz to meet and escort them. But it was the cumulative effect of a series of small delays which proved fatal: the royal troops stood down in succession before the 'treasure' they had been told to expect could arrive.

In twenty-four hours' continuous travel the royal party nevertheless reached Varennes, within easy reach of safety, before they were brought to a halt. At Ste-Ménehould, a few miles back, Louis had been recognised, and the posting-master, Drouet,[1] riding in pursuit, had learnt the coach's route by chance and had galloped across country quickly enough to close the road. The pitiful process of return by a roundabout route took three and a half days, and the party, escorted by National Guards with their arms reversed, re-entered Paris through great crowds of silent citizens. The queen's hair, it is said, was turned grey in the course of the week. Bouillé, a man already damned by the radicals for his ruthlessness in suppressing a serious mutiny at Nancy in the previous August, meanwhile deserted his command and crossed the frontier into Austrian territory.

Three weeks before this fiasco, French representatives abroad had been instructed in the king's name to deny reports that he was not free, and to assert his delight in the Constitution. When he fled he left behind him a

---

[1] Drouet subsequently became a violent deputy for Marne in the Convention. Being captured by the Austrians, he was exchanged for Madame Royale, Louis XVI's daughter, and returned to France to be implicated in Baboeuf's conspiracy. After helping to repel Nelson's attack on Teneriffe he returned to France again to become sub-prefect of Ste-Ménehould. Exiled in 1815, he remained quietly in the country until his death in 1824.

signed declaration condemning the measures he had accepted during his 'captivity'. From this it is clear that Louis was well aware that government had been destroyed in the name of popular sovereignty. The king complained that the Assembly, 'by denying him any control of the legislation it quite arbitrarily classified as constitutional' had placed him 'entirely outside the constitution' and reduced the crown to 'a vain semblance of monarchy'. In the royal analysis, indeed, all authority had been reduced to confusion; Louis saw his ministers as frustrated by the Assembly's committees and by the local authorities, which were also thwarting one another everywhere; he saw the licence of the press and the spirit of the clubs causing universal anarchy and discontent; and he saw grave perils in the growth of the Friends of the Constitution, 'an immense corporation, more dangerous than any that existed formerly'.

Despite this document, which of course furnished first-hand evidence of the king's insincerity in the past and undermined all possibility of faith in his word for the future, the Assembly from the beginning to the end of the crisis maintained the fiction that the Royal Family had been abducted by the enemies of the people. In short, it temporised, for it was confronted by a highly dangerous situation. On the one hand the king's flight made a royalist rising and a foreign attack, which had long been feared, seem imminent. On the other, political excitement in Paris flared up in a republican form. *Fleur-de-lys* were defaced in the streets and the Cordeliers Club led a campaign to decide 'what should be done about the executive'. Thus to renounce the monarchy seemed a certain way of precipitating war with Europe, and perhaps with half of France as well, while to renounce republicanism was to risk a new rising in Paris. The Assembly concentrated upon keeping control of France and providing for its defence. Meeting in permanent session, the deputies despatched representatives to the frontier areas, ordered the National Guard to furnish 100,000 volunteers for full-time service in the emergency, and exhorted all men to maintain law and order. They also assumed full sovereignty, proclaiming their decrees to have the force of law and authorising the ministers to take complete charge of the executive. The king was, by implication, suspended, and France became a republic *de facto* while remaining a monarchy *de jure*.

The Royal Family's ignominious return to Paris simply prolonged the dilemma. The republican movement gathered strength and the radical press demanded the deposition and even the execution of the king. The rulers of Europe, meanwhile, were compelled to abandon the convenient pretence that their brother of France was free. On 5th July Leopold of Austria bestirred himself to ask his fellow sovereigns to sign a common declaration demanding that Louis should be set at liberty and threatening vengeance for any further offence against him or his family. The Assembly still kept to its middle

course, merely confirming its first decrees, but behind the scenes the Triumvirate drew closer to La Fayette and the court, believing that they all had a
common interest in re-establishing constituted authority. Barnave, who had
been one of those sent by the Assembly to escort the Royal Family back to
Paris,[1] even entered into correspondence with the queen. He apparently
convinced himself that Leopold could be calmed, and the aristocratic Right
in the Assembly won over, if the king were restored and the Constitution
revised in order to strengthen the position of both the crown and the
middle-class.

When in mid-July the Assembly eventually opened its debate to regularise
the situation, Barnave therefore urged it to recognise that the Revolution was
over. 'If you lose faith in the Constitution,' he asked, 'where will you stop?
Where will your successors stop? This revolutionary movement has destroyed
all that it set out to destroy, and has brought us to the point where it is
necessary to halt . . . one step further towards liberty must destroy the
monarchy, one more towards equality must abolish private property'.
The Assembly, well aware of the risk of war and most unwilling to begin all
its work again, accepted the point. Despite the opposition of Robespierre and
a small minority, a decree was passed on 16th July which in effect provided
that the king should be reinstated as soon as the Constitution could be
completed and presented to him for acceptance.

The Cordeliers' republican campaign now became a dangerous one, and
the first effect of their persistence in it was to complete the breach that had
already opened between the democratic and the more conservative deputies
of the Left. On 15th July, before the Assembly's decision was taken, the
Cordeliers swept the Jacobins into joining them in a petition demanding the
deposition of the king and his 'replacement by constitutional means'. Next
day many Jacobins resigned in protest, and these soon afterwards established
a rival 'Society of the Friends of the Constitution', led by the Triumvirate
and known from its place of meeting as the Feuillants. On 17th July the
remaining Jacobins withdrew their support from the Cordeliers' petition,
which was now clearly contrary to the Assembly's decision. The Cordeliers,
however, had meanwhile found it necessary to promote a still more drastic
version of the document. This denied the validity of the Assembly's decree,
as contrary to the will of the sovereign people, and demanded that Louis
should abdicate and that a new constituent body should be called to reorganise the executive. After 6,000 people had signed this on the Altar of the
Country in the Champ de Mars, where 14th July had just been celebrated a
second time, the National Guard appeared in force. It was led by La Fayette
and Bailly, with the red flag displayed, for martial law had been proclaimed

---

[1] The others were Pétion and La Tour-Maubourg.

that morning after two men, found hiding beneath the planking of the altar steps, had been lynched in the streets. Firing almost inevitably followed, and some fifty people fell.

This use of force was but the beginning of a period in which the Municipality and the Assembly tried with considerable success not only to secure the safety of the streets but also to silence criticism and to end all popular political activity. The Feuillants were not sufficiently reactionary to 'crush the clubs', as some wished, but many radicals were arrested and several democratic papers were proscribed. Desmoulins, Robert and Marat went into hiding, and Danton fled to England for a time. Even Robespierre, who held a handful of Jacobins together in non-committal meetings, thought it well to move his lodgings to the Rue Saint-Honoré, close to the Assembly and the Club. Barnave and his associates could now hope to consolidate the Constitution without challenge from below—but in asserting their authority they had sundered themselves from the *menu peuple* of Paris. The 'massacre' of the Champ de Mars was not forgotten, and in the course of time Bailly was to be guillotined on the same spot, while the red flag was burnt before his eyes. However accidental the bloodshed may have been, the display of force from which it arose was a facet of a policy of reaction, and this could only be justified by the hope that the Revolution would be stabilised and an opportunity provided for peaceful development.

Even before the Assembly dissolved itself at the end of September the hollowness of any such hope, and the futility of relying upon the court instead of on the people, had become apparent. The queen, who at the behest of the Triumvirate wrote reassuringly to Leopold, secretly repudiated her letters and implored him to save the monarchy by armed intervention. The emperor, rightly judging that moderation was in control in France, was content to restrain Frederick William of Prussia and the *émigrés*, but he nevertheless supposed that his earlier threats had been of good effect, and so joined Frederick William in publishing the Declaration of Pillnitz on 27th August 1791. In this the two sovereigns undertook to take joint action to restore order in France if other monarchs would join them. Leopold knew well that the condition would not be fulfilled, and Marie-Antoinette at once recognised that 'the emperor has betrayed us'. To the people of France, however, the Declaration was a real threat, an ultimatum and an insult. The policy of the moderates was thus swiftly associated with dishonour, and one means of securing stability was soon proved unsuccessful.

The attempt to strengthen the monarchy by revising the Constitution was also a failure. The intransigents of the Right, whom the court either could not or would not control, simply refused to support proposals intended to consolidate the constitutional régime. The Left, for their part, were not unnaturally convinced that it would be folly to strengthen the hand of an untrustworthy king. Proposals such as those for a second chamber or for the admission of deputies to ministerial office had therefore to be abandoned. All that the Feuillants could do was to clamp the completed Constitution firmly upon France. Any future revision was made as complicated and protracted a process as possible, and middle-class control was reinforced by a further restriction of the franchise. As a concession to Robespierre and the democrats, the hated *marc d'argent* was dropped, so that any 'active' citizen could become a deputy; but at the same time the franchise was so restricted that the right of election to any office of real responsibility was confined to a very few substantial property owners. In practice even these amendments proved futile and dangerous, for the first Legislative Assembly was already being elected on the existing franchise, and within a year the rigidity of the Constitution was to make a new revolution unavoidable. As the Assembly also failed to revoke the rule established on Robespierre's proposition on 16th May by which no deputy was eligible for re-election, responsibility for the future was deliberately handed over to new men.

On 13th September 1791, Louis accepted the Constitution at a ceremony which also marked his own reinstatement. On 30th September, after he had reaffirmed his loyalty, the Assembly dissolved. Pétion and Robespierre alone received an ovation from the people, who saw in them the most stalwart champions of democratic rights, and perhaps recognised that for Robespierre the Revolution was still a positive movement. The departing Assembly, for whom it was already over, had helped to destroy an ancient order and to bring a free society to birth, but the very magnitude of its task had driven it to formulate and apply the new principle of power, the sovereignty of the people. This the Assembly fondly fancied it had confined within the clauses of an immutable Constitution, but it was not to be so easily restrained. The new parliament had inevitably to assert it against the ancient rights and powers upheld by the hostile kings of Europe. The nation itself, now free but deeply divided and quite ungoverned, would soon assert it also, in the clubs and in the streets, against both crown and parliament.

4

The Collapse
of the Constitution

In October 1791, when the Legislative Assembly first met in the Manège, the great majority of Frenchmen, though troubled by the attacks on the Church and disillusioned by the advantages afforded to the well-to-do, were still loyally attached to the Constitution and the monarchy. The majority of the new deputies, too, were men who had served the new régime successfully in its local courts and councils: they were moderate lawyers who desired above all to make the new Constitution work. Even the Feuillants, who now sat on the Right in considerable strength,[1] were ready to co-operate in this in order to achieve that conservative revision which the National Assembly had had to abandon. The deputies, however, were by no means in full control of the destinies of France. The king still retained the right to appoint and dismiss ministers as he chose, and since only the decision of three successive parliaments could invalidate his veto, his power to block decrees was almost absolute. Moreover, rival political authorities—the political clubs, and particularly the Jacobins, throughout France, as well as the sections and the municipality of Paris—were fast acquiring power outside the walls of the parliament, and the active minority which controlled these bodies was far from satisfied with the Constitution of 1791. To these men the general principles proclaimed in 1789 had come to mean that the nation ought to be a truly democratic, and preferably secular, state, in which all patriots could co-operate as equals to secure the common good. Even after Varennes the existence of an emasculated form of monarchy was just compatible with this attitude, but the royal veto and the obnoxious distinction between 'passive' and 'active' citizens, which symbolised the effective restriction of political power to the propertied classes, could only be accepted temporarily and on sufferance.

The Jacobin Club was by now fast regaining the power it had almost completely lost to the Feuillants in July. At first the Feuillants, having some control of the government's means of communication with the provinces,

---

[1] The fact that 264 of the new deputies registered as Feuillants and 350 remained uncommitted, whereas only 136 registered as Jacobins or Cordeliers, gives some indication of the balance of forces in the Assembly.

and having money to spend on propaganda, had won the support of many of the affiliated societies; the Jacobin remnant, meanwhile, had fast run into debt and had even been reduced to debating national affairs the day *after* their appearance on the agenda of the National Assembly. The resolution of Robespierre, however, had prevented any sacrifice of independence. Under his guidance the Jacobins had emerged from the crisis on the right side of the law, untainted either by the initial republican agitation or by the conservative reaction which rapidly destroyed the reputation of the Feuillants.[1] By September their membership had risen to almost 800, individual Feuillants were trying to return to the parent society, and some 500 new clubs were seeking affiliation with it. The admission of 'passive' citizens to membership of the Club, and the opening of its meetings to public audience, also greatly strengthened the Jacobins' position. Public galleries were installed in their hall in October, and the openness of their proceedings was ever afterwards the basis of their potent claim to be nothing more or less than a section of the people holding common council. On 28th October, when Robespierre returned to the Club after a short retirement to Arras, he was acclaimed and offered the chair in recognition of his part in this reconstruction, and under his direction more stringent tests of patriotism were soon being applied to applicants for membership or affiliation.[2]

Yet despite this recovery, which made the Jacobins more than ever a rival parliament to that in the Manège, their democratic and egalitarian suspicion of both king and parliament was restrained for a surprisingly long period by the respect generally afforded to the Constitution, which was regarded as law established by the power of the nation in assembly. Moreover, although only a minority of the new deputies had become members of the Society, some of these men were so outstanding in debate that they were for some months able to impose their policy on both the Society and the Assembly, and this too delayed the development of conflict between the two.

The most influential of the newcomers was Jean Pierre Brissot, a well-meaning but self-satisfied busybody who had raised himself from humble origins by prolific journalism and had acquired a wide reputation as an authority upon political and international affairs. As a co-opted member of the Municipality of Paris and as founder and first secretary of *Les Amis des Noirs*, a society for the emancipation of negroes, Brissot could claim acquaintance with liberal nobles like La Fayette as well as with radical democrats like

---

[1] The Jacobins' brief support for the Cordeliers' petition before the Champ de Mars 'massacre' was eventually to be represented as part of a plot by Brissot to bring about an Orléanist Regency.

[2] A campaign for the purification of affiliated societies was conducted in the winter of 1791–92, and some evidence suggests that a central training school for Jacobin agents might have been established in Paris. See J. M. Thompson, *Robespierre*, Vol. 1, p. 200.

8 Pétion

From a lithograph
by F. S. Delpech

9 Brissot
From a lithograph
by F. S. Delpech

10 Robespierre

From an engraving by Geoffroy

Robespierre. As editor of the *Patriote Français*, the most popular of the more earnest journals of the day, he also exercised considerable influence throughout France. He was in reality a man of words without wisdom, impulsive and irresponsible, and his background could easily be represented as one of dubious intrigue. His bustling activity and genuine idealism nevertheless enabled him to become the central figure of a group of friends which included the great mathematician and philosopher Condorcet, as well as three notable Jacobin barristers from Bordeaux. These were Gensonné, grave and severe; Guadet, savagely sarcastic in debate; and Vergniaud,[1] the greatest orator of them all, who was often statesmanlike but still more often indolent. Outside the Assembly all these deputies were associated with the friends of Madame Roland,[2] the attractive and ambitious wife of an elderly official from Lyons, a woman possessed by the dream of romantic republicanism. With some other deputies, like the violent and utterly irresponsible Isnard from Marseilles, these men formed a loose-knit group which became known as the Brissotins. Since Robespierre, who soon challenged their lead, was at first discredited in the ensuing conflict, they represented the majority of the Jacobins for the next six months, and although they were heavily outnumbered in the Assembly by more moderate men, they were able to dominate it by demanding vigorous action against counter-revolution at home and abroad.[3]

This demand was not unjustifiable. Far from ending the emigration, the amnesty which had accompanied the completion of the Constitution had

---

[1] Vergniaud (Pierre Victurnien), b. 1753, was the son of a minor army contractor who became bankrupt. Befriended by Turgot, he was educated at the College du Pléssis at Paris and was called to the bar in 1781; Guadet (Marguerite Élie), b. 1755, the son of the mayor of St.-Émilion, was leader of the Bordeaux bar in 1789 and president of its criminal court in 1791; Gensonne (Armand), b. 1758, the son of an army surgeon, was *procureur* of the Municipality of Bordeaux in 1790 and an appeal judge in 1791: having sent a report on Negro emancipation to the National Assembly, he was invited to investigate the religious question in western France, and presented this report to the Legislative Assembly. Vergniaud and Gensonné were executed at Paris on 31st October 1793, Guadet at Bordeaux on 20th June 1794.

[2] Manon, Jeanne Philipon, Madame Roland, b. 1754 at Paris, was brought up in the country by an uncle and married in 1780 Jean Marie Roland, b. 1734, a conscientious and hard-working civil servant who had acted as inspector of commerce in Paris and Amiens and who was appointed inspector-general of manufactures at Lyons in 1786. She established a salon at Paris in 1791, and he was appointed Minister of the Interior 23rd March–13th June 1792 and 10th August 1792–22nd January 1793. Madame Roland was imprisoned after the Revolution of 2nd June 1793 and executed 9th November 1793; Roland, who had fled from Paris, left his hiding place at Rouen and killed himself on hearing of her death, 10th November 1793.

[3] Brissot and his friends appear to have had some contact with Sieyès, who was now receding into the background of events; there seems no reason to think he influenced them much. See P. Bastid, *Sieyès et sa pensée* (Paris 1939), p. 124 *et seq.*

facilitated a massive new exodus of intransigent noblemen, whose womenfolk commonly sent little dolls to titled gentlemen in France in token of their contempt for those cowardly enough to compromise with the Revolution. Trade, employment and the administration were inevitably affected, but more important was the great loss of officers in the army: by 1792 two-thirds of the 9,000 officers of the line had left their regiments. *France extérieure*, as the emigrants called their court and company, certainly encouraged these desertions, as well as inciting the orthodox clergy in France to prevent the peasantry from purchasing nationalised land or even paying taxes. More violent resistance to the constitutional Church was also frequent, particularly in the Vendée, and as early as 9th October Gensonné had to tell the Assembly that the situation there would be most difficult to control. It is small wonder that the deputies and a great many other Frenchmen believed that Coblentz, where the Count of Provence now called himself Regent of the Kingdom, was the centre of a vast network of royal conspiracy, or that they ascribed every ill to the activities of agents who were financed and directed from beyond the frontier.

The Brissotins' first remedy for this evil, particularly advocated by Brissot himself and by Isnard, was that of drastic repression. As Isnard put it in a phrase which acquired dreadful and enduring popularity, 'We must amputate the gangrened limb to save the rest of the body'. On 31st October Provence was ordered to return to France within two months, a command which he treated as a joke, and on 9th November the Assembly decreed that all Frenchmen assembled beyond the frontiers would be treated as traitors unless they returned by the end of the year. Further, on 29th November the non-juring clergy were ordered to take the ordinary oath of civic allegiance within a week, under pain of being deemed unpatriotic and liable to deportation if any disturbance should occur in the places where they lived. The king for his part aggravated the situation by vetoing both decrees, conditional though they were—a fact which did not prevent many Jacobin-controlled authorities from enforcing them later.

Brissot, however, had meanwhile won widespread support for what he believed to be the fundamental solution to all the problems of France—the adoption of a much more aggressive foreign policy. In a bellicose speech on 20th October he argued forcibly that since the source of counter-revolution was at Coblentz, it was against Coblentz that blows must be struck. On 29th November, therefore, a deputation from the Assembly called upon the king to instruct him in the new diplomacy: he was to summon the Elector of Trier and other princes of Germany to disperse the *émigré* forces within a prescribed time, so that the nation might know its friends from its enemies, and he was to do so in language appropriate to 'the grandeur of an outraged nation'.

This was in effect a challenge to the Austrian Emperor, to whom the Elector was bound to turn for support: but Austria, since 1756 France's nominal ally, was almost universally hated as the hereditary enemy, and war against her seemed to Brissot and most of the Jacobins—though not to such men as Robespierre and Danton—to be positively desirable. They believed that it would strengthen credit and the economy by providing a demand for supplies of all kinds; they were convinced that it would end the disorder which was troubling France by destroying foreign support for sedition and by forcing those who opposed the Revolution to show themselves in their true colours. 'War', cried Brissot, 'is actually a national benefit. . . . A people which has won its freedom after ten centuries of slavery needs war; it needs war to purge away the vices of despotism, it needs war to banish from its bosom the men who might corrupt its liberty.' Again he declared: 'We need treachery on a grand scale; our salvation lies that way, for strong doses of poison remain in the body of France, and strong measures are necessary to expel them.' In particular, Brissot believed that war would compel the king to show where his loyalty lay: 'The chief executive officer will be forced to rule in accordance with the constitution. If he does his duty, we will support him whole-heartedly; but if he betrays us, the people will be ready.' Insurrection could not have been more obviously implied.

Despite the almost incredible stupidity of these views, Brissot and his supporters seem to have held them sincerely, preferring the prospect of open war to that of further fighting with a hidden enemy. Their critics have of course ever since asserted that their prime purpose was to storm the citadels of power: yet the whole situation was one in which war was implicit. The early idealism of May 1790, when the National Assembly had formally renounced all wars of conquest and declared that France would never take up arms against the liberty of any people, had not previously been put to any serious test, for Austria and Prussia were preoccupied with their own problems and had little thought for a France which seemed too disorganised either to assist or to injure them. The Emperor Leopold, who had succeeded Joseph II in 1790, had inherited an Empire apparently on the verge of dissolution, and he had had to patch up an agreement with Frederick William of Prussia and pacify both the Netherlands and Hungary. In 1791 and 1792, moreover, both he and Frederick William were much concerned about the danger that Catherine the Great of Russia would annex part or all of Poland, a state which perpetually invited partition. The plight of Marie-Antoinette, Leopold's sister, and the appeals of the French *émigrés* therefore had little effect upon Austrian policy before the flight to Varennes, and even after that the general growth of anxiety in western Europe only led Leopold to try the effect of threats of intervention. These, however, merely made matters worse. Frenchmen, who naturally knew nothing of the emperor's mental reservations at Pillnitz, failed to appreciate that the Austro-Prussian rapprochement was directed at least as much against Russia as against France, and they were convinced that the whole power of Europe was being arrayed against them in support of the king and the *émigrés*—whose armies, though ludicrous in retrospect, were regarded as a very real menace at the time. A threatening letter from Provence and Artois in September 1791 had confirmed this impression, and Brissot's call for a preventive war won a ready response from French opinion.

Nor were the Brissotins alone in their campaign. Barnave and the Lameths, the founders of the Feuillants, warned the Court and the Right that a military adventure could only benefit the extremists and identify the monarchy with a foreign foe; but their influence was soon superseded by that of La Fayette and the Count of Narbonne.[1] These militant nobles supposed that a swift and successful war, preferably limited to an assault upon the Elector, would enhance the prestige of the monarchy and enable them to effect a conservative revision of the Constitution. Their group maintained contact with Brissot and Condorcet by way of the salon of Madame de Staël, Narbonne's mistress, and it secured the appointment of Narbonne (who was reputedly an illegitimate son of Louis XV) as Minister for War.[2]

The king and queen, for their part, did all in their power to ensure that the emperor would resist French pressure. On 14th December 1791 Louis announced that the summons to the Elector had been sent, and Narbonne presented plans for the formation of three armies, one of which was to be commanded by La Fayette: but on the same day, Louis wrote privately to the emperor to explain that the ultimatum should be rejected. The king had already appealed secretly for armed intervention by a congress of the powers —'the best method', as he told the King of Prussia, 'of checking the factions here . . . and of preventing the evil which torments us from overcoming the other states of Europe'—but he was fully prepared to play along with the Feuillants to precipitate a conflict in which he felt sure the enfeebled French forces would be swept aside. 'The fools!' wrote Marie-Antoinette to Fersen,

---

[1] Louis, Comte de Narbonne-Lara, b. near Parma 1755, educated at Versailles 1760 onwards, was the dashing colonel of the Royal Piedmont Regiment; escorted the king's aunts to Rome, 1791, appointed Minister of War, probably through the influence of Madame de Staël, 6th December 1791–9th March 1792; able, sincerely tried to rally nation to throne, but offended Louis by tactless presumption; escaped from France, came to England, returned after Brumaire, d. 1813.

[2] Barnave soon afterwards retired to Dauphiné, as his old friend Mounier had done before him: arrested in September 1792, he was executed in November 1793. The Feuillant Club itself was closed down in the winter of 1791–92 on the pretext that it was within the precinct of the Assembly, although the name was long applied generally to the consti-tutional royalists.

'They can't even see that they are serving our purposes! . . . the best way they (the Powers) can help us is to fall upon us with the full weight of their forces.' Thus the royalists and the conservatives alike identified themselves exclusively with France, held their own interests to be those of the state, and proved themselves as politically bankrupt as were most of the Jacobins.

So assiduously sought, war approached inexorably. Ignoring Louis's injunctions, Leopold advised the Elector to order the émigrés to disperse, but he accompanied the concession with a show of force. As 1792 began, France learnt from an imperial despatch that although the émigrés' armies were being disbanded, Austrian troops had been ordered to protect the territory of Trier, 'since events give little evidence of stability or moderation in French affairs'. On 13th January Gensonné proposed that a new ultimatum be sent, this time to the emperor, and on 25th January the Assembly resolved that he should be required to give by 1st March 'a full and satisfactory reply' to the question whether he would renounce every treaty and convention directed against the sovereignty, independence and security of the nation. Austria and Prussia now drew still closer together, signing a defensive alliance on 7th February and beginning to prepare plans for joint action against France, and although the Austrian Chancellor, Kaunitz, sent only an indignant reply to France on 17th February, this inflamed opinion further by its arrogant denunciation of the Jacobins as the people most responsible for the crisis.

The deputies of the 'pernicious sect', as Kaunitz called the Jacobins, now seemed to be carrying all before them. Already spokesmen for a campaign which concentrated many divergent interests in a single channel, they also represented all those who resented foreign interference in French affairs, whether this sprang from jealousy of the ancient honour of France or from fervent belief in the virtue of the Revolution. These men, and most of those to whom they spoke, believed France and the Revolution to be in danger, believed France and its Constitution to have been slighted, and believed above all that France and freedom were identical and invincible. Encouraged in their illusions by a considerable number of democratic refugees from the Netherlands, Germany and Switzerland—men whom France could apparently shelter without inconsistency—Brissot and Isnard[1] encouraged others to

---

[1] Isnard (Maximin), b. 1751 near Nice, son of a merchant. A fiery and irresponsible deputy for Var in the Legislative Assembly and the Convention, he gave great offence to the Parisians in defending the independence of parliament, and retired after the Revolution of 2nd June 1793. Proscribed in the following October, he passed the Terror in hiding and eventually returned in February 1795 as one of the most violent enemies of the Terrorists. After being a member of the Council of Five Hundred he became a local official in Var, died 1825.

believe that in the impending war the armies of tyranny would melt away as the forces of freedom went forward, while the peoples would rise everywhere in welcome to their liberators. Nor, in this war of peoples against kings, in Brissot's crusade for universal freedom, were the possibilities of French expansion overlooked: Liège was to be liberated first, and if the Low Countries and the Rhineland then chose to associate themselves with France, her increased greatness could only help her to contribute the more to the happiness of mankind. Never can a war have been more joyfully fostered than in the atmosphere which enabled Isnard, ever incurably dramatic, to flourish a presentation sword in the Jacobin Society and to cry 'Gentlemen, this sword shall be for ever victorious! The French people will utter a great shout, and every other nation will answer to its call!'

Success came to the Brissotins in the spring of 1792. Maintaining their reputation as 'patriots' by vociferous criticism of the king and his more pacific ministers, they renewed, not without reason, the allegation that an 'Austrian Committee' at Court was trying to betray the Revolution. Delessart,[1] the Minister for Foreign Affairs, was a particular target for these attacks, and when on 9th March the king suddenly dismissed Narbonne, who had proved impossibly arrogant in office, Brissot and the deputies of the Gironde raised a mighty cry in the Assembly. The Tuileries being visible from the windows of the Manège, Vergniaud threatened those in the palace who misled the king, pointedly reminding 'all its inhabitants'—and, by implication, particularly Marie-Antoinette—that only the king himself was held inviolable by the Constitution. Delessart was impeached, the other ministers resigned, and a 'patriot' ministry was appointed. Led by Dumouriez,[2] an ambitious military adventurer, this included Roland and Clavière, both friends of Brissot. Dumouriez then continued Narbonne's policy, hoping like him that a successful campaign would serve to restore the royal authority. Preparations were made for an early invasion of the Netherlands,

---

[1] Lessart (Antoine de Valdec de), b. 1742, served under Necker, 1789–90, Minister of Finance 1790, of the Interior 1791 and of Foreign Affairs 30th November 1791–17th March 1792. Impeached, sent before High Court at Orléans, massacred at Versailles 9th September 1792.

[2] Dumouriez (Charles François Dupérier), b. 1739, served with distinction in the Seven Years War and being wounded and pensioned became a secret diplomatic agent. When his patron, Choiseul, fell he was sent to the Bastille, but being released on the accession of Louis XVI he became commanding officer at Cherburg. Able and confident, he welcomed the Revolution, brought himself to the notice of the king and became Foreign Minister and leader of the 'Patriot' ministry on the fall of Delessart in March 1792. Resigned 16th June 1792, became Commander of the Army of the North, won battle of Valmy 20th September 1792 but was defeated at Neerwinden 18th March 1793 and fled to Austrian lines on 5th April. After years of fruitless exile in Germany and Switzerland he came to England, lived at Acton 1803–1807 and Ealing 1812–22, died at Henley 1823.

and French diplomats made vain efforts to detach Prussia from Austria, although Frederick William was in fact far more belligerent than Leopold. The sudden death of the emperor on 1st March, and the accession of the more warlike young Francis II, brought matters to a head. A final ultimatum sent by Dumouriez was left unanswered, and on 20th April the Assembly approved a declaration of war, only seven contrary votes being recorded.

The war was justified at the time principally as a necessary preventive measure against foreign-based counter-revolution, and although the fears of the French are now known to have been exaggerated, it is still possible to suggest that Austrian intimidation and imminent Prussian aggression were real contributory causes. Indeed, the Austrian court finally committed itself to supporting a Prussian invasion of France shortly *before* news of the French declaration of war reached Vienna. France, however, obviously courted the conflict, and the few who opposed it were discredited as faint-hearts. French historians have therefore tended both to condemn the irresponsible folly and short-sightedness of the factions concerned, and yet, in the tradition of Michelet—and, indeed, of the Brissotins themselves—to exalt the popular demand for war by implying that the masses were moved by a passionate desire to extend the benefits of freedom to all mankind.

Fervent idealism undoubtedly inspired the men who made the Revolution, but it was ever allied to a new intransigence. This had become apparent even in the days of the pacific National Assembly, which had disowned war as a by-product of despotism but had also made it plain that the nation could not be considered bound by treaties made by the old monarchy. In the debates of May 1790, de Broglie had demanded that the deputies, the representatives of the sovereign nation, should demonstrate that their conduct would be based on principles very different from those of the past, and in the few matters of foreign policy which arose in 1790–91 they indeed did so. The various rulers of the Rhineland, whose seigneurial rights in their estates in French Alsace had been guaranteed by successive treaties since 1648, protested to the Assembly in February 1790 against the loss of these rights by the decrees of August 1789; they were offered an indemnity, but encountered a flat refusal on the matter of right, since 'throughout the French Empire there can be no other sovereign power than the general will of the nation' and since the people of Alsace were united to the French people by their own will and not by 'diplomatic parchments'. The new principles were also applied to the Papal city of Avignon and the adjacent area of the Venaissin, which were eventually annexed in September 1791 after repeated appeals from the revolutionary party there had been shelved so that pressure might be maintained on the Pope to accept the Civil Constitution of the Clergy. Violent civil war in the enclave, and the complete inability of the Papal

95

authorities to restore order, justified the French intervention, but the rights of the Papacy were nonetheless over-ridden in the name of the will of the people, as Robespierre had demanded in November 1790.

The rights of both Rome and the Rhineland rulers were represented by the emperor as war approached, and although these were perhaps pretexts rather than causes of the conflict, the exchanges about them reveal the real issues involved. If Austria recognised only rights established before the Revolution and maintained by the monarchy, and provoked the French assemblies intolerably, these on their side recognised no right other than the present will of the people of France, and so identified negotiation with dictation. The Legislative Assembly might assert that 'the war . . . is not a war of nation against nation, but the just defence of a free people against the unjust aggression of a king'; but war with both the kings and the peoples of Europe was inevitable while France spoke only the language of sovereignty.

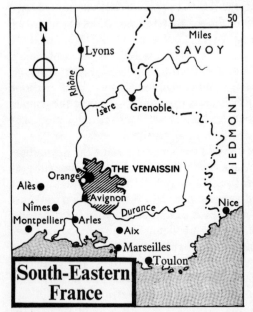

South-Eastern France

The war which was to last for the next twenty-three years was thus really nationalist from its beginnings: but at first its ideological implications were more obvious, and, as Barnave had anticipated, the crisis immediately intensified the conflict between the more ardent revolutionaries and all those whom they regarded as fellow-travellers with the court and the kings of Europe. This was most apparent in the bitter quarrel which divided the Jacobin Society between a minority which stood by Robespierre in opposition to the war, and the majority which at first favoured the policy of the Brissotins. Robespierre was no pacifist, but he was quick to realise that the Brissotins were playing the court's game by promoting a war which must put great power into the hands of the ministers and the generals, the very men who were most hostile to the Revolution. Seeing the terrible danger of treason in high places, he saw also the folly of those who pretended that they would welcome its exposure and that some spontaneous insurrection would suffice to thwart it. Since in Robespierre's view the real source of the troubles of France was in counter-revolution at home, since the real Coblentz was in

Paris, 'in a place not far from here', he held it to be imperative that counter-revolution should be crushed in France before it was attacked abroad. 'You propose to give supreme power to those who most want your ruin', he declared on 12th December, and he protested again and again that 'the only way to save the state and to safeguard freedom is to wage war in the right way, on our enemies at home, instead of marching under their orders against their allies across the frontiers.'

Robespierre's great attempt to expose the shallow optimism of Brissot, to remind men that 'no one loves an armed missionary' and that to declare war is not to dispose of all the problems of government, nevertheless failed completely. Even Danton and Marat, who had at first supported him, fell silent, and as he became more isolated and unpopular he became increasingly convinced that those who accused him of lack of patriotism were in reality in conscious collusion with the court, and were deliberately betraying the Revolution into the hands of Louis and La Fayette. Profound suspicions and bitter personal attacks thus poisoned relationships between the Brissotins and the Robespierrist Jacobins.

This division did much to impair the success the Brissotins had gained in securing the appointment of their friends to the ministry, for these appointments, apparently arranged by backstairs intrigue, seemed to confirm all Robespierre's suspicions that their whole policy was governed by base ambition for personal power.[1] The names of Roland and Clavière[2] were certainly put forward from Vergniaud's salon in the Place Vendôme; but Dumouriez, who dominated the ministry, owed his appointment quite as much to his own careful cultivation of royal favour as to an acquaintance with Gensonné, and an assumption of Jacobinism. Moreover, even when Duranthon and Servan two more of Madame Roland's friends, were also given office, the group had little real power. The Brissotins, despite their success in promoting the war, remained a loose radical minority in an overwhelmingly conservative Assembly, and in the council chamber the 'patriot' ministers could not prevail upon the king to do more than a bare minimum of business with them.

[1] According to Dumont, Brissot openly admitted that the original attack upon Delessart, which brought his friends to office, was a party move, an attempt to steal a march upon Robespierre. *Souvenirs sur Mirabeau* (ed. Paris 1951), p. 203.

[2] Clavière (Étienne), b. 1735, a prominent Swiss banker who was exiled from Geneva after the French minister Vergennes sent troops to suppress the democratic revolt there in 1782; as a financier he promoted various enterprises in France before the Revolution and was then partly responsible for the introduction of the *assignat;* as a reformer, he provided a link between the Swiss exiles and the friends of Brissot, whom he had met in Switzerland. He became Finance Minister in the Patriot or Brissotin ministries 23rd March–13th June 1792 and 10th August 1792. Retaining office until the Revolution of 2nd June 1793, he was then arrested. Tried before the Revolutionary Tribunal, he committed suicide 8th December 1793.

Louis, indeed, could scarcely conceal his contempt for Roland's parade of republican simplicity of dress and manner, and although it is sometimes said that there was here an opportunity for the development of effective government based upon parliamentary support, the king's disdainful acceptance of the nominations[1] suggests that he was really only awaiting the arrival of the allied armies.

The war, too, increased the Brissotins' embarrassment by revealing the fearful weakness of the French forces. Revolutionary propaganda and the wholesale emigration of officers had destroyed the discipline of the regulars, and the 'blues' (the volunteers of 1791) had only reached the front at half their strength, and were neither trained nor equipped to fight. The aged Rochambeau's feeble attempt to execute Dumouriez's orders for a general offensive was therefore a tragic fiasco. On 29th April, as one of his divisions advanced towards Tournai, the men cried treason and broke before the Austrians' eyes, soon afterwards murdering their general, Dillon, in the streets of Lille. Next day the second division, that of Biron, began to move to Mons, only to fly back to Valenciennes at the first encounter. Within a month of the outbreak of war, the War Minister, de Grave, and Rochambeau had both resigned, and the generals in council had advised the king to make peace immediately, military operations being impossible. The French at this time were saved only by the inertia of Prussia and Austria, who were ponderously preparing for war and anxiously watching Catherine of Russia —whose armies entered Poland in strength on 18th May.

All this was of course ascribed to treason, and treason was not lacking. On 26th March Marie-Antoinette had sent details of the French plans across the frontier, and now La Fayette, who commanded the Army of the Centre, was approaching the Austrians for an armistice: detesting Dumouriez and convinced that the Jacobins were threatening the Constitution, he meant to march on Paris and close down the clubs. Suspicion of these things, and news of the disastrous beginning of the fighting, naturally stimulated passions in Paris and vindicated Robespierre in his criticism of the Brissotins. They were rightly held responsible, and as Robespierre was constantly at the Jacobin Club while they were at the Assembly, he attacked them there relentlessly, as well as driving home his attacks in his new journal, *The Defender of the Constitution*. Marat and Desmoulins, Billaud-Varenne,[2] Collot d'Herbois,

[1] 'I had previously chosen men commended by their sound opinions and high principles. . . . I have now thought it my duty to replace them by men whose title to office is that their views are those of the popular party. . . .' J. M. Thompson, *The French Revolution*, p. 258.

[2] Billaud-Varenne (Jean-Nicholas, b. at La Rochelle 1756), and Collot d'Herbois (Jean-Marie, probably b. at Paris 1750), were to become the two most violent members of the Committee of Public Safety 1793–94. The former, an unsuccessful lawyer, made himself

Couthon and other influential men of Robespierre's mind added their denunciations to his, and in the early summer of 1792 opinion in the Club
slowly but steadily swung against the Brissotins. The conflict thus became
one between the Society on the one hand and the Assembly on the other,[1] a
development which was to have enduring effects upon the Revolution and
upon the growth of the new democratic tradition.

Economic insecurity now combined with political and military perils to
produce a second and a greater Revolution in France, that of August 1792.
Although the Assembly had done something to strengthen the *assignat* by
sequestrating the estates of *émigrés* on 9th February, its repeated issues of the
new paper money—which totalled an additional 800 million livres by April
1792—had depreciated it to 57 per cent of its face value by June. The cost of
living rose correspondingly, and despite the good harvest of 1791 the peasants
were reluctant to sell their grain. Shortages of all sorts, greatly aggravated by
hoarding and speculation, consequently caused widespread disorders, which
amounted to an agrarian revolt in the corn lands round Paris.

The difference between the popular reaction to this situation and that of
the politically predominant middle-class was first apparent early in the year,
when a sudden shortage of sugar occurred in Paris.[2] Rioters seized stocks and
sold them off at popular prices; deputations went to the Assembly demanding
to know how profiteering in the necessities of life could be reconciled with
the Declaration of Rights; and the deputies showed only a general devotion to
the principles of free trade and anxiety about the threat to property, law and
order. In May, after Simoneau, the Mayor of Étamps, had been lynched while
trying to suppress a food-riot, a petition was presented to the Assembly by a
local *curé*, Dolivier, which showed the growing popular demand for the
reimposition of the price-controls once maintained by the monarchy, and

known as a violent radical and anti-clerical writer and was elected member of the Commune
of 10th August 1792 and deputy for Paris to the Convention; the latter, in turn actor,
playwright and theatre-manager, made his reputation by a series of revolutionary plays
1789–91 and by organising the fete in honour of the Nancy mutineers in March 1792,
becoming deputy for Paris to the Convention. Both were exiled to Cayenne in 1795,
Collot to die within the year and Billaud to marry a native girl and to settle after 1815 in
Haiti where he died in 1819. Georges Couthon, born in 1755 in Auvergne and also a member
of the Great Committee, was a successful lawyer and a mild humanitarian who was a
paralytic cripple by 1793. A leading Jacobin at Clermont-Ferrand in 1790, he was deputy
for Puy-de Dôme to the Legislative Assembly and the Convention and a close friend of
Robespierre, with whom he was executed 28th July 1794.

[1] This distinction was not, of course, absolute at this stage: Brissot still had supporters
in the Jacobins, and some deputies, such as the *trio cordelier*—Chabot, Basire and Merlin
de Thionville—represented the extreme Left in the Assembly.

[2] A consequence of the bloody revolt which the conflict of idealism and self-interest
on both sides of the Atlantic had occasioned in the French West Indies.

which even implied that property right was relative and not absolute. At the same time another priest in Paris, Jacques Roux,[1] called for the death penalty for hoarders. As the war intensified the patriotic ardour of the people, as men adopted the red cap of liberty and as the *ça ira* acquired a wilder rhythm and still wilder words, Roux and his followers, the *enragés*, or Wild Men, began to acquire importance. The Paris radicals' first demands, however, were still political, and these were voiced by a conference of the sections convened on 5th May on the initiative of the journalist Chaumette: all citizens ought to be armed at once with pikes, and all, not merely those called 'active', should be admitted to the assemblies of their sections, which should be allowed to meet in permanent session to deal with the emergency.

Although the Jacobins were as yet just as averse as the Assembly to any form of state regulation of the economy, their democratic approach to both political and social questions, as well as their increasingly puritanical type of patriotism, meant that they were the quicker to condemn the iniquities of the profiteers. More particularly, Robespierre's real sympathy for the poor, and his remarkable political prescience, helped him now to retain his association with the working people of the towns, on whose power and willingness to volunteer for military service the Revolution at war must increasingly depend. He took a prominent part in the popular fête held on 15th April in honour of the Swiss soldiers of Chateauvieux's Regiment, who had mutinied at Nancy in 1790 and were now hailed as heroes after their release from the galleys at Brest: but he was careful to disassociate himself from the honours afforded to the memory of Simoneau, the murdered mayor, whom the Brissotins and the Feuillants of the Assembly together belauded by a counter-demonstration on 2nd June—an occasion on which the 'throne of the law' was significantly inscribed with the words '*Liberté, Egalité, Propriété*'. As their assumption of trivial territorial titles and their proclivity for the salons indicates, the Brissotins' social sympathies were much more patrician than plebeian, and under the increasing pressure of the Jacobins they moved appreciably to the Right in May and early June.

The development of the split between the two 'patriot' groups was, however, delayed by the growing danger to them both of a strong conservative reaction. As the Brissotins became conscious of this, and of their own unpopularity, they began a new attack upon the 'Austrian Committee' and promoted a new series of emergency measures. On 27th May a decree

---

[1] Jacques Roux, whose early life is obscure, was at this time a middle-aged priest, *vicaire* of Saint-Nicolas-des-Champs, who preached open-air sermons advocating political terrorism and extensive economic measures for the welfare of the poor. Continuing this campaign after the victory of the Montagnards in June 1793, he was treated as a counter-revolutionary, driven from the Cordeliers and finally arrested on 5th September 1793. He killed himself in prison in February 1794.

provided for the deportation of non-juror priests on the denunciation of twenty 'active' citizens; on 29th May the king's Constitutional Guard of 1,200 men was dissolved; and on 8th June Servan,[1] the Rolandist Minister of War, won the Assembly's approval for his proposal to establish a permanent camp near the capital for the 20,000 men of the National Guard called to Paris for the approaching fête on 14th July. Although both Right and Left feared that such a force might be used against them, its value for the defence of the city and as a training school for the army outweighed all doubts, and even the sections accepted the plan as a temporary substitute for their own programme. Louis, however, approved only the dissolution of his own Guard. Roland, as Minister of the Interior, then sent him an open letter, undoubtedly written by Madame Roland, which warned him, amidst much patronising reproof, that by opposing essential measures of public security he ran the risk of a new revolution. Deeply offended, Louis took Dumouriez's advice and dismissed Roland, Clavière and Servan on 13th June. When Dumouriez discovered that the king was still not prepared to pass the other decrees, he resigned and departed for the front, and the king formed a new ministry of Feuillant nonentities.

The situation was now similar to that of July 1789. Though Robespierre might maintain that the safety of the state was of more importance than the fate of a ministry, though Desmoulins might sneer at the Brissotins as dupes of the royalists, it seemed that patriots had been dismissed and a patriotic programme halted at the caprice of the king. Moreover, the growing expectation that the reaction would culminate in a military *coup d'état* was confirmed by a letter from La Fayette, read on 18th June, in which he demanded that the Assembly should act to end the rule of the clubs, since the Jacobins were fast establishing a state within the state. Next day the king formally announced his veto on the decrees, and on 20th June there occurred the first invasion of the Tuileries. In defiance of the law, two armed processions from the Faubourgs Saint-Antoine and Saint-Marcel marched up the Rue Saint-Honoré, accompanied by vast crowds of men and women bearing weapons and banners. Admitted to the Assembly, their orator, Hugenin, a customs clerk, assured the deputies that they were ready 'to use every means to avenge the majesty of the outraged people'. His 'petition' clearly threatened revolution: if necessary, the executive power would have to be destroyed, for 'a single man must not influence the will of twenty-five million men. If out of respect we maintain him in his position, it is on condition that he will fill it constitutionally'. The people then paraded through the

[1] Joseph Servan de Gerbey, an elderly, rigid and upright soldier and a Jansenist, was appointed Minister of War in May 1792 on the recommendation of his friends the Rolands. Dismissed with them in June, he was reappointed on 10th August 1792, and retired in October when Dumouriez invaded the Low Countries.

101

Chamber to the strains of *ça ira*, and proceeded to plant a tree of liberty in the gardens of the nearby Capucin monastery.

The day, however, was not over. As the crowds began their return journey, accident or design directed them across the Tuileries Gardens, along the riverside and into the Place du Carrousel, where they pressed against the Palace gates. The National Guardsmen on duty, fearing violence, gave way, and a multitude surged into the palace in search of the king. Louis and the queen, pinned for hours into the window embrasures of adjacent rooms, were beset by the shifting throng and assailed by repeated cries of 'Sanction the decrees!' 'Recall the ministers!', and 'Down with the veto!' The king, who had both to don the cap of liberty and to drink to the health of the nation, owed his life to his own composure, and it was he who eventually persuaded the people to disperse by suggesting that other rooms in the palace might be opened for their inspection.

These dramatic events have never been wholly explained. Once the monarchy had been overthrown, the Brissotins' enemies asserted that on this occasion they had tried to mount a revolution in their own interest, and had failed. The explanation accords so well with Brissot's earlier threats, and Roland's more recent warning, that many historians, as hostile to these repentant Jacobins as were their own contemporaries, have accepted it without question. There is, however, no positive proof that the Brissotins did more than smooth the path for the petitioners in the Assembly, and the man whose connivance with the crowd is most obvious, Pétion, since the previous November Mayor of Paris, was still as close to Robespierre as to Brissot, and was before all a Pétionist, principally interested in his own popularity. Nor does anything suggest that more than a warning of revolution was intended. The crowds, ostensibly gathered to commemorate the anniversary of the Tennis-Court Oath, were in holiday mood, the weight of the national crisis resting surprisingly lightly on their shoulders, and it would seem that several obscure adventurers and some popular leaders, particularly the brewer Santerre,[1] very successfully contrived to use the occasion as a cover for a major political demonstration.

This was welcome enough to all shades of 'patriotic' opinion: on 17th June the deputy Lasource, who can safely be called a Brissotin, had told the Jacobin Club that the Assembly, being bound by the Constitution, could not act until the people's will had been made manifest. On 21st June, too, the Club informed its affiliated societies that 'a great and salutory movement, from which patriotism may expect the happiest results, has just occurred in

---

[1] Santerre (Antoine Joseph), b. 1752, a wealthy brewer of the Faubourg Saint-Antoine, prominent 14th July 1789, 20th June 1792, appointed c.-in-c. National Guard of Paris 10th August 1792, served against the Vendéans, arrested after defeats, released after Thermidor, d. 1809.

the capital'. But if the Assembly and the Club were alike in following events rather than in controlling them, the men of the sections had certainly learnt much about their own power and the weakness of both the parliament and the monarchy—as, indeed, did the young officer Bonaparte, an eye-witness of the affair.

The immediate consequence of 20th June, however, was that reaction was reinforced. The Court determined that in future the Tuileries would be defended. Almost all the departments' directories demanded that those who had abused the king should be found and punished, and in Paris alone 20,000 signatures were quickly collected for a petition to this effect. Preliminary enquiries and a few arrests were made, and the Department of Paris suspended Pétion and Manuel, the procureur of the Municipality, from office. All this activity caused great alarm even to moderate men, and when on 28th June it became known that La Fayette, who was now generally regarded as a would-be Cromwell, had suddenly arrived in Paris, the long expected counter-revolution seemed imminent. For the first time for months Brissot appeared at the Jacobin Club, and patched up an agreement with the Robespierrists by promising to prove to the Assembly that the general was a traitor. Yet in fact La Fayette's attempt to coerce the capital was an utter failure. The Assembly did not censure him for leaving his post, as Guadet demanded, but neither did it authorise him to act against the Jacobins, as he himself had hoped. The Court, moreover, was obtuse enough to disdain his aid: despising him as a constitutionalist, and convinced that foreign intervention would soon restore its full independence, it received him coldly, and the queen prompted Pétion to prevent the National Guard from assembling for his review. On 29th June, therefore, when he attempted to lead a march against the Jacobins, only thirty officers answered his call. Next day he left the city, his opportunity lost.

Fear nevertheless remained, growing ever greater. Men ignorant of the royal attitude assumed that plans had been concocted in the palace for a royalist march on Paris by La Fayette's forces, and in the background the Prussian army was moving into position alongside that of Austria in preparation for the invasion. The Brissotins, caught between the peril of counter-revolution and that of a new insurrection, strove to ward off the more immediate danger. On 3rd July Vergniaud, in one of his greatest speeches, demanded that a state of emergency should be proclaimed and that the king, in whose name France's enemies were closing about her, should be required to give 'a plain statement of his intention to triumph or perish with the people'. Brissot soon went further, openly naming the king as the source of national paralysis and declaring that the invaders could be conquered by a blow struck at the Tuileries. This intimidation was to some extent successful. On 10th July the new ministers resigned, and the Directory of the Paris

103

Department also did so when the Assembly decided to reinstate Pétion and Manuel. The balance of forces was swayed in favour of the Revolution by orders for the re-election of all staff officers of the National Guard, who were notoriously conservative, and for the removal from Paris of all regular troops except a few Swiss Guards. The veto, too, was evaded, for after 14th July the contingents of the National Guard from the provinces were to be established in a camp at Soissons. The state of emergency demanded by Vergniaud was also organised: when the word was given, all administrative authorities and all National Guards would be required to remain on continuous duty to effect the defence of the nation.

France, however, was not to be saved by stretching the Constitution, which had already, as Morris wrote after 20th June, 'given its last groan'. Louis attended the fête on 14th July wearing a breastplate of taffeta beneath his coat, but he was not to be frightened into forming a second 'patriot' ministry. Appointing another make-believe government of unimportant loyalists, he spent money freely on propaganda and on the enlistment of para-military bodies which might keep control until help arrived from Austria. Plans for a new escape from Paris, pressed upon him by La Fayette and others, he rejected in the confident belief that some loyal gentlemen and the few Swiss who remained to him could if necessary 'drive back to its faubourgs all that *canaille* in insurrection'.[1]

Real revolution was now in preparation. On the morrow of 20th June a handsome young man from Marseilles, Charles Barbaroux,[2] had sent a notable letter to his municipality, which then stood at the forefront of the Revolution. The Jacobins of Marseilles had had to fight desperately to overcome counter-revolution in the city in 1789 and 1790, and since then they had taken the lead in considerable military operations against royalist forces in Arles and Avignon. Barbaroux, the secretary-general of their National Guard, who had been sent to Paris to represent their interests and discredit some of the official deputies of the department, knew their quality well, and he now wrote: 'It is no use hoping that the court will change its policy unless we give it something more to be afraid of than any insurrection of the Faubourgs Saint-Antoine and Saint-Marcel. . . . The simplest way

---

[1] The words of the Baron de Vioménil as reported by the Marquis de Puységur to Mathieu Dumas, who was pressing La Fayette's plan.

[2] Barbaroux (Charles J. Marie), b. 1767, had come to Paris in February 1792 to represent the interests of the patriots of Marseilles against their royalist opponents at Arles and had established many contacts with the Jacobins and the deputies of the left. Elected deputy to the Convention for Bouches-du-Rhône, he soon became associated with the Rolands and was an impetuous opponent of Robespierre and the Parisian delegation. Proscribed in the Revolution of 2nd June 1793, he fled to Caen and thence to the Gironde, where he was executed at Bordeaux after attempting suicide in 1794.

of frightening it is to put into effect of our own will the decree for the formation of a military camp at Paris, increasing very considerably the number of
citizen-soldiers proposed in the decree.' In consequence of this letter, Marseilles formed a *corps d'élite* of 516 volunteers, men selected for their patriotism as well as their physique, men who, in Barbaroux's words, 'knew how
to die'. On 2nd July they marched for Paris, proudly man-handling their
cannon and teaching France as they advanced the song which immortalises
their name. The Municipality meanwhile despatched a petition to the
Assembly, directing it to recognise that 'the law relative to the monarchy'
was incompatible with freedom and equality and was invalidated by the
national will.

As the Marseillais moved towards Paris, the majority of the federal forces
sent to the capital for 14th July departed for the camp at Soissons, among
them men like Masséna and Soult, who were one day to lead Napoleon's
armies as marshals of France. Others, however, remained in the city in
defiance of the law; these formed a central committee at the Jacobin Club,
and organised petitions calling upon the Assembly to act against the king.
In their manifesto of 20th July, they bluntly informed the Assembly and the
nation that they would not leave the capital until the treacherous court had
been overcome. Robespierre was certainly in close touch with the five
obscure men who directed these operations from the lodgings which one of
them shared with him, and the language of their demands reflects his own
programme, expressed at the Club by Billaud-Varenne on 15th July, for the
overthrow of the monarchy and the formation of a new national assembly,
a Convention which should be elected by the people as a whole.

The *fédérés'* initiative was followed by the sections of Paris, which profited
greatly from the proclamation of the state of emergency, *La Patrie en Danger*,
on the city squares on 22nd to 24th July. As several thousand volunteers
enrolled and went into camp in the Champ de Mars, the Assembly recognised
the right of the sections to meet in permanent session; by 27th July their
central committee was sitting alongside the Municipality in the Hôtel de
Ville. Their delegates, men like Chaumette, the journalist Carra, Fournier
'the American' and the giant soldier Westermann, were soon joined with the
five *fédérés* in a secret Directory of Insurrection. Moreover, the distinction
between 'active' and 'passive' citizens was now swept aside. On 30th July,
the day the Marseillais reached Paris, the Théâtre-Français Section, which
included the old Cordeliers District, announced that 'passive' citizens would
henceforth be admitted to its assembly. Others soon followed suit, and at the
same time a new decree, proposed by Carnot to create 'a nation in arms',
permitted all men to enroll in the National Guard and to carry pikes. The
middle-class control established in 1789 thus crumbled away, and popular
democracy, the forces of the *sans-culottes*, stood in arms in the capital.

Until lately, little was known about the *sans-culottes*, who were sometimes identified with the Jacobins, occasionally idealised as 'the People' in the abstract, and more often treated as an insensate and brutalised rabble. Detailed research has now given them identity as an important independent element in the Revolution. In the more general sense of the word, the *sans-culottes* were the ordinary working people of the towns, as distinct both from the very poor, the vagrants and the ne'er-do-wells, and from the better educated professional people and those prosperous enough not to have to work with their hands. They were therefore the great majority of the urban population; but in the complex society of the time, in which a few large 'manufactories' stood amidst a multitude of tiny workshops, and in which many gradations of status separated the wage-earning labourer from the independent master-craftsman, they could not constitute a coherent economic class. Predominantly small shop-keepers, and tradesmen and artisans of infinitely varying occupation, their greatest common economic interest was to ensure that the cost of living was controlled (although even here the attitude of the shop-keepers towards regulation might soon differ sharply from that of the craftsmen). While their anger and suspicions were easily aroused against those who seemed to possess too much, they were ultimately as interested as the peasantry in the preservation of small property.[1]

Used more particularly, however, the name of *sans-culotte* was a political one, a title of honour for the truly active citizen, the man whose patriotism was to be measured not by some arbitrary tax-qualification, but by his regularity in attending the assembly of his section, by his readiness to turn out for service with the National Guard, and by his zeal to maintain the principles of the Revolution in every possible way. A man of substance, like Santerre, could be a good *sans-culotte* if his conduct came up to this standard. Such men as these, fiercely proud of their independence and of the fact that they did not speak or dress like gentlefolk, were the militants of the Revolution, who saw all problems in terms of black and white, and were quick to demand immediate and violent remedies for their ills. They were thus in some respects much more radical in attitude than the more cautious, economically conservative and socially respectable Jacobins, for whom the Revolution was fast becoming a matter of moral doctrine, and from whom they may broadly be distinguished as 'the people in the galleries'. They stood nonetheless for a solid social interest, the desire of the small man of the towns to preserve his freedom and his livelihood from the old power of

---

[1] 'Let no one have more than one workshop, more than one shop': address of the Sans-Culottes Section to the National Convention, 2nd September 1793, cited by A. Soboul, *Les Sans-Culottes Parisiens en l'An II* (Paris 1958), p. 468. The Section envisaged a similar restraint upon the size of farms: *ibid.*, p. 469. and note.

privilege and the new power of money, and were far removed from the criminal riff-raff of legend.

These militants, and the men they could in emergency bring in from their workshops in answer to their section's call—for even when their organisation was fully developed, the full power of men mainly concerned with making their living could only occasionally be made manifest—were of course a minority of the population of France. They were, however, a minority on whose power the Revolution depended for its very existence so long as the army was unreliable, disorganised, or stretched to its limit in defence of the frontiers. Since even the illiterate rank and file of the townsmen were far more politically conscious than the normally inert masses of the peasantry, their conception of democracy was to be a matter of great consequence. Fundamental to this was a deep-seated belief in the imprescriptable sovereignty of the people, whose will could be ascertained only in assemblies of the people. Laws were held valid only if, and only as long as, they received the sanction of public consent; officials, including members of parliament, were no more than the agents of the people, empowered only to do their bidding and subject to recall so soon as they failed to effect the popular will.

In practice this meant that democracy was to be direct and decentralised among a multitude of local assemblies, whose powers would be absolute. Of these, the sections of Paris were some, and they held that although their rightful power had been in abeyance under the Constitution, the exercise of it must naturally revert to them in time of crisis. It was in accordance with this belief that the Théâtre-Français Section on 30th July called upon those hitherto 'aristocratically known as passive citizens' to share in 'the exercise of the portion of sovereignty which belongs to the section'. Since the sans-culottes were by this time fully convinced that the king was the first enemy of the Revolution, their intervention could only mean his deposition, if necessary by insurrection. On 31st July the Mauconseil Section resolved that it would no longer recognise Louis XVI as King of the French, and invited the other sections to support its decision, of which the Assembly was informed.

The great tension which now gripped the city is apparent in the fact that between 26th July and 5th August there were at least three false starts to the impending insurrection. Active minorities succeeded in dominating some of the more conservative sections, and the news of the Prussian declaration of war and the publication of an ominous manifesto by the allied commander, the Duke of Brunswick, ensured that the most drastic measures would have general support. Officially published in Paris on 1st August, the manifesto derived from proposals first put forward by the king and queen themselves. Contrary to their wishes, however, the émigrés had drafted it and foisted it upon the Duke, omitting all that was conciliatory.[1] In its final form it declared that the aim of the allied sovereigns was to end anarchy in France. It threatened all civilians, including the National Guard, with immediate execution if they opposed the allied advance, and it ordered Paris to submit at once to the king, upon pain of 'an exemplary and ever-memorable vengeance' and the delivery of the city to 'military punishment and total destruction'. Nothing could have been more effective in identifying the monarchy with the invader and concentrating anger against the throne.

Moreover, after mid-July it became increasingly clear that there was little to be hoped for from the Legislative Assembly and the Constitution of 1791. As the threat of a new revolution came nearer, the Brissotins changed their front and did their best to hold back the whirlwind they had done so much to sow. Twice Vergniaud wrote to the king reproaching him for his inaction and urging him while time remained to appoint a patriot ministry to meet the crisis. Guadet and Gensonné joined him in writing one of these letters, and some accounts say that Gensonné actually went to the Tuileries. These secret overtures were only suspected, but on 26th July Brissot and Guadet openly repudiated the republican movement and threatened republicans with the same treatment that would be meted out to the counter-revolutionaries at Coblentz. Lasource,[2] too, tried on 29th July to persuade the Jacobins to disperse the *fédérés* 'lest they excite a tumult which can serve no useful purpose'. That these men should cling to the Constitution as the crisis approached is comprehensible, but that they should still have supposed that Louis could ever identify France with the Revolution seems almost incredible. On the most charitable interpretation, political realities passed them by, whereas Robespierre saw that: 'The state must be saved. Nothing is unconstitutional, except what ruins it.'[3]

The Brissotins now seemed close to counter-revolution, and the frail alliance made between them and the Jacobins at the end of June now fell asunder. Even so, the Club and the sections awaited the outcome of two final tests of the Assembly's attachment to the Revolution. One was the impeachment of La Fayette, which Brissot had promised in June. The delay was already damning. On 20th July Robespierre had declared that 'if La Fayette remains unpunished we have no constitution'; but one

---

[1] It was known in the Jacobin Club on 28th July, and its general nature was common knowledge in informed circles weeks beforehand. On the royal proposals, see, e.g. J. H. Clapham, *The Causes of the War of 1792* (Cambridge, 1899), pp. 210, 221.

[2] Lasource (Marc David Alba), b. 1763, a Protestant pastor, deputy for Tarn to the Legislative Assembly and the Convention, an advocate of the war with Austria and later an opponent of the Montagnards, proscribed in the Revolution 2nd June 1793, executed Paris 31st October 1793.

[3] *Défenseur*, No. 11.

chance remained, a debate arranged for 8th August. In the meanwhile another clear-cut choice appeared: on 3rd August all but one of the sections adhered to a petition, which Pétion himself presented, calling upon the Assembly to decide by 9th August whether or not the king was to be deposed. Next day a separate address from the Quinze Vingts Section (the southern half of the Faubourg Saint-Antoine) made it clear that this was an ultimatum and that insurrection would follow failure or inaction. The Assembly, and the Brissotins in particular, failed both these tests. The impeachment of La Fayette was moved on 8th August only to be defeated by 406 votes to 224. That night a member of the Jacobin Club declared: 'it is madness to trust further in the Assembly. The people must be told that the Assembly cannot save them and that only a general insurrection can.' On 9th August, more-over, the Assembly on Condorcet's proposition suspended all further dis-cussion of petitions about the deposition of the king. The insurrection which began that night in Paris was consequently quite as much a repudi-ation of parliament as of the throne, and it was supported by patriotic bourgeois as well as by working people.

The Tuileries was not ill-prepared for the trial of arms to which Louis's well-meaning weakness and impolitic obstinacy had now reduced the ancient monarchy of France. Some 200 to 300 loyal gentlemen, Chevaliers de Saint Louis, stood beside 900 men of the Swiss Guard. Mandat, the aged but resolute commander of the National Guard, had also assembled about 2,000 men of his more loyal battalions. Their artillery was carefully posted to command the extensive courtyards of the palace, and other guns were placed on the bridges to keep the forces of south-eastern Paris from joining those of the Faubourg Saint-Antoine. As Pétion, the Mayor of the city, and Roederer, the *procureur* of the Department of Paris, were also present in the palace, the court felt reasonably secure. All was, however, vain, for the resolution of a few determined men at the Hôtel de Ville outweighed the king's infirmity of purpose, and the defence was undermined before a blow was struck.

In response to the call of Quinze Vingts Section, delegates from other sections gradually assembled at the Hôtel de Ville in the early hours of the morning of 10th August, and formed a committee under the chairmanship of Hugenin. These men pushed the Municipality into acting as they wished until they felt strong enough to suspend it and declare themselves a new Commune, acting 'by virtue of the insurrection'. Their first care was to disarm the enemy. Soon after midnight three members of the Municipality went to the Pont Neuf to order the National Guardsmen there to with-draw their guns. When, at about one o'clock, they had succeeded in this, the alarm gun on the bridge was fired. In the silence which followed its single report, the deep toll of the tocsin rang out from the Cordeliers Monastery. Other bells took up the tale, and the men in the Tuileries stood to their arms:

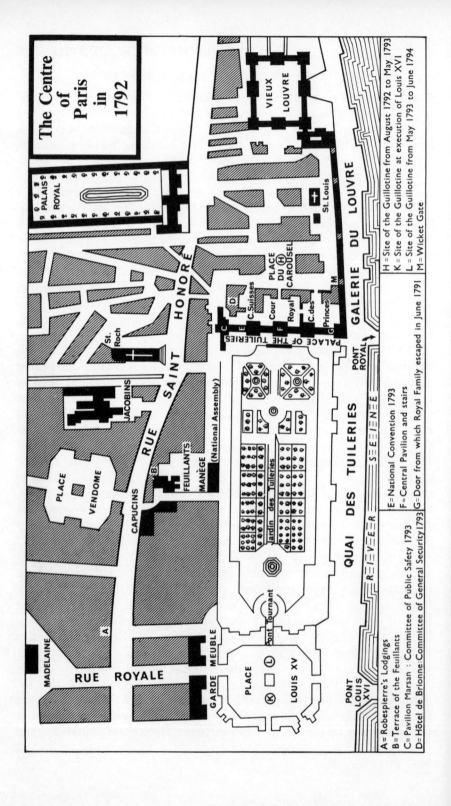

The Centre of Paris in 1792

A = Robespierre's Lodgings
B = Terrace of the Feuillants
C = Pavilion Marsan : Committee of Public Safety 1793
D = Hôtel de Brionne: Committee of General Security 1793
E = National Convention 1793
F = Central Pavilion and stairs
G = Door from which Royal Family escaped in June 1791
H = Site of the Guillotine from August 1792 to May 1793
K = Site of the Guillotine at execution of Louis XVI
L = Site of the Guillotine from May 1793 to June 1794
M = Wicket Gate

but the attackers were not yet ready. Their next step was to make the Municipality agree to recall Mandat from the palace 'to account for his command'—to which Santerre was at once appointed. Persuaded by Roederer to obey this summons, Mandat was arrested at the Hôtel de Ville and despatched to the Luxembourg as a prisoner, only to be shot down by a youth with a pistol as he was leaving the building. Pétion, meanwhile, had slipped quietly from the Tuileries, cheerfully consenting to protective arrest by an inordinately strong force of *sectionnaires*. By daybreak it was evident that the National Guards at the Tuileries could not be relied upon to fire upon their fellows. After a pathetic attempt to review them, Louis yielded to Roederer's insistence that it would be best to avoid bloodshed by abandoning the Tuileries and taking refuge with the Assembly.

Much blood, however, was now to flow to no purpose in a terrible demonstration of the power and determination of the people. As the Royal Family were being escorted by some loyal soldiers across the Tuileries Gardens to the Manège, the forces of the *fédérés* and the sections, about 20,000 strong, were converging on the palace. The first of them to arrive, a force principally composed of the men of Marseilles and Brest, thrust their way through the crowd in the Carousel, entered the palace courtyard and began to fraternise with the defenders: but some fool fired on them from a window, a volley followed, and a charge by the Swiss cleared both the courtyard and the Carousel. Hearing this firing, Louis belatedly wrote a hasty note from the Manège ordering the Swiss to lay down their arms and return to their barracks. The insurgents, however, were maddened by the belief that they had been led into a trap, and before the king's order was delivered they had begun to attack in earnest. Against all precedent, the Marseillais rallied and returned to the assault, with all the weight of Santerre's forces beside them. All but a few of the National Guards of the garrison deserted. The Swiss, caught in flanking fire from the Long Gallery of the Louvre, were soon forced into the palace, where they fought fiercely to hold the foot of the great stairs. At this point Louis's order was at last produced. The drum beat retreat, and the Guard fell back fighting through the Gardens until they were broken and slaughtered near the Round Pond. The palace itself was sacked, many of those within being hunted down and slain remorselessly, combatants or not. Some sixty Swiss, taken as prisoners to the City Hall by the Marseillais, were massacred[1] by the mob there. In all, there were killed or wounded that day about 800 of the king's men, including 600 of the Swiss, and nearly 400 of the insurgents, of whom some ninety were *fédérés* and about 300 were ordinary people of Paris, no less heroic than the Swiss.

[1] The word is used deliberately in the belief that it may legitimately be applied to a crowd which, however provoked and whatever its social composition, behaves on a particular occasion in a savage and uncontrolled manner.

This great rising, like that of 1789, was primarily defensive: at a critical moment a blow was struck to prevent the king from triumphing over the Revolution with the aid of foreign arms. Since no single stroke could suffice to dispel all danger, the insurrection in itself was inconclusive. The court was indeed overcome: the Feuillants disintegrated, and La Fayette, failing miserably in an attempt to move his army to march against Paris a few days later, fled across the frontier with the last hopes of the liberal aristocracy.[1] The Prussians, however, still approached the frontier with the *émigré* princes in their wake. Even in Paris the Commune and the Jacobins had to clothe their victory in compromise, for although the *fédérés'* participation in the insurrection ensured that it had a national character, the assent or acquiescence of the majority of the population of France had still to be secured. The Legislative Assembly, reduced by the defection of the Right to a Brissotin remnant, had therefore to be maintained on condition that it recognised the existence of the Commune and provided for the election of a National Convention. In the meanwhile its own proposals—moved, to his cost, by Vergniaud—for the re-appointment of the 'patriot' ministers and for the suspension, instead of the deposition, of the king, had also to be accepted. At the insistence of the Commune, the Royal Family were surrendered to its custody, and their long ordeal in the cramped accommodation of the Manège ended in confinement in the grim tower of the Temple.[2] The immediate result of the insurrection was that authority in France was fearfully divided between the conflicting forces of the Assembly and the Commune.

Despite this, 10th August 1792 was a decisive date, on which a second Revolution, of profound significance, occurred in France. In this respect the king's hostility and the Prussian invasion did little more than provide an occasion for the victory of a democratic nationalist movement, with which compromise was practically impossible. The rising, in effect, inaugurated the Republic, and it marked the immediate advent of complete political democracy to the most powerful and influential country in Europe. When on 11th August the Assembly made arrangements for the elections to the Convention, universal suffrage was recognised and all distinctions between citizens disappeared.[3] There were also even further steps towards social

---

[1] Arrested and treated as a revolutionary, La Fayette spent five years in the Austrian cells and dungeons before Napoleon secured his release.

[2] Louis was first seated beside the president, while the queen remained at the bar of the House, but all the Royal Family were soon removed to the reporters' box, a room twelve feet square and separated from the Chamber by a grill. There they remained for most of the two days of turbulent session, until they were transferred first to the Feuillants' monastery buildings, and then to the Temple on 13th August.

[3] All Frenchmen over the age of twenty-one who were self-supporting and not domestic servants were enfranchised.

11 Danton

From an engraving by P. F. Bertonnier

12 The Storming of the Tuileries, 10th August 1792

From a painting by Jean Duplessi-Bertaux, exhibited at The Salon of 1793

equality, and later in the month legislation, intended to purchase the support of the peasants, swept away much of what remained of seigneurial payments and facilitated the purchase of *émigré* property in small lots.

The forcible destruction of the monarchical constitution left no shred of ancient authority to sanctify a new régime: continuity with the past was broken, and as endless addresses from the Commune to the Assembly soon testified, the sovereignty of the people now stood as the only source of law. Indeed, in its electoral proposals the Assembly itself was constrained to admit its own incompetence and to 'invite' citizens to conform to its regulations. Thus while the new Revolution consolidated the unity of the nation by abolishing old distinctions, it intensified disunity and sharpened the concept of the nation by compelling men to choose between the old authority and the new. Their choice was not to be a simple one. When on 4th August Vergniaud had moved the rejection of the resolution taken against the monarchy by the Mauconseil Section, he had argued that sovereignty belonged to the people as a whole and not to any single section of it. The identification of 'the sovereign people', with whom the revolutionaries as distinct from the royalists identified France, had already become a matter of interpretation.

5

The Elimination of the King

The fall of the monarchy on 10th August 1792 at first aggravated the situation of France. While invasion still impended, a royalist reaction like that which had followed 20th June seemed likely, and it was quite possible that the state, so suddenly bereft of its ancient centre of unity, might disintegrate in civil war. Already La Rouerie's attempt to raise revolt in Brittany was known, and within ten days an early rising in the Vendée gave the royalists brief control of Châtillon. Even the army's reception of the news of the republican insurrection was unpredictable, and La Fayette in fact tried to turn his men against Paris before he deserted to the Austrian lines on 19th August, the day that the Prussians at last began their advance. In Paris, moreover, all was provisional. As the nation waited to elect its new Convention, government was divided and disputed between different authorities —the Executive Council of ministers, the Assembly's principal committee (the Committee of Twenty-one), the Commune of the Insurrection, and the general assemblies of the sections of Paris.

The Brissotins, who had profited from the insurrection by the reinstatement of Roland, Clavière and Servan as ministers, and who dominated both the Committee of Twenty-one and the depleted ranks of the Assembly, could do little to restore unity to government. Their apparent protection of the monarchy had earned them the implacable hostility of the Commune, a very formidable body. Increased by election to 288 members, principally artisans, shop-keepers, obscure journalists and lawyers of the lower middle-class, the Commune reflected the great increase in *sans-culotte* influence that had been brought about by the insurrection. Although it consisted wholly of delegates sent to it daily by the sections, each of which remained an autonomous democracy with its own military force[1] and security committee, the Commune had general direction of the police and the National Guard of the capital, and it unhesitatingly assumed that the people had invested it with full authority to protect and preserve the Revolution. Deeply suspicious of the Brissotins' sincerity, the *sans-culottes* in the sections and in the Commune were determined that ruthless action must be taken to crush counter-

---

[1] The military strength of the sections was increased in September by a reorganisation of the National Guard. This restored control of battalions to the local assemblies, which had largely lost such control when the districts were suppressed in 1790.

114

revolution and to beat back the armies of the enemy. Their identification of popular sovereignty with the continuous practice of direct democracy, as well as their social and economic radicalism, led them now to challenge and encroach upon the authority of the middle-class parliament. In their eyes the Assembly was no more than the rump of an out-dated institution, preserved purely for its convenience value; it might rubber-stamp the actions of the Commune, and even the insurrection itself, for the benefit of provincial opinion, but it had no authority to call the Commune to account. As Hugenin, president of the Commune, told the deputies when he led a delegation to the Assembly immediately after the palace had fallen, 'The people has charged us to inform you that it has reinvested you with its confidence, but also to declare that it can only recognise the people of France, your sovereign and ours, as fit judge of measures imposed by the necessity of resistance to oppression.'

To the Brissotins, however, the Legislative Assembly remained the national assembly, and even though it was reduced to only 284 of its 749 deputies, they regarded it as holding authority in trust for the whole nation until a Convention could assemble. When the king had been suspended on 10th August, Vergniaud replied to the further demands that he should be completely deposed by asserting that no final decisions could be taken before the Convention had met, and he again reminded the demonstrators that 'Paris is no more than a part of France'. Thus even before the king had been conveyed to the Temple, a grievous dispute had begun among the revolutionaries. Implicit in this were such great questions as the relationship of Paris and the provinces, and the conflicting interests of the wealthier and the poorer classes in both town and country, but at root the conflict was one between popular and parliamentary democracy, conceptions which were irreconcilable since each was seen in terms of indivisible and inalienable sovereignty.

At this time the Jacobins of Paris stood shoulder to shoulder with the Commune. Differences of outlook between the members of the Society and the men of the sections, though discernible to the historian, remained submerged, it being a cardinal point of the ever-evolving Jacobin interpretation of the Revolution that the Society was identical with the people. Any expression of anxiety about 'the exaggeration of principles' or about the policies advocated by '*têtes exaltées*' thus amounted to heresy and was swiftly suppressed. The insurrection was also a major victory for the Society, which in September became that of 'the Friends of Liberty and Equality'. Although neither Danton nor Robespierre had led the people in the streets, both had contributed directly to the success of the revolt,[1] and on its morrow

[1] Robespierre's part in the preparation of the insurrection is well summarised by J. M. Thompson: 'It was not his work . . . but no single man had hoped for it, worked for it, or

THE ELIMINATION OF THE KING

both acquired positions of the first importance. Danton, who was made Minister of Justice so that his prestige could protect Roland and his friends, made himself the mainspring of resistance to the invader, personifying for ever the determination of revolutionary France to outface disaster and defy defeat. Robespierre, elected a member of the Commune on 11th August, attended its meetings assiduously for a fortnight, until the elections to the Convention became his main concern. Although he was certainly not in control of the Commune, his influence there was clearly considerable. Believing as he did that all true patriots should support the men of Paris, who alone could speak and act for the people as a whole, he had no doubt that the Jacobins and the sections were as one. Indeed, on the evening of 10th August he even exhorted the Commune to ensure that the Assembly was kept under close control, so that it could not harm the cause of liberty.

Almost all that happened in the tremendous weeks that followed served to force these two sides further asunder. Convinced that the danger of counter-revolution was greater than ever before, the various authorities adopted drastic measures of security, anticipating much of what was later called the Terror. The Assembly's Security Committee, indeed, eventually evolved into the Committee of General Security, and its Committee of Twenty-one prepared the way for the Committee of Public Safety. Deputies were despatched to the armies with plenary powers over both military and civil officials, while the municipal authorities—who had now, like the clergy and everyone else of importance, to swear to uphold liberty and equality—were empowered to search out suspects and imprison them without reference to the law-courts. The Commune, meanwhile, rounded up such suspects, imposed a severe censorship on press and post, and sought to control movement in and out of the city by requiring travellers to produce a *certificat de civisme*—a document the citizen had to obtain from the security committee of his own section. Arms, too, were requisitioned and redistributed to patriots, railings were ripped up to be turned into pikes, and images, crucifixes and bells were taken from the churches for conversion into cannon.[1]

---

talked about it as he had.' (*Robespierre*, Vol. 1, p. 258.) Danton's activities on the night of 9th–10th August remain almost unknown; long hailed as the hero or damned as the villain of the day, he is now generally written down, as Robespierre is written up. He was, however, certainly in an influential position, being a member of the Municipality—and one of the three officials who were maintained in office by the delegates of the sections (Pétion and Manuel being the other two). For a summary of the relevant references, see Lefebvre, *La Révolution française*, pp. 260–261, note.

[1] 'Considering that much material of great value for the defence of *la patrie* may be found in the multitude of images which exist only because the people are simple and the priests are rascals. . . .' Resolution of 17th August, cited Mathiez, *La Révolution française*, p. 238.

116

All this improvised activity, however, increased confusion and multiplied antagonisms. Agents sent out by the Commune to explain the insurrection to the people of France sometimes rallied provincial patriotism by wild talk which gave great alarm to the wealthy. Sometimes, too, they came into conflict with other delegates from the Executive Council or the Assembly. The Commune itself became convinced that the Assembly's respect for legality was but a cover for unpatriotic procrastination, and the Assembly saw the Commune as intolerably dictatorial and criminally careless of the rights of person and property.

Dispute developed particularly about the treatment to be afforded to those regarded as royalists. The Commune made no bones about this: now that the era of equality had arrived, there could be no discrimination between citizens, but the lack of civic virtue could of course make a man ineligible for citizenship. All those who had shown such a deficiency, particularly the Feuillants and those who had signed petitions against the 20th June and other patriotic causes, were promptly disenfranchised 'as unworthy to fulfil any civic function', and priests were arrested more or less on sight. Further, the *sans-culottes* regarded those who had been captured during the fighting at the Tuileries as proven public enemies, fit only for immediate trial and exemplary execution. On 11th August, while the Commune urged the sovereign people to suspend its vengeance 'since all the guilty men will perish on the scaffold', Santerre warned the Assembly that he could not answer for law and order if the surviving Swiss guards remained unpunished. The Assembly agreed to establish a court-martial, but since no officers could be found to form such a court, it decided on 14th August that all those accused of crimes committed on 10th August should go before the ordinary criminal courts.

Next day Robespierre came at the head of a delegation from the Commune to remind the deputies that 'the people may be calm, but they are not asleep'; he demanded that all the guilty men, and particularly those who, like La Fayette,[1] were behind the conspiracy, should be tried by an extraordinary tribunal. This, he insisted, must be composed of commissioners elected by the sections to form a sovereign body from which there could be no appeal. The Assembly conceded that verdicts relating to 10th August should not be subject to appeal, 'lest the judgments be too numerous to have the deterrent effect society expects', but ordinary procedure was otherwise maintained, and Brissot presented an address to remind the people of the original principles of the Revolution. The sections nevertheless began to elect jurymen, and on 17th August another delegation came from the Commune to inform the deputies that there would be a new insurrection that night

---

[1] It was on this day that La Fayette repudiated the Revolution by arresting representatives sent to his camp by the Assembly. This, however, was not yet known.

117

unless a popular tribunal was created at once. Although even the 'monta-gnard' minority, the deputies who were most sympathetic to Paris, protested indignantly against this coercion, the Assembly was forced to yield. The Tribunal of 17th August was created to legalise extraordinary judicial action by judges chosen *ad hoc* by the sections of Paris alone.

Beginning its work in the Tournelle in the Palais de Justice on 21st August, the Tribunal the same day condemned Louis Conolot d'Angremont to death for raising irregular forces for the royal service, and he died on the Place du Carrousel that night, the first political victim of the guillotine.[1] In general, however, the new court simply reflected the feebleness of the authorities which had created it. In default of vigorous direction, its organisation re-mained embryonic and its procedure orthodox. After a week only two more men had been sent to the scaffold, and in the next three days two acquittals followed. Agitation for far more drastic action than this consequently continued. As early as 11th August there had been rumours of a plan to purge Paris of counter-revolutionaries by putting the prisoners to the sword, and on 19th August Marat openly advocated such a massacre as a preferable alterna-tive to slaughtering the members of the Tribunal and the deputies who had passed the 'fraudulent decree' of 17th August.

Each succeeding day now added some great new strain to the tension in the capital. The funerals of those who had died on the 10th were accompanied by wild calls for vengeance, particularly at a provocative ceremony at the Tuileries on 26th August. On that same day, as the sections began to choose their delegates for the election of the deputies to the Convention, men learnt that Longwy had fallen to the Prussians after resisting bombardment for less than a day. Brunswick's advance, if painfully deliberate, nevertheless appeared inexorable, and Paris prepared desperately to resist assault. The Assembly decreed that the death penalty should be imposed on all who should speak of surrender in besieged cities. It ordered non-juror priests to leave France within a fortnight under pain of deportation to New Guinea, and it called for the immediate levy of 30,000 men from Paris and its en-virons. The Commune similarly redoubled its efforts, summoning the citizens to work on the fortifications as they had once worked on the arena of the Champ de Mars. It hurried on the manufacture of pikes and the enlistment of volunteers, and it organised a general search of the houses of suspected persons for fire-arms. At Danton's demand, these general household visits were also authorised by the Assembly on 28th August. For two days,

---

[1] On 20th March 1792 the Assembly had ordered the use of this instrument as a method of humane execution. Known as the Louisette, or Guillotine, from the names of Dr Louis and Dr Guillotin who had recommended it, its first victim was a highwayman executed on 25th April. The Carrousel was used as a place of execution in the belief that punishment should be exacted on the scene of the crime.

118

therefore, from the morning of 30th August onwards, the shops were shut and the people were confined to their homes. Soldiers guarded the streets and thirty commissioners from each section combed their own localities for weapons and for suspects. Few arms were found, but some 3,000 people, including many priests, were arrested. Although most of these had to be released for want of accommodation in the over-crowded prisons, alarm prevailed everywhere. At this moment, with incredible ineptitude, the Assembly attempted to strike down the rival authority of the Commune.

This action was justified on the ground that protests against the Commune's conduct had been expressed by some of the sections, particularly the Lombards Section, in which Louvet de Couvrai,[1] a close friend of Brissot and Roland, was influential. Its immediate occasion, however, was an attempt by the Commune to arrest Girey-Dupré, co-editor with Brissot of the *Patriote français*, who had dared to imply in his edition of the 28th that the domiciliary visits were really intended to terrorise the electorate. On 30th August complaints from Roland about the Commune's arbitrary abuse of its authority were echoed by a succession of speakers. The news that the Ministry of War had been besieged by an angry crowd, while the Commune's commissioners searched the building for Girey-Dupré, led directly to the decree which ordered the sections to proceed at once to the election of a new municipality. The Assembly's anger was certainly stimulated by the Brissotins' direction of developments, but the Commune's provocation was considerable and the deputies' indignation was general.

Such a decree at such a moment was nevertheless disastrous. Its immediate result was to set popular and parliamentary authority in direct defiance of each other and to rip the ranks of the revolutionaries permanently apart. On 31st August Tallien[2] came from the Commune to tell the Assembly that

---

[1] Louvet (Jean Baptiste de Couvrai), b. Paris 1760, book-seller's clerk and author of the romance *Faublas*, became political pamphleteer and playwright after 1789, and supported Roland in the Lombards Section and as editor of *La Sentinelle*. An impetuous opponent of Robespierre, he was proscribed in the Revolution of 2nd June 1793, fled to Normandy, the Gironde and eventually Switzerland. Returning to the Convention in 1795, he was more moderate and statesmanlike, became a member of the Council of Five Hundred and died in obscurity in 1797.

[2] Tallien (Jean Lambert), b. 1767, lawyer's clerk and revolutionary journalist (*L'Ami des Citoyens*), active in Revolution of 10th August 1792, member of the Commune of 10th August, deputy to Convention for Seine-et-Oise, responsible for the repression of counter-revolution in the Gironde during the earlier part of the Terror, one of the chief conspirators against Robespierre in Thermidor 1794. Married Theresa Cabarrus (*vide* p. 195, n.), from whom he was divorced in 1802. One of the principal figures of the Thermidorian reaction, Tallien was present at the defeat of the royalists at Quiberon by Hoche in 1795 and ordered the executions which followed. One of the Council of Five Hundred, he was captured at sea by the British at the time of Napoleon's Egyptian expedition. Released

to strike at the saviours of the country was to repudiate the Revolution: 'Everything we have done . . . has had the people's sanction. If you attack us, you attack the people, who made the Revolution on 14th July, who consummated it on 10th August, and who will maintain it in the face of every danger.' In reply, the President of the Assembly, Lacroix, told the deputation that if the Commune did not obey the law it would show the whole of France that a single city was in rebellion against the general will. The decree was maintained that day, and on the evening of 1st September the Commune formally resolved to remain in office in defiance of it. Robespierre, who advised against this, nevertheless openly denounced his enemies in the Assembly, ('the *liberticide* Brissot, the faction of the Gironde, the villainous Committee of Twenty-one') as having sold France out to Brunswick, and he repeated this accusation in unmistakable terms on the evening of 2nd September. In consequence, the Commune's Security Committee issued warrants for the arrest of Brissot, Roland and at least eight others. Only the personal intervention of Danton next day prevented the execution of these warrants, which would undoubtedly have sent the Brissotins to their deaths in the prison massacres that began on 2nd September. The Brissotins had every justification for believing for the rest of their lives that Robespierre had done his best to have them murdered.[1]

All authority being now diminished, the swiftly mounting national crisis brought forth the best and the worst of Revolution. On the morning of Sunday, 2nd September, word reached Paris that Verdun, the last fortress blocking Brunswick's way to the capital, was about to fall. The Commune promptly called the citizens to arms, prematurely proclaiming that the enemy was already at the city gates. The red flag of emergency flew at the Hôtel de Ville. Delegates were despatched to rouse the sections to full awareness of 'the imminent danger of the country, and the treasons which surround us', and the order was given to fire the alarm-gun and ring the tocsin. Learning of these things, the Assembly abandoned its attempt to annul the Commune's authority, and Danton, in immortal words, called upon his countrymen to conquer by their courage and to triumph by their daring. In the days that

---

in 1802, he became consul at Alicante, contracted yellow fever and was retired on half-pay, dying in obscurity in 1820.

[1] In the notes which Robespierre later gave to Saint-Just as a basis for the indictment of Danton, one of the charges was that Danton had opposed Robespierre's attempt to 'prevent Brissot from renewing his plots' at this time. See J. M. Thompson *Robespierre*, Vol. I, p. 274 (where the second denunciation is mistakenly printed as 4th September) and Vol. II, p. 153. Robespierre's own reply on 5th November 1792 to the charge of promoting the assassination of the Brissotins, made against him by Brissot in the press and Louvet in the Convention, was at best evasive, and—in his denial of his presence at the Commune—untrue.

followed, thousands of volunteers were assembled and rushed away to rein-
force the army, while women worked with the men on the ramparts and met
in the churches to make clothing and equipment. But in this splendid time of
spontaneous patriotism, self-sacrifice marched hand-in-hand with murder.
Scarcely had the tocsin rung before priests, who were being sent under
escort to the Abbaye prison, were assaulted and murdered in the streets
near Saint Germain-des-Prés. Soon afterwards a band of men burst into
the Carmelite seminary in the Rue Vaugirard, which was being used as a
prison for priests. They slew some indiscriminately, and then improvised a
popular tribunal to sift the innocent from the guilty according to the people's
perception of justice and their ultimate right to execute it. The same form was
next observed for other political prisoners at the Abbaye, where Maillard
presided over the swift proceedings of the people's court. Those who were
acquitted were hailed as patriots and offered escort to their homes; the others
were 'released' or 'transferred'—and cut down by the self-appointed
executioners who awaited them in the courtyard. The prison massacres
continued for five days, until the night of 6th–7th September, and in all nine
prisons were invaded. Some 1,500 prisoners were released or returned to their
cells, and between 1,100 and 1,300 others, including thirty-seven women,
were killed. Although only one-quarter of the victims were political prisoners,
the Tribunal of 17th August was practically left without employment.[1]

The true history of these September Massacres still remains unknown.
Allegations of responsibility abound, but so little is certain that even in 1796
official proceedings could only elicit sufficient evidence to condemn three
obscure men as murderers. Historians generally agree that it was predominantly the public temper which made the massacres possible, and that
the weakness of authority and the over-riding needs of defence prevented
any effective intervention. According to Madame Roland, Danton—
nominally Minister of Justice, but in reality solely concerned with defence—
replied to a remonstrance with the robust exclamation: '*Je me fous bien des
prisonniers, qu'ils deviennent ce qu'ils pourront!*'[2] Certainly the situation
would suffice to explain still more wholesale slaughter. Men were generally
convinced that counter-revolution, defeated in the palace, was lurking in the
prisons. The captive priests and royalists were believed to be biding their
time while the volunteers marched away, waiting until they could break out

---

[1] The proceedings of the Tribunal in the trial of Major Bachmann of the Swiss Guard
were interrupted in the late afternoon of 2nd September by an incursion of killers from
the courtyards of the Conciergerie. They retired before the authority of the law, and later
Bachmann passed through their shambles unharmed on his way to the scaffold. A few days
later the judges also condemned the aged Caxotte, chief clerk to the intendant of the civil
list, who had been spared by the murderers when his daughter cast her arms around him.

[2] 'To hell with the prisoners! They must look after themselves!'

in company with a horde of common criminals and sack the city before delivering it to Brunswick. Nor was this fear altogether far-fetched: prison breaks had occurred before, and the prisons were notoriously over-crowded, under-staffed and so easy of access that the counterfeiting of *assignats* was almost an industry within them. Many therefore condoned the massacres, like the young Parisian who wrote on 2nd September: 'Necessity has made this execution inevitable. . . . It is sad to have to go to such lengths, but it is better (as they say) to kill the devil than to let the devil kill you.' Nevertheless, the killings were not the work of a maddened multitude. Although the matter remains controversial, it seems rather that they were carried out by a comparatively small number of *sans-culottes* and *fédérés*, who were convinced that their work was just and that they were serving the city by ridding it of priests and prostitutes, aristocrats and forgers, all alike in being enemies within the gates. As the massacres were in this sense the counterpart of patriotism, so the men of September were—and are—said to be indistinguishable from the men of 10th August. Similar smaller episodes in the provinces—particularly the killing at Versailles on 10th September of fifty-three political prisoners, including Delessart, who were being brought to Paris from Orléans for trial—occurred both before and after the events in Paris, and these suggest that the Parisians' attitude of mind was common to the whole country and was ultimately responsible for what happened.

To explain, however, is not necessarily to exonerate. Although the massacres were the product of fear and hatred, although they seem to have been spontaneously effected, it is hard to believe that they were wholly unpremeditated. In the paralysis of government, small groups were naturally driven to independent action, and on 2nd September several sections passed resolutions like that of the Section Poissonnière, which declared: 'that there is only one way to avert danger and stiffen the citizens' resolution to march to the frontier, and that is to execute immediately justice upon evil-doers and conspirators in the prisons.' Men such as Marat and Fabre d'Eglantine,[1] however, had long been actively inciting just such an act of violence—as, indeed, they continued to incite the provinces to emulate Paris.[2] Appointed

[1] Fabre d'Eglantine (Philippe François Nazaire) b., 1750 at Carcasonne. The son of a draper, he adopted the name *d'Eglantine* after taking part in a literary competition at Toulouse in 1771; thereafter became a strolling player, settled in Paris 1787 and produced a series of political plays and comic operas. A member of the Cordeliers Club, active on 20th June and 10th August 1792, he became secretary to Danton as Minister of Justice and had considerable control of patronage and secret funds. Elected deputy to the Convention for Paris, responsible for the nomenclature of the Revolutionary Calendar, implicated himself and compromised Danton in financial scandals, executed with Danton 1794.

[2] On 3rd September a letter was drawn up by the Security Committee of the Commune to be sent to the local authorities of France. It informed them that 'some of the ferocious conspirators detained in the prisons have been put to death by the people', and expressed

on 2nd September to the Commune's Security Committee, which was reconstituted that very day, Marat and his colleagues met that morning at the mayor's residence, and the priests who were imprisoned there were then sent openly across Paris. Their deaths began the more general bloodshed. Deliberate provocation here seems more probable than mere negligence. The best that can be said for the Commune is that its members allowed their authority to be exercised by a violent minority, and that its Security Committee tried to keep the killings under some sort of control through the establishment of the popular tribunals. These, however, practised only lynch law. The slaying, at best no more than butchery, inevitably bred bestiality: isolated individual atrocities, like the torture of Marie Gredeler at the Conciergerie and the mutilation of the body of the Princesse de Lamballe, led to the cold-blooded clubbing of boys at the Bicêtre and the sabring of women at the Salpêtrière. The Commune, however, saw that the mess was cleaned up and that the murderers were compensated for their loss of earnings.

Some days before these horrors occurred, Roland, Clavière and Servan had considered the advisability of abandoning Paris and establishing a new line of defence along the Loire. Learning of this proposal, Danton had firmly repudiated it, exclaiming that he had brought his aged mother and his young children to Paris and that he would rather perish with them in the ashes of the city than see it delivered to the Prussians. Defiance incarnate, Danton may really have believed, as he soon afterwards told the young duc de Chartres, that the fidelity of the volunteers of Paris would be assured if the Revolution released a river of blood to sever them from the *émigrés*. Some historians, indeed, still suggest that the massacres may be justified by their contribution to the defeat of the Prussians; but this seems no more than supposition. The invaders had already encountered a peasantry resolute to defend their homes and to prevent any restoration of the old régime, and the 20,000 volunteers who were hurried out of Paris in September, untrained, undisciplined and almost unarmed, were in fact kept as far from the fighting as possible by generals who had troubles enough already. Other factors, like the foul weather, the fundamental weakness of the enemy and the efficiency of the French cannon, swayed the fortunes of war far more than did the massacres.

The allied attack on France was in truth far less formidable than it appeared. Supposing that they would be welcome in France as liberators, Austria and Prussia had kept strong forces back in the east, where the

the hope that 'the entire nation . . . . will hasten to adopt this necessary measure of public security'. Printed in all probability on Marat's press, this message went out under the seal of the Ministry of Justice, probably with the connivance of Fabre, Danton's secretary. The comment of some historians that the letter had little actual effect seems inadequate.

123

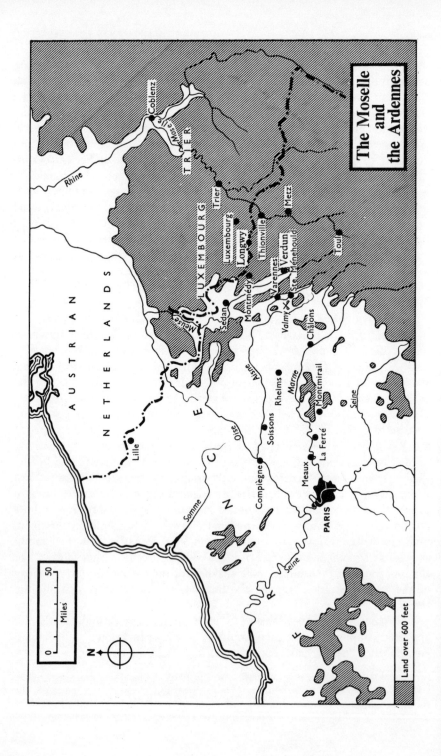

The Moselle
and
the Ardennes

Coblenz

Rhine

TRIER

Moselle

Trier

Luxembourg

LUXEMBOURG

Longwy

Metz

Thionville

Verdun

Ste. Menehould

Toul

Meuse

Sedan

Montmédy

Varennes

Valmy

Châlons

AUSTRIAN

NETHERLANDS

Aisne

Rheims

Marne

Montmirail

Lille

Oise

Soissons

Seine

Somme

Compiègne

Meaux

La Ferté

PARIS

Seine

FRANCE

N

Miles

50

0

Land over 600 feet

development of the Polish situation was still their principal concern. Unity of purpose, too, was lacking: their advance began before their diplomats had reached agreement about territorial acquisitions and exchanges. While the cautious Brunswick wanted only to secure advanced bases for a final campaign in the spring of 1793, Frederick William of Prussia, who accompanied the army, was anxious to press on to Paris and so free himself to deal with Russia. On the other hand, Brunswick's army was comparatively compact, and his line of advance was strategically dangerous. Having 42,000 Prussians and 5,600 Hessians under his personal command, with 15,000 Austrians on either side of his army and 4,500 *émigrés* under Provence in his rear, he threatened to pass between the French Army of the Centre, now commanded by Kellermann, and that of the North, led since La Fayette's defection by Dumouriez. That ex-minister had been a troublesome subordinate, but he now revealed remarkable ability and astonishing confidence in command.[1] Believing that a move into Belgium would bring Brunswick hurrying home, he remained in the north until pressure from Paris compelled him to defer any offensive and to come southwards to block the road to the capital. With great boldness he then stripped his frontier in order to concentrate about 20,000 men in the hill forest of the Argonne, some five miles east of Verdun, swearing that he would hold its passes as the Thermopylae of France. Even when on 14th September an Austrian thrust penetrated a minor northern pass and enabled the allied army to turn the whole position, Dumouriez did not retreat, but only reversed his front to stand at Sainte-Ménehould, with his back to the hills and Brunswick between himself and Paris—a position that Napoleon later said he would never have dared to hold.

Just before Brunswick attacked, Beurnonville arrived with more reinforcements from the north, and Kellermann came up with 16,000 men of the Army of the Centre, so that on 20th September 50,000 French confronted 34,000 Prussians. The full brunt of the battle, however, was borne by Kellermann's army, which consisted not, as is still alleged, of *sans-culottes*, but of the best troops of the old regular army and two battalions of the volunteers of 1791, trained soldiers of good quality.[2] Stationed on the rising ground at Valmy, to the east of Sainte-Ménehould, these endured prolonged bombardment without flinching, while their own artillery, the

---

[1] Servan's suggestion that, since powder was scarce, Dumouriez should only allow his men to take part in hand-to-hand fighting, illustrates the atmosphere in which he had to work.

[2] The spirit of the volunteers of 1792, who are sometimes represented as stern and severe republicans, and sometimes as a wild and lawless rabble, is not here in question, although it may be said that even the best of them were so completely independent that they were hardly of the army at all. Seven battalions of them, brought up by Beurnonville from Châlons 'to get accustomed to an army', were kept well in the rear at Valmy.

product of pre-revolutionary reforms, proved itself immeasurably superior to that of the Prussians. Eventually Frederick William himself ordered an advance, but his parade-ground formations made no progress against mud and musket-fire, and had soon to be recalled. Though the Prussians continued their cannonade until dusk, their failure to win the day sufficed to end their invasion. Torrential rains, the ravages of dysentery, and a severe shortage of supplies compelled Brunswick to seek Dumouriez's sanction for a retreat, and Dumouriez quietly agreed to shadow the Prussians back to the frontier so that he might be free to attack the Austrians in Belgium. The encounter at Valmy thus ended all immediate danger of the Revolution being still-born. As the young Goethe, who was present in the Prussian camp, perceived, it opened a new era in the history of the world.

The war now went wonderfully well for France. As the Prussians fell back in increasing distress and disruption, French forces under the generals Montesquiou and Anselme replied to Sardinia's declaration of war by completing their triumphant occupation of Savoy and Nice, and the Army of the Rhine, under the command of Custine, took Spires, Worms and Mayence from the Rhenish princes. The Austrians, too, were forced to abandon their siege of Lille, which had held out heroically under heavy bombardment, and Dumouriez came to the north again and hit them hard. At the battle of Jemappes on 6th November a strong French army, again composed of the best of the regular troops and three battalions of the volunteers of 1791, successfully stormed the Austrian positions in front of Mons. A week later Dumouriez entered Brussels as a conqueror, and throughout the winter of 1792–93 Belgium was entirely in the hands of the French.

These victories were not to prove permanent, but they gave France security until the spring of 1793, and they occurred just as the formation of a new parliament offered her people fresh hopes of stability at home. The Convention met for the first time in the Tuileries on the afternoon of 20th September, the day of Valmy.[1] This new assembly was really only directly representative of the actual minority of Frenchmen who had bothered to vote in the primary and secondary electoral assemblies, but it was nevertheless regarded as possessing an unprecedented moral authority. Elected by universal manhood suffrage, and untrammelled either by constitutional limitations or by royal rights, it was a constituent power as conceived by Sieyès, a body invested with the sovereign power of the nation and fully competent to lay down the foundations of law and establish institutions de novo. In acknowledgment of this authority, the Commune of the In-

---

[1] Although permanent accommodation was being prepared for the Convention in the Tuileries, it was not to be ready for use until the following May. After this first formal meeting, the Assembly met as before in the Manège.

surrection accepted without demur a decree by which the rump of the Legislative Assembly on 19th September ordered the election of a new municipality in Paris. Moreover, when on 21st September the new deputies moved into the Manège, they inaugurated the new régime in enthusiastic unanimity. Their first decrees declared that the constitution they were to draft would be submitted to the people for approval, and that persons and property were now under the protection of the nation. Amidst great enthusiasm, too, they pronounced the abolition of royalty, ending the ancient monarchy of France and establishing the Republic, as they thought, for ever.

This time of concord seemed to offer the possibility of orderly freedom and a profitable peace with foreign enemies. Within a week, however, the Convention became the scene of bitter conflicts, and within a month its authority was being openly challenged by that of the sections. By the beginning of November civil war seemed about to begin in the streets of Paris, and the Jacobin Club had again become identified with militant dissidence. When new dangers threatened the nation in the spring of 1793, parliamentary government had become so paralysed that yet another revolution was necessary to save the state.

This dangerous situation developed in part because the deputies felt themselves bound not only to provide France with a constitution, but also to govern the country as a senate and a final court of appeal. At the day of their first meeting they repudiated a suggestion which seemed to presage the growth of a presidential system, and thereafter they tried both to legislate for the nation and to adjudicate upon the minutiae of local and even personal matters. No assembly of more than 700 men could have done this without acrimony, even if procedure and party organisation, as well as a committee system and an effective means of liaison between the legislative and the executive, had been far more fully developed than they were in 1792. Moreover, until new accommodation became available in the Tuileries in May 1793, the Convention worked without respite in the unhealthy atmosphere of the Manège, a narrow amphitheatre with high tiers of seats at either end. The cramped conditions of this building and its unhappy associations with past controversy naturally fostered faction.

At best, however, the Convention could hardly have been more than a battleground for forces already aligned by earlier events. There being now no bar to the re-election of members of previous assemblies, both the Brissotin and the Robespierre Jacobins had secured seats, each group being convinced of the ambition and duplicity of the other. Thanks to Robespierre's skilful management, the electoral assembly of Paris had met in the Jacobin Club, deliberating in public and voting aloud. Various measures of disenfranchisement and intimidation, and the fact that the September massacres

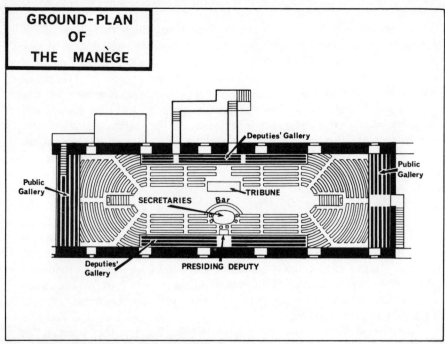

GROUND-PLAN
OF
THE MANÈGE

Deputies' Gallery

Public Gallery

Public Gallery

TRIBUNE

SECRETARIES

Bar

Deputies' Gallery

PRESIDING DEPUTY

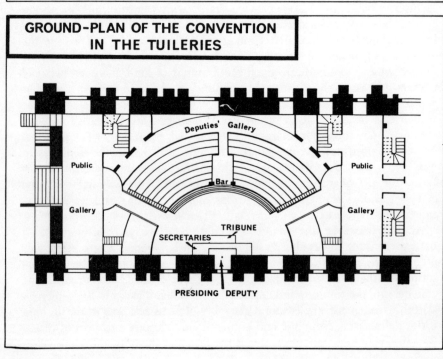

GROUND-PLAN OF THE CONVENTION
IN THE TUILERIES

Deputies' Gallery

Public

Public

Gallery

Gallery

Bar

TRIBUNE

SECRETARIES

PRESIDING DEPUTY

were then proceeding, had ensured that all twenty-four of those chosen as deputies for Paris were men of Robespierre's mind. He himself was the first to be elected, and Danton, Marat, Billaud-Varenne, Collot d'Herbois, Camille Desmoulins and the Duke of Orléans—now officially re-named *Citoyen Égalité*—were with him. The Brissotins, on the other hand, had been returned by the departments, for their reputation as the patriots of the Legislative Assembly was far better known in the provinces than was their recent repudiation by the radicals of the capital.[1] Their connection, though still as loose as ever, was now rather larger than it had been before, for a number of new deputies were closely associated with them. Louvet, for example, was elected for the Loiret, although he had never been there, and both Barbaroux and Buzot—once Robespierre's colleague in the Constituent Assembly—had become devoted to Madame Roland. Pétion, too, was now of their number: being bitterly resentful of the way in which he had been thrust aside by the Commune after 10th August, he had broken with Robespierre, and won a seat for the Eure et Loir after being rejected in Paris. The two groups took their seats on opposite sides of the Assembly, the Brissotins sitting on the Right and the Jacobin deputies of Paris and their supporters taking the highest seats on the Left, and so being known by the name Montagnards, or men of the Mountain.

The exact nature of the dispute which ensued has long been debated by historians, who have usually made the mistake of supposing that each of the two sides was united and organised as a large and coherent party. This idea, which is as convenient in writing as it is in argument, was popularised in the middle of the nineteenth century by the brilliant but unreliable *Histoire des Girondins* by Lamartine: it derives, however, from the political propaganda of 1792–93, which was of course intended to mislead. In fact, the deputies of the Convention were quite remarkably disunited, the very term 'party' being one of opprobrium. It was generally believed that in a democracy affairs of state ought to be directed according to the general will of the people, and it was thought that this could only be ascertained if each of the people's deputies freely and independently expressed his own perception of it. Any form of private or preliminary agreement was thus regarded as a deliberate attempt to distort the truth and to promote some particular

---

[1] This, at least, is the usual explanation of their success, which is also ascribed to the preponderant influence of their newspapers—some of which were certainly subsidised by Roland's Ministry of the Interior. The Jacobins of Paris, on the other hand, seem to have concentrated on winning the capital: their circular to their affiliated societies on 12th September apologises for an interruption of correspondence since 10th August. Even so, something seems unexplained, and one may well wonder whether the split in the Society was even now so clear-cut and complete as it was later alleged to be. The alternative explanation, that the provincial Jacobins knew all about the dispute but deliberately chose men opposed to Robespierre, is of course heretical.

partial interest to the detriment of the public good. It was for this very reason that the disputes in the Convention became so bitter: every difference of opinion underlined the Assembly's failure to achieve the 'terrible unanimity' which everyone thought to be essential.

The Brissotins themselves were never much more than a small group of friends, and if their support of one another sometimes seems preconcerted, their complete independence as individuals is demonstrably the real reason for their complete failure to govern France. Their association was hardened only by the opposition of the Montagnards—who were peculiarly strong and united in the parliament for the simple reason that their differences were very largely reconciled in advance of debates. The Montagnards' general attitude was pre-determined by preliminary discussion at the Jacobin Society, from which dissidents were soon expelled as public enemies. Although they were as hostile as anyone to the idea of 'party', they in fact formed one within the Convention by claiming that they alone represented the people, in whose hearing at the Jacobins their views were decided. As Robespierre's brother Augustin wrote in April 1793, 'the Jacobin Society is by its very nature incorruptible. It deliberates before an audience of four thousand persons, so that its whole power lies in public opinion and it cannot betray the interests of the people'. The disruption of the Convention was not due to a conflict between two parties, but to one between the Convention, the national parliament itself, and those of its members who were the spearhead of an extra-parliamentary movement, that of the Jacobins.[1]

Appreciation of this point makes much else clear. Since there was in reality only one political party involved, it is hardly surprising that those who have attempted to determine fundamental differences of origin, outlook and policy between the Montagnards and the 'Girondins' have only produced contradictory definitions. Thus although it is likely that the Montagnards were more responsive to popular opinion, and particularly Parisian opinion, than were the majority of their colleagues, and although in time widely differing social groups gathered behind the Jacobins and behind the Convention, there was little or no social distinction between the deputies themselves. Indirectly elected, the new assembly contained only one or two men who can be considered working-men, and as wide a gulf separated Vergniaud from Louvet as from Desmoulins. The quarrel which broke out in the first week between the Brissotins and the Montagnards was certainly a continuation of that which had begun in the Legislative Assembly over the question of

[1] The unity of the Montagnards must of course be recognised as relative rather than absolute: their most prominent speakers sometimes differed in the parliament, but they were far more of a coherent force than any other group. Augustin's letter (to the Society in Arras) is cited in the Appendix of Georges Michon, *Correspondance de Maximilien et Augustin Robespierre*, Paris, 1926.

the war, and had later been aggravated both by the Brissotins' ambiguous attitude towards the deposition of the king and by their resentment of the Commune's assumption of dictatorial powers. By the beginning of September 1792, Robespierre had convinced himself that the Brissotins were fully prepared to betray the Revolution, and that only Paris could prevent them from doing so, while the Brissotins believed that Robespierre had tried to have them killed in the prisons. Irreconcilable hostility consequently divided them, and petty personal rancours, like Pétion's resentment of Robespierre's pre-eminence or Madame Roland's genteel repugnance for Danton's vulgarity, inflamed the antagonism.

This personal quarrel gained new significance from the reaction that followed the September massacres. Although, like everyone else, the Brissotins had at first averted their eyes from the killing, they were genuinely shocked by its extent,[1] and they were quick to stigmatise the whole capital and all their opponents in the Commune and the Jacobins as anarchists and *septembriseurs*. Even Danton, whose intervention had saved them, was castigated as a man of blood. In the last days of the Legislative they condemned disorder, renewed their attacks upon the power of the Commune and demanded that forces should be sent from the provinces to protect the Convention from Paris. They thus identified themselves with the maintenance of law, the rights of the provinces and the sovereignty of parliament, and when the Convention met it was almost completely united in their support. The new deputies, principally professional men from the provinces, were suspicious of Paris and horrified by the apparent danger of lawlessness and looting. They showed their feelings by appointing Pétion as their first President,[2] by affording Brissot, Condorcet, Vergniaud and Lasource the honour of acting as secretaries, and by confirming the authority of the Committee of Twenty-one and of the Rolandist Executive Council.

The Brissotins, however, showed neither wisdom nor magnanimity in their use of this commanding position. Twice within a month they attempted to legislate against Paris and to incriminate Robespierre as a would-be dictator. On the first occasion a report from Roland reiterated his opinion that the Convention ought to have a military force at its own disposal, the 'departmental guard'. Buzot then succeeded on 24th September in securing the appointment of a commission to enquire into the state of Paris, to draft a law

---

[1] Roland's attitude is representative. On 3rd September, in a famous letter, he told the Legislative that a veil should be drawn over the events of the previous day, since the people tempered its vengeance with a kind of rough justice. But he also urged the Commune to prevent further violence, and ten days later he explained: 'I did not hastily condemn the terrible initial upheaval. . . . I did believe its continuation had to be avoided'.

[2] As in earlier assemblies, the honour of acting as President was afforded by election for a fortnight at a time.

against incitement to murder, and to examine means of providing the assembly with an armed guard drawn from the departments. Next day, after Lasource had won general approval by asserting that the power of Paris must be restricted to that of any other one of the eighty-three departments of France, Barbaroux and his friend Rebecquy openly attacked Robespierre. At this point, however, the attack became diverted. To the horror of all, Marat avowed that he believed some form of dictatorship to be imperative; but he claimed that this opinion was his alone, and he threatened, pistol in hand, to blow out his brains on the spot if freedom of opinion was to be denied. An earlier move by Danton decided the debate: his proposal that the assembly should renounce both dictatorship and federalism gave rise to the celebrated resolution: 'The French Republic is one and indivisible.' From this time onwards the Montagnards could easily represent the Brissotins' attacks on Paris as part of a 'federalist' design to disrupt the unity of the nation. In reality, only Buzot seems seriously to have favoured a federal form of government, but the allegation injured the Brissotins. It became still more damaging when Danton, who had resigned from the Ministry of Justice in order to take his place in the assembly, became irritated by the deputies' support of Roland, who had refused his seat and remained Minister of the Interior; for Danton now revealed that the old man and his associates had considered the possibility of abandoning Paris when Brunswick was advancing towards it.

A month later, when the conflict had become further embittered by a series of attacks upon Danton, who could not account for all the monies that had been entrusted to him as Minister of Justice, the Brissotins made a second attempt to crush their opponents. On 29th October a report from Roland again attacked the Commune—which still survived, thanks to the complex processes of electing a new one—and repeated the allegations about Robespierre. On this occasion the disunity of the Brissotins was particularly evident. While Buzot was waiting to present his proposals for the capital punishment of sedition, Robespierre demanded to know who would dare accuse him to his face—and a single voice cried 'Moi!'. Louvet then unexpectedly strode forward to the rostrum to pronounce a long philippic against him, which was not pressed to a division. Buzot was again frustrated next day, when attention was distracted from his proposals by Barbaroux's demands for such drastic measures as the abolition of the permanence of the sectional assemblies and the replacement of the Commune by commissioners designated by the departments.

Thus on each of these two occasions the Brissotins failed to achieve their objective, partly because their efforts were not adequately co-ordinated, and partly because they wearied and antagonised the rest of the Convention by their persistent pursuit of what seemed only a personal quarrel. Moreover, they made the great mistake of attacking Paris, and all those associated with it, indiscriminately. In the Convention, this drove Danton into opposition, and in the city it destroyed the goodwill with which the Convention had been welcomed. The sectional assemblies, most of which were at first resentful of the Commune's arbitrary actions, and which were as alarmed as anyone by the possibility of violence and pillage, were potential allies, but the possibility of their support was heedlessly cast away. When they protested against the law which bound them to elect their new municipality by secret ballot and when they expressed their determination to vote orally in the way 'worthy of free and virtuous men', they were condemned as rebels by the Brissotins.

The Brissotins' campaign to secure a departmental guard naturally intensified the sections' suspicions of them, particularly when Buzot's committee attempted to initiate an enquiry into the strength of the armed forces that existed in Paris. By 19th October the sections and the Commune had drawn together sufficiently to present a joint protest to the Convention. The purpose of this, as Chaumette put it in a preliminary address, was to ensure that the delegates (*mandataires*) of the people should know the will of 'an integral portion of the sovereign (people)'; the deputies were to understand that, if necessary, an appeal would be made to the people as a whole to judge between its delegates and Paris, the home of enlightenment and the proven bulwark of the Revolution. In this way the sections, which had always assumed that they had the right to sanction the Convention's decrees, soon began to question the validity of its authority. Guadet, condemning the address of 19th October as unconstitutional, might assert in the Convention that 'it is here that the exercise of the sovereignty of the French people resides', but in reality direct democracy and parliamentary government were again in open conflict.

The opposition of Paris, and their reverses in the Convention, compelled the Brissotins to give up their efforts to obtain approval for a departmental guard. They did not, however, abandon the plan itself. In general they seem to have been convinced that the fall of the monarchy had really ended the Revolution, and that any new discontent or opposition must be malevolent. As Brissot wrote at this time, 'Before 10th August the disorganisers were real revolutionaries, for a republican had to be a disorganiser. But today the disorganisers are counter-revolutionaries. They are anarchists and levellers.' Many deputies probably shared this opinion, but Brissot and his friends were apparently also convinced of their own worldly-wisdom and intellectual superiority. According to Pétion the real conflict of the time was that 'between light and darkness, between knowledge and ignorance'. Brissot did not hesitate to assert that a third revolution was necessary to suppress anarchy, and his associates had no qualms in calling upon their constituents to send armed forces to Paris on their own initiative. As early as 24th September Barbaroux had announced in the Jacobin Club that a second battalion of Marseillais was on the march to Paris, and on 20th October its arrival was marked by the presentation of an address against anarchy and dictatorship. By the middle of November, when conservative addresses from the provinces were reaching the Convention in ever-increasing numbers, there were some 12,000 of these 'federal' troops in Paris, and for a time there was serious friction between them and the forces of the sections. Many of the newcomers, however, were no more than volunteers on their way to the front, and these were more concerned with finding board and lodging than with politics. The aid offered to them by the Commune soon pacified them and Jacobin propaganda rapidly won over most of those who stayed long in Paris. The danger of violence passed, but the Convention remained defenceless.

By now the Brissotins' intransigence had begun to affect the balance of forces in the Assembly. On 24th October Fabre d'Eglantine remarked at the Jacobins that although at first the whole Convention had been united in hostility to the deputies of Paris, something more like equilibrium had begun to appear. For a short time, indeed, it even seemed that a centre party might emerge between the Brissotins and the Montagnards. But although Camille Desmoulins referred to the appearance of such a group of moderates, whom he called the *Phlegmatiques*, early in November, this development was short lived. The Convention did not divide, as is usually supposed, into three parts, for no sooner had the relatively obscure men of the centre begun to assert themselves than they were subjected to an alarming assault by the Jacobin deputies, and this re-established the division between these Montagnards and the majority. Thanks to the Brissotins' own mistakes, the Montagnards were now still more closely associated with Paris, and during October they also secured complete control of the Jacobin Society. Brissot, who was formally expelled from the Society on 10th October, had apparently advised his friends to affect disdain of its activities, and his subsequent appeal to the affiliated clubs evoked but little response. The Montagnards also became much more aggressive in the Convention, contesting debates by systematic interruption, appealing to their supporters in the public galleries and repeatedly demanding the *appel nominal*—a vote taken by roll-call, in which each deputy in turn was required to pronounce his opinion aloud from the rostrum.

Montagnard pressure, however, was not merely a matter of turbulence. On 5th November Collot d'Herbois answered the Brissotins' allegations about the September massacres by openly avowing that these had been essential to the survival of the Revolution and were 'an integral part of our creed of liberty'. On the same day, Robespierre made a masterly reply to

Louvet's earlier denunciation, boldly reminding the Convention that to attack the men who had made the insurrection of 10th August was to repudiate the Revolution and liberty itself, both of which had always been illegal. In this way the Montagnards identified themselves with both Paris and the Revolution, deliberately accepting responsibility for the best and the worst of the immediate past. Thus by the beginning of November, some six weeks after the Convention first assembled, the majority of its deputies found that the principle of parliamentary democracy was being strongly challenged by two alien forces in alliance, the extra-parliamentary Jacobin movement and the popular democracy of Paris.

It was no accident that this situation coincided with the Convention's first steps towards the indictment of the king, for the Jacobins' attitude implied that their opponents were—and always had been—counter-revolutionaries and enemies of the people. As Chabot put it at the Jacobins on 7th November: 'By the Brissotins we mean those who opposed the insurrection of 10th August.' Moreover, the Montagnards probably calculated that ruthlessness towards the king would win much support, for many moderate men were afraid lest delay in dealing with him might lead to a new outbreak of popular violence at the Temple. Furthermore, the *sans-culottes* of Paris, on whose support the Montagnards depended, saw the deputies' attitude towards Louis as the supreme test of their sincerity. Holding him responsible for the blood that had been shed in the attack on the Tuileries and in the defence of the frontier, they regarded his trial and execution as the Convention's first duty. To substantiate their claim to represent the Revolution, the Montagnards had therefore to demand that Louis should die ,and this again implied that all who opposed them were really more royalist than republican at heart.

The Brissotins were particularly vulnerable to this charge, for the record of their relationship with the Court was rich in ambiguity, and even their suspension of the king on 10th August was commonly regarded as an attempt to preserve the monarchy instead of abolishing it completely. Moreover, despite all that they could do, the development of the debate diminished their reputation as republicans, for their hostility to the Montagnards inevitably became entangled with the Assembly's very real reluctance to send Louis to the scaffold. Although a preliminary report on 8th November by the Legislative Committee had asserted that the Convention, as an assembly embodying all the constituent power of the people, was fully competent to try the king, most deputies had grave doubts about proceeding further. Some privately sympathised with the man they called the tyrant. Many were concerned about the consequences of regicide, fearing royalist rebellions in the provinces and foreseeing, like Danton, that peace negotiations would become impossible and that new wars might well ensue. As lawyers, too

135

almost all disliked confusing the legislative and the judicial powers and being both prosecutors and judges in a single cause. The indictment of the king for crimes he had committed before his deposition, and for which he had some claims to constitutional inviolability, also had a regrettable appearance of retrospective law. The debates which began on 13th November and which lasted for two months were therefore at first as serious as they were inconclusive. On 20th November, however, the sudden discovery of many of Louis's private papers in a secret cupboard in the Tuileries (the *armoire de fer*) provided new proofs of the king's duplicity. Now Mirabeau's venality was revealed and La Fayette's royalism confirmed. A trial became inevitable: but Roland and all his friends were compromised by his stupidity in removing the contents of the cache before witnesses were present to see that no documents had been abstracted.

On the first day of these debates, 13th November, a maiden speech by the youngest of the deputies, Antoine de Saint-Just,[1] established the foundation of the Montagnard position. Too young to sit in earlier assemblies, Saint-Just had followed the Revolution as an ardent admirer of Robespierre. Now, at the age of twenty-five, he was to stand beside him, a proud and handsome intellectual, coldly self-contained and completely fanatical. The Convention, he claimed, should not concern itself with the king's guilt or innocence, for kingship was itself a crime; it should not consider a trial, for there could be no common law between a prince and the people whose power he had usurped; Louis had but to be executed as an enemy, according to the laws of war. For Saint-Just, the Republic was already 'the total destruction of everything opposed to it'.[2] A fortnight later, on 3rd–4th December, after the *armoire de fer* had been discovered and a delegation had come to the Convention to protest against delays, Robespierre himself developed Saint-Just's thesis in rather less abstract terms. The Convention, he said, was not a court sitting in judgement, but a responsible parliament, required to take a step essential to public security; since the people had already condemned Louis for past crimes by rising in revolt against him, the Assembly had not to try him but simply to order his immediate elimination as a present menace to the tranquillity of the Republic.

These terrible assertions served their purpose. Many who had doubted the morality and legality of a trial were prepared to accept a measure of political expediency, and those who continued to oppose the Montagnard minority seemed to be shielding royalism and reaction. When Buzot, at this time probably the most active opponent of the Montagnards, tried to escape

---

[1] Saint-Just (Antoine Louis Léon de Richebourg de), b. 1767 at Decize, Nivernais, deputy to the Convention for Aisne, executed with Robespierre 28th July 1794.

[2] The definition made by Saint-Just in his speech of 8 Ventôse (26th February) 1794.

13   Saint-Just

From a drawing made by Charles Guérin at Strasbourg, 1793

14   The Execution of Louis XVI, on the Place de la Révolution (the present
Place de la Concorde), 21 January 1793

From a closely contemporary water-colour by an unknown artist

from this dilemma by moving legislation against the Orléanists—the Duke of Orléans being now the Montagnard 'Égalité'—he only exposed himself and his friends to accusations of attempting to save the king by procrastination, and his more disciplined antagonists soon forced the majority to revoke the decrees which Buzot had proposed. On 8th December the Assembly ended its general discussions and ordered an indictment to be prepared, and it also accepted Marat's proposal that all the decisions arising from this should be reached by *appel nominal*, 'so that the traitors in this Assembly may be known'. As Danton had long since perceived, once matters reached this point the king's fate was sealed. The indictment, essentially the charge that Louis had consistently encouraged counter-revolution, was practically unanswerable in its own terms. When on 11th December Louis was brought to the bar of the Assembly to hear and reply to the charges, he bore himself with quiet dignity, and only displayed indignation when he was accused of shedding the blood of Frenchmen. His replies, however, were equivocal and evasive, and he failed either to challenge the competence of the Convention or to appeal to principles older or greater than those of the Revolution. All heard him in respectful silence, but none doubted his guilt.

The Montagnard minority, however, had still to win its first victory over the rest of the Convention. Far from surrendering to their leadership, the Brissotins sought desperately for some 'patriotic' way of frustrating Robespierre without openly opposing the condemnation of the king. A second attack upon Orléans was one such move, and even after the king's counsel, de Sèze, had vainly advanced a formal defence of inviolability on 26th December, Buzot and Salle succeeded in delaying a decision by proposing that there should be a referendum, an appeal to the sovereignty of the people. These expedients proved as vain as the secret attempts of the Spanish chargé d'affaires to purchase support for Louis by bribery. Opposing them with disciplined clamour, the Montagnards dismissed them all as disguised royalism. Robespierre reiterated the assertion that the people had already made their will manifest on 10th August, and added the decisive argument that a referendum could only cause royalist agitation and even civil war. At the same time, increased pressure was brought to bear. On 30th December a deputation of the citizens of Paris appeared at the bar, complete with representatives of those wounded or bereaved on 10th August, and four days later the Mountain suddenly revealed their knowledge of the letters Vergniaud and his colleagues had written to the king just before the insurrection, 'in the days when the Montagnards alone were guided by instinctive patriotism'. In this atmosphere, uproar and disorderly scenes became commonplace, and on more than one occasion deputies streamed across the hall behind such fire-eaters as Barbaroux and Louvet in attempts to compel the Montagnards to be silent. 'We are here under an oppressive majority',

137

declared the Montagnards;[1] but Vergniaud protested that 'the majority of this Assembly cannot remain for ever under the domination of a seditious minority'.

On 14th January 1795, after a week had been allowed to enable deputies to print and circulate their opinions, the final voting began. Since the Assembly had accepted Marat's proposal that this should be by *appel nominal*, it was a protracted process. For five days each deputy in turn had publicly to pronounce his decision on each of four separate questions, each declaration being both officially recorded and unofficially ratified or repudiated by the crowded public galleries. During this terrible time, when some stories suggest that almost every deputy was carrying concealed arms, the king was judged guilty by an overwhelming majority. The referendum was rejected by a majority of 139 (425 votes to 286); the sentence of death was accepted by a majority of 53 (387 votes to 334);[2] and a stay of execution was rejected by a majority of 70 (380 votes to 310). Two days later, on 21st January, Louis was brought from the Temple to the Place de la Révolution, and there beheaded by the guillotine, his last words being lost amid the rolling of the drums.

This was, as it was intended to be, an irrevocable act. The king, himself a worthy and well-meaning gentleman, died as Saint-Just had said he must, not for what he had done but for what he was. In order to identify themselves with the Revolution, the Montagnards deliberately severed the present from the past, committing themselves and their nation to new causes in defiance of the whole of Europe and the greater part of France. Still more important was the manner of the act. The sovereignty of the nation and the will of the people—in reality the marginal majorities of a far from representative Assembly—were shown as superior to both ancient right and new enlightenment, and justice was made to appear as a mere instrument of policy. Although the Montagnards had yet to secure permanent power and coordinate an apparatus of government, the whole of the Terror was implicit in the killing of the king.

---

[1] The speaker, probably Thuriot, is referred to in the *Moniteur* as Tureau (Vol. XIV, p. 866). Thuriot de la Rosière (Jacques Alexis) member of the Legislative Assembly and the Convention for Marne, associated with Danton, died 1829.

[2] Twenty-six deputies voted for an amendment which linked their preference for execution with their desire for a reprieve. The one was not, however, conditional upon the other, and it is inaccurate to cite the figures as showing a majority of one (361 to 360).

6

The Purging of Parliament

After the execution of Louis XVI, France was indeed two nations, and effective power eluded everyone. 'The truth is', wrote Burke in 1793, 'that France is out of herself. The master of the house is expelled, and the robbers are in possession. If we look for the corporate people of France . . . they are in Flanders and Germany, in Switzerland, Spain, Italy and England.' Promising to restore the old order in its entirety, the Count of Provence declared himself Regent for His Most Christian Majesty, Louis XVII, King of France and Navarre; but Provence was in exile in Germany, his subjects were outlawed Frenchmen, and his master, the eight-year-old Dauphin, was a closely-guarded captive in the Temple. On the other side, the republican government at Paris was weak and divided. Constant attacks drove Roland to resign on 22nd January, and although his friends Clavière and Lebrun remained at the Ministries of Finance and Foreign Affairs, they were now isolated. Pache,[1] whom Roland had helped to become Minister of War, had soon shown himself an ardent Jacobin, and Garat, who succeeded Roland, was only appointed because he was too colourless a character to offend anyone in the Convention. An attempt by that assembly to co-ordinate the work of government by creating a Committee of General Defence did nothing to mend matters: large in numbers, but limited in its powers, this Committee merely mirrored the disunity of the deputies.

Political disunity, with the general distrust of any strong executive power, was indeed the real weakness of the revolutionary nation. The Montagnards, who had gained greatly from their attacks upon the king, could brand all who opposed them as *appellants*[2] and conspirators, but they were nevertheless still a minority and could seldom do more than obstruct the proceedings of

---

[1] Jean Nicolas Pache, a Swiss, was a protégé of Necker's and a friend of the Rolands. Helped by them to the Ministry of War after the retirement of Servan in October 1792, he clashed with Dumouriez about the methods of supplying the armies and became a strong Jacobin. When displaced from the War Office in February 1792, he was elected Mayor of Paris by an overwhelming majority against the more moderate candidate and stayed in office until arrested in May 1794 for supposed Hébertism, being then replaced by Robespierre's nominee Lescot-Fleuriot. Tried and acquitted in the Year IV, he survived the Revolution and died in Ardennes in 1823.

[2] The name given to those who had supported the proposal to decide the king's fate by a referendum, supposedly part of a royalist plot.

the Convention. On the other hand the majority—from which the Brissotins were now distinguishable only by their prominence—was also quite unable to govern effectively. Although at least half its leaders, including Brissot, Barbaroux, Buzot, Vergniaud, Gaudet and Gensonné, had voted for *la mort*, they were all damned as moderates by the Mountain, and they remained hopelessly independent and individualistic. Even when Buzot, on 13th January, at last persuaded the assembly to accept his proposals for drawing an armed guard from the provinces, his friend Boyer-Fonfrède intervened to prevent further action being taken. Moreover, the introduction of any proposals displeasing to the Mountain invariably led to denunciations and organised uproar. By the dictation of disorder, the Montagnards were making majority government impossible, and since there could be no constitutional solution, a new Revolution became unavoidable.

Circumstances determined that this should again take the form of popular insurrection, for by the spring of 1793 the danger of military defeat and counter-revolutionary conquest had recurred. In September 1792 the Convention had hesitated to approve any measures likely to extend the war. When the people of Savoy had sought union with France, a decision had been deferred, despite Danton's assertion that all liberated peoples ought to repudiate royalism and adopt French forms of government. After Valmy there were even negotiations for peace, but Austria and Prussia, which were now chiefly interested in the dismemberment of France, soon made it clear that they would require the Revolution to recognise all the rights of the old régime. France would have to evacuate all imperial territory, restore the papal authority in Avignon, compensate the Rhineland princes for their feudal rights in Alsace, grant some territories to the king's brothers, and guarantee the safety of all the Royal Family. As these terms were of course incompatible with the revolutionaries' conception of the sovereign rights of the nation, the war went on, and the French were soon tempted to commit themselves far beyond their effective strength. Influential foreign refugees like Anarcharsis Cloots, the Prussian who called himself the Orator of Humankind, still fostered the illusion that their peoples awaited liberation, and in Nice and the Rhineland and Belgium the minorities which had welcomed the French forces were soon clamouring for permanent protection. 'Such is our position', the delegates of Nice explained to the Convention on 4th November, 'that we can only be Frenchmen or slaves.'

Above all, the astonishing success of French arms inspired elation, and after Jemappes had been won on 6th November doubts quickly disappeared. Henceforth caution was swept aside and policy was determined by a mixture of interest and ideology. Despite the fact that the final course of the River Scheldt ran through Dutch territory and had been closed to commerce by repeated international agreements,[1] the Executive Council on 16th November attempted to conciliate opinion in Belgium by declaring it open to shipping. This unilateral decision, commercially advantageous to Antwerp but injurious to both Amsterdam and London, was then enforced by a squadron of ships of the French fleet. At the same time the Convention enthusiastically approved the famous decree of 19th November by which France promised *'fraternité et secours'* to all peoples who wished to recover their liberty, and on 27th November it accepted, with only one dissident vote, the annexation of Savoy. As Grégoire exclaimed on this occasion: 'Our lot is cast: we are launched upon our course, all governments are our foes, all peoples are our friends.' In Brissot's words, written on 27th November: 'We can never enjoy our liberty while a Bourbon remains enthroned . . . we cannot rest until all Europe is ablaze.'

Soon, however, it became apparent that this widening war would be expensive, and Cambon[2] then introduced the crucial decree of 15th December. In this the Convention, 'faithful to the principles of the sovereignty of the people, which do not permit it to recognise any institutions detrimental thereto', ordered its generals to suppress feudal institutions in occupied territories. They were to confiscate the property of all who opposed them, including that of the Church, and to supervise the election of friendly administrations to govern at the expense of the dispossessed. Thus France announced her intention of ruling conquered territories by revolutionary minorities, and of strengthening her economy by forcing foreigners to accept the *assignat* in exchange for their wealth and their property.

Taken together, these various measures amounted to a declaration of war on Europe. Having made herself, by virtue of the Revolution, the arbiter of right and wrong in international affairs, France was led by victory into aggrandisement. Other annexations followed the first, and on 31st January 1793 Danton demanded that of Belgium also, since the limits of the Republic were 'defined by nature' as 'the four corners of the horizon: the banks of the Rhine and the Ocean, and the foothills of the Alps'. The opening of the Scheldt and the occupation of Belgium inevitably antagonised Great Britain, and as early as 13th November Pitt promised Holland to support her if she should be attacked. The execution of the king, which Pitt called

[1] Since the Treaty of Munster in 1648. France and Holland had reaffirmed their agreement to keep the Scheldt closed as recently as 10th November 1785, when they signed the Treaty of Fontainebleau.

[2] Cambon (Pierre Joseph) b., Montpellier 1756, deputy for Hérault to the Legislative Assembly and the Convention, in both of which he was particularly concerned with finance. Attacked by Robespierre as a reactionary just before Thermidor, he contributed to the overthrow of his accuser, but was subsequently accused of malversation by Tallien and retired from political life soon afterwards. Twenty years later he was again elected by Hérault to Napoleon's Chamber and opposed the Bourbon restoration. Exiled to the Netherlands in 1816, he died in 1820.

'the foulest and most atrocious deed which the history of the world has yet had occasion to attest' was marked by general mourning in London, and the French declaration of war on Britain and Holland on 1st February 1793 probably only anticipated similar action against her. The conduct of France, as Pitt told the House of Commons on the same day, was inconsistent with the peace and liberty of Europe, for her new criterion of conduct, the will of the people, was no more than the power of the French. 'Unless she is stopped in her career', he said, 'all Europe must soon learn their ideas of justice—law of nations—models of government—and principles of liberty from the mouth of the French cannon.' A month later, on 7th March, the Convention also declared war on Spain, one more enemy for France being, according to Barère,[1] 'no more than another triumph for liberty'. Within a short time all the European states save those of Switzerland and Scandinavia were at war with France and were being united by Britain into a great coalition against her.

Well before this could be effective, however, the Convention's early over-confidence had led the French directly to disaster. At the end of 1792 their armies were over-extended. As they had advanced, so they had separated, and a particularly dangerous gap had opened between Dumouriez's forces in Belgium and those of Custine on the Rhine. Moreover, although Dumouriez realised that it was of the first importance not to alienate the Belgians, neither he nor his Brissotin friends[2] could prevent the Convention from putting the decree of 15th December into effect there. By 1st February Cambon estimated that property to the value of sixty-four million livres had been obtained from Belgium. This exploitation and the attack upon the Church aroused deep antagonism to France, and on 17th February the French commissioners in Belgium warned the Convention that the country would revolt at the first news of a French defeat. In these circumstances, Dumouriez's advance into Holland on 16th February was as much a result of

---

[1] Barère de Vieuzac (Bertrand), b. 1755, lawyer of Toulouse, member of the National Assembly for Third Estate of Bigorre and of Convention for Hautes-Pyrénées, and a notable orator, he became a member of the Committee of Public Safety, for which he often acted as spokesman during the Terror. Exiled with Billaud-Varenne and Collot d'Herbois in 1795, he remained in hiding in France and lived on the fringe of politics from 1798 until he was exiled at the Restoration. Returning to France from Belgium after 1830, he died in 1841.

[2] While he was victorious, Dumouriez had general support. Robespierre, however, seems always to have distrusted him, and the Montagnards had long supported Pache, the Jacobin Minister of War, in his running fight with the general over supplies. The Brissotins, who had broken with Dumouriez when he remained in office after Roland was dismissed in June, 1792, had by now resumed friendly relations with him, supporting his case against that of Pache until the latter left the Ministry on 4th February 1793.

despair as of obedience to orders. His initial success there went for nothing when, on 1st March, Coburg's Austrians struck out from their salient and overwhelmed the weakened army of occupation. Within a few days all Belgium was in revolt, Liège had been recaptured and the French forces in Holland were falling back in disorder.

To make matters worse, the France which heard these evil tidings was once again disturbed by serious social unrest. Although the insurrection of 10th August had been followed by legislation intended to reconcile the peasantry to the new Revolution, the economic situation had steadily deteriorated. A decree of 25th August had carried the legislation of 1789 closer to the peasants' objective by declaring that no manorial dues need be redeemed unless the landlord could show an original title, and after 14th August the property of *émigrés* could be purchased in small lots. Other legislation in September authorised local governments to control the distribution of corn by requisitioning. None of these measures, however, touched the real problem: neither the Legislative Assembly nor the Convention could prevent prices from rising. So weak was the central government that the departments and communes behaved as so many independent republics, competing for supplies with each other and with the commissioners charged with supplying the armies. The farmers themselves, as distrustful of authority as they were of the *assignat*, usually did their best to hold on to what they had. During the autumn, riots and demonstrations for price-control grew more and more serious, until in November the area of the Île de France and the Beauce was almost in rebellion. The Convention's only answer to this situation was repression. Confronted in November by appeals for price-control from several departments as well as from the Commune and sections of Paris, the Assembly voted money to increase imports, but reaffirmed its faith in complete freedom of trade. 'Government', wrote Roland, 'consists primarily in anticipating and preventing the undesirable in a negative way. . . . Perhaps the only action the Assembly can allow itself to take about food supplies is to announce that it should take no action.' On 8th December the requisitioning laws were repealed and interference with the distribution of corn was made a capital offence. As for the countryside, troops were used to restore order there.

Paris, however, could not be controlled so easily. As always, the capital attracted the hungry and the unemployed. A prolonged attempt to provide work by extending the fortifications of the city only aggravated the evil: still more men came forward to claim the comparatively high wages offered by the Commune, and regular labourers in Paris became more restless than before. Moreover, when winter gave way to spring, the general rise in prices caused real distress to all those wage-earners, shop-keepers and craftsmen who normally lived at little more than subsistence level. As Saint-Just had

143

clearly stated in the debates in November, the real cause of the trouble was inflation: once war had begun, *assignats* had been issued in ever-increasing quantities to finance it,[1] and in January and February 1793 their value, which had long been declining gradually, suddenly fell sharply to 50 per cent of the nominal. In these circumstances the influence of the extremists increased sharply, and the sections of Paris made repeated appeals to the Convention to adopt one or more of the solutions which were constantly canvassed by Jacques Roux and the *enragés*. These called particularly for the control of corn-prices (which was probably intended to be a first step towards more general controls) and for the withdrawal of all metal currency in favour of the *assignat*. The Convention, however, remained devoted to the doctrines of economic liberalism. Even Marat, whose constant demands for the ruthless proscription of hoarders and speculators had made him a popular hero, described the sections' petitions as outlandish and subversive. The result was that on 25th February the ordinary people took the law into their own hands, and throughout the city shops were raided and their contents sold off at popular prices. Although order was restored next day by Santerre and some of the National Guard, the situation remained highly explosive.

On none of these matters was the Convention clearly divided. Although Robespierre had again expressed his sympathy for the poor in December, maintaining that the necessities of life ought to be as sacred as life itself, the Montagnards were one with the rest of the Assembly in disliking any interference with economic freedom. They and their opponents accused each other of encouraging disorder for political purposes, but in reality the unrest in Paris revealed that there was general popular discontent with the rule of the middle-class. Nor is it sound to suggest, as historians of the Montagnard school usually do, that 'the Girondins' had been particularly responsible for the adoption of the policy of revolutionary war in the autumn of 1792. If anything Brissot and his friends had been more hesitant about this than had the rest of the deputies, and the Montagnards had done much to make peace impossible by their insistence upon the execution of the king. Nevertheless, when social distress and military defeat afflicted France in the spring of 1793, the *sans-culottes* of Paris at once held the Brissotins to blame.

On the night of 9th March, when the news from Belgium became known, the Commune again sent out a general call to arms. One crowd at once surrounded the Manège. Another invaded the Jacobin Club to demand a purge of the Convention, and then went on to destroy the printing presses of Brissot's *Patriote français* and Gorsas's *Courrier*. Throughout the night many

---

[1] By the middle of October, 1792, *assignats* to the value of 2,400 million livres were in circulation. When war was declared on Britain and Holland on 1st February 1793, 800 millions more were issued.

THE PURGING OF PARLIAMENT

deputies sat in their benches in hourly expectation of insurrection and massacre. Their fears were exaggerated, but for the first time some of the sections demanded that certain 'unfaithful deputies' should be expelled from the parliament. Two days later the Section Bonconseil specifically named 'Brissot, Pétion, Buzot, Guadet, Vergniaud, Gensonné, Barbaroux, Gorsas, Rebecquy, Lanjuinais, etc.'[1] Such was the result of the Brissotins' folly in antagonising Paris and in allowing the Montagnards to identify themselves exclusively with the Revolution. In the clubs and in the popular press of Paris, criticism of the Mountain had become synonymous with moderation, reaction, and treason.

On this occasion the storm subsided, for neither the Commune nor the Jacobin Club was yet willing to approve action against the Assembly. The sorry story of disunity and defeat, however, was still far from being told. On 24th February the Convention had ordered the conscription of 300,000 men, but this attempt to anticipate the nation's needs gave rise to widespread resistance in the following months. In the remote countryside of the Vendée, demonstrations against taxation and conscription for an alien cause flared into open rebellion in the middle of March. The nobility and the clergy in the area soon proclaimed the cause of Church and king in this civil war, which the raw national militia were quite unable to control. At the same time Dumouriez, who had always resisted restraint, suddenly showed himself to be a second La Fayette. Returning almost alone from Holland, he tried desperately to placate the Belgians by reversing the course of the revolution in their country. French commissioners were arrested, clubs of collaborators were closed down and a restitution of property was promised. Having sent an abusive letter to the Convention, the general then tried to drive back the Austrians with what forces he could muster in Belgium. He was twice defeated, at the battle of Neerwinden on 18th March and before Louvain on 21st March. Then for the third time in as many years France suffered the shock of seeing a commander-in-chief go over to the enemy. By offering to march against Paris, Dumouriez secured an armistice from Coburg, the Austrian commander, and on 27th March he undertook to restore the Constitution of 1791, with Louis XVII as king. When the Convention sent Beurnonville, the new Minister of War, and four deputies to his headquarters, he arrested them and handed them over to the Austrians as prisoners. Only the doubtful morale of a defeated army now stood between Dumouriez and his objective. For all its incompetence, however, the Convention commanded immense respect. Once it was known that Dumouriez had arrested the deputies, his appeals went unanswered, and on 5th April he and his principal staff-officers galloped into the Austrian lines under the

[1] Author's italics.

N

0   50
Miles

The Hague

NETHERLANDS

UNITED

AUSTRIAN

Dunkirk
Hondschoote
Calais
Ypres
Boulogne

Antwerp

R. Maas

NETHERLANDS

R. Scheldt
R. Lys
Tourcoing
Brussels
Louvain
Maestricht
Neerwinden
Liège
Lille
Tournai
CONDE
MONS
Fleurus
VALENCIENNES
Charleroi
Namur
MAUBEUGE
Jemappes
LUXEMBOURG
Abbeville
Cambrai
R. Sambre
Wattignes
Amiens
Sedan

Compiègne
R. Meuse
Soissons

F R A N C E

Paris

R. Seine

**The North-East
Frontier**

⊙ FORTRESSES OF THE QUADRILATERAL

fire of his own soldiers.[1] The army, however, had to fall back to the fortress of Valenciennes, within the frontier of France, and Custine had simultaneously to abandon the Rhineland to advancing Prussian forces. Leaving 20,000 men besieged in Mainz, he halted only at the Wissembourg lines, which barred the road into Alsace.

Practically paralysed as it was by its own disputes, the Convention nevertheless did much to meet this mounting crisis by finding new ways of making its will known and its orders obeyed. On 10th March it decided to despatch eighty of its own members to the provinces with full powers to overcome opposition to recruitment at any cost. On 11th March, before these deputies left Paris, it also approved the establishment of a new extraordinary criminal court to deal with counter-revolution, since, as Cambacérès said, 'ordinary principles no longer suffice'. Within a month both these devices were developed further. Early in April, when Dumouriez's defection was known, the powers of the public prosecutor in the new Revolutionary Tribunal were considerably increased, and the parliamentary immunity of the deputies was abolished.[2] More commissioners were also sent out from the Convention, these being attached to the armies and invested with unlimited powers to expedite military expansion. On 19th March, moreover, a decree that was to have terrible consequences was passed unanimously: all those accused of participating in rebellions or in demonstrations against recruitment were declared *hors de la loi*, and all rebels taken in arms were to be executed within twenty-four hours on the summary judgment of military commissions. A decree on 21st March also provided for the creation in every commune throughout the country of security committees of twelve men each. On 6th April the central government was further strengthened by the formation of the Committee of Public Safety, the nine members of which were to be elected monthly. This committee was nominally empowered only to 'supervise and speed up' the work of the Executive Council, and it was initially a comparatively cautious body which was greatly influenced by Danton. The Convention had nevertheless taken a decisive step by entrusting executive authority and adequate funds to a small number of its own members.

From all this *ad hoc* legislation there gradually evolved a system of government that was at once unusually flexible and exceptionally powerful. As their tricolour sashes signified, the commissioners of the Convention, or 'representatives on mission', embodied all the sovereign power of the people, and they could exercise that authority wherever it was needed most. Acting

---

[1] He took with him Égalité's son, the future King Louis Philippe.

[2] Deputies, however, could only be indicted by the Assembly itself, a reservation which was jealously guarded.

through the local security committees, which were variously called *comités de surveillance* or Revolutionary Committees, as well as through the local Jacobin Clubs, they could become immensely effective pro-consuls for the Convention. In the long run, however, the Committee of Public Safety could keep most of them under a fair measure of control, for all their authority was delegated and they were as accountable to the Revolutionary Tribunal as any of those they found false or faint-hearted.

None of this was easily achieved. The two sides in the Convention were intensely suspicious of each other's motives, and almost all the deputies except Danton disliked any infringements of the sacred doctrine of the separation of powers. Every tentative step towards stronger government was consequently taken amidst allegations and counter-allegations about 'dictatorship' and 'anarchy', and every new institution had to be established as a temporary departure from normal practice. In the course of these conflicts, moreover, the distinction between the Montagnards and their opponents became more and more a matter of principle. Being, as it were, in opposition, the Montagnards were prepared to respond to popular pressure for 'revolutionary'—that is, for speedy and effective—action to control both the political and the economic crises, and they became increasingly associated with the idea that strong government was necessary to save and consummate the Revolution. The majority of the Convention, however, regarded the Revolution as complete, and the Brissotins, who were of course compromised by the consequences of their earlier radicalism, were in general reluctant to accept further innovations. In opposing the Montagnards, therefore, the Brissotins tended to become still more representative of the authority of parliament and of the liberty of the individual, causes with which Vergniaud and his colleagues from Bordeaux now became particularly associated. The fact that Isnard, who was undoubtedly a Brissotin, was as responsible as anyone for the creation of the Committee of Public Safety, shows that this distinction between the majority and the minority was not an absolute one; but the difference in attitude was often apparent. When the first disasters in Belgium became known, Vergniaud and his colleagues strove for two days to modify the Montagnards' proposals for the organisation and procedure of the Revolutionary Tribunal. They objected, *inter alia*, to the idea that the jurymen should vote aloud and in public. On 13th March moreover, Vergniaud made a great speech in condemnation of the disorders that had occurred on the night of the 9th, deploring the development of a 'new mode' of liberty in which public licence was tolerated as if it were the necessary counterpart of patriotism. Although the Convention did not adopt the firm measures he advocated on this occasion, it shared his fears, and its anxiety was reflected even in its emergency legislation. Several clauses of the decree which created the local Revolutionary Committees, for example,

148

were obviously intended to prevent the domination of the general assemblies of the sections by minority groups of extremists.

Political antagonism was of course further inflamed by the defection of Dumouriez, which redoubled distrust even as it made drastic measures still more necessary. Most men had trusted the general far too long, but none would admit that all had been equally deceived. As Dumouriez had eventually announced that he proposed to prune the Convention down to its healthy stock, all became convinced that he must have had accomplices in the Assembly. Philippe-Égalité, and all of the Orléanist family who could be found, were arrested and imprisoned, first in Paris and then in Marseilles. The Brissotins, who had been the general's warmest supporters, were most seriously injured by his actions. Danton, however, was apparently more directly implicated. Although he had hurried to Belgium at the first alarm, he was suspiciously slow to reveal the full truth when he returned to Paris, and it was not difficult for Buzot and others to suggest that he had tried to cover up for Dumouriez because he was involved with him in a plot to establish Orléans as king.

As the Convention stood thus appallingly divided in the face of grave national danger, two significant developments occurred. Danton, whose prestige might have sufficed to hold the Assembly together in moderate courses, was again driven into the arms of the Montagnards, whose superior wisdom he now openly acknowledged. Moreover, both he and Robespierre avowed that the safety of the Revolution depended above all else upon the aid of the people. This meant, in effect, that the Montagnards and the Jacobins were now prepared to renew their working alliance with the masses, and particularly with the *sans-culottes* of the sections of Paris, against the rest of the Convention. To secure power so that they could save the country and effect their own interpretation of the Revolution, they would sanction a new insurrection, this time directed against parliament itself.[1]

A first attempt to implement this policy began at once. On 5th April Robespierre's brother Augustin called upon the sections to come to the bar of the Convention and 'force us to put disloyal deputies under arrest'. The same day the Jacobins of Paris sent a circular to their affiliated societies, signed by Marat, asserting that as the centre of counter-revolutionary conspiracy was in the Convention itself, the men of France must force the expulsion of the leaders of the faction of the *appellants*, 'a sacrilegious cabal directed by the English court'. The sections of Paris naturally responded first. On 8th April a deputation from Bonconseil urged the Montagnards 'to wage war to the death on the moderates' and to cleanse the Assembly of

[1] This may be something of an anticipation, since Robespierre at least hoped that public opinion could be so stimulated that the parliament would purge itself without having to bow to force. The threat of force was nevertheless used, and force itself was eventually employed.

the accomplices of Dumouriez, '*les Brissot, les Guadet, les Gensonné, Vergniaud, Barbaroux, Louvet, Buzot, etc*'. Two days later the Section Halle au Blé demanded the arrest of twenty-two deputies. This figure, becoming a sort of magic number, was reiterated in an address presented on 15th April in the name of thirty-five of the forty-eight sections, which was endorsed by both the Jacobins and the Commune. At this point, however, action was deferred on Robespierre's advice, and the Commune withdrew its support. In practice, the Montagnards' position was proving very delicate. If the sections were given their head, they might well so weaken the parliament that even the Montagnards themselves would be compelled to obey their orders; but if they were held back too much, the provinces might rally to the support of their elected representatives. There was not much room for manoeuvre between the rough revolutionaries of Paris and the reactionary forces which were influential in France.

The shadow of civil war was now indeed deepening across the country. Royalists, and all who, by conviction or interest, considered that the Revolution should be stayed before order was destroyed and property imperilled, drew together in opposition to the Mountain, although in truth many of them cared no more for the majority than for the minority of the Convention. On the other hand, the more militant patriots, who feared for the safety of the Revolution and hoped to purify society still further, opposed all who were hostile to the Montagnards. The masses, who suffered ever more severely from the constant increase in prices, also held these more moderate deputies responsible for all their hardships. The opposing sides in the Convention thus inadvertently became identified with different social interests, and their disputes reflected the increasing antagonism between the rich and the poor of France. Although there could not be in the society of that time a class-war of the type supposedly implicit in that of the industrial age, the Revolution and the economic crisis had clearly sharpened the ancient struggle between the 'have-nots' and the 'haves', and the question of conscription precipitated open conflict between them. This, the Convention's first real call for positive sacrifice, was naturally unpopular, for much of the country was still apathetic or hostile to the Republic. It was, indeed, conscription which goaded the peasants of the Vendée into the bloody war which began in March. The law of 24th February, which at best had moral authority only for an ardent minority, was moreover a bad one. Since each locality was left to decide for itself how to raise its quota of men, local issues affected the incidence of the levy. Patriotic districts, which had already sent many volunteers to the army, found the new demand inequitable, and everywhere the people who happened to be in power found that they had a wonderful opportunity to rid themselves of some of their political opponents. Further, as the burden of service was commonly passed to the poor, there was a general demand that

150

the rich should be made to prove their patriotism by paying additional taxation and subscribing to forced loans. Contention was consequently general.

In this situation the Montagnards came to realise that the country could only obtain recruits if something was done to meet popular needs. Reports from the representatives on mission, most of whom were Montagnards, made this quite clear. As Saint-André[1] wrote to Barère, 'if you want the poor to help you to make the Revolution a reality (*achever la Révolution*), it is absolutely essential to keep them alive'. For this reason, as well as because they had to consolidate their alliance with the *sans-culottes*, the Montagnards sacrificed their free-trade principles and accepted the idea that the price of corn must be controlled. The alliance was probably sealed on 20th April, when the Convention learnt that the Commune had declared itself to be 'in a state of insurrection' until food supplies were assured. The Montagnards then rose from their seats to cheer, and they offered to associate themselves with the sections and the popular societies in an oath of mutual support. The majority of the assembly maintained its opposition to any economic legislation through long and stormy debates, but on 2nd May it was overawed by a great demonstration of 10,000 men of the Faubourg St-Antoine, who threatened immediate insurrection if the *maximum* was not accepted. The law was passed on 4th May, each department being made responsible for fixing a maximum price for grain from the average prices of the past few months. The Montagnards, who had re-aligned themselves with the opinion of the *sans-culottes* by this change of front, also tried at this time to associate themselves still more closely with the popular revolutionary movement. In his proposals for a new Declaration of Rights, Robespierre on 24th April allowed property right to be relative to the general welfare, and he asserted the principle that the state must force the rich to aid the poor. On 8th May, too, he advised the sections to form and arm, at the expense of the rich, a new revolutionary militia—*une armée révolutionnaire*—one of the main purposes of which would in fact be to compel the peasantry to part with their grain.

In March, Carnot had written: 'We need expect no peace from our enemies, and those at home are worse than those abroad. We must smash them, or they will crush us.' By May, the country was on the point of

---

[1] Saint-André (André Jeanbon), b. 1767; a Protestant pastor from Montauban who had previously been a merchant and a sea captain, member of the Convention for Lot; an able administrator though a poor speaker, he became a member of the Committee of Public Safety and was entrusted with a series of missions which kept him largely apart from the politics of the Terror. Responsible for the reorganisation of the French navy, he survived Thermidor, was given further missions, captured by the Turks in Algeria and eventually became prefect of Mainz for Napoleon, where he died of cholera while visiting the sick survivors of the retreat from Moscow (1813).

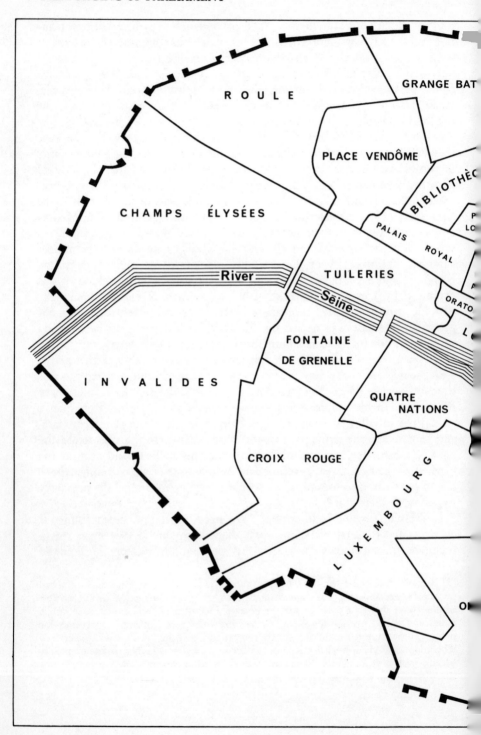

ROULE

GRANGE BAT

PLACE VENDÔME

BIBLIOTHÈC

CHAMPS ÉLYSÉES

PALAIS

P
LO

ROYAL

River

TUILERIES

ORATO

Seine

L

FONTAINE
DE GRENELLE

INVALIDES

QUATRE
NATIONS

CROIX ROUGE

LUXEMBOURG

O

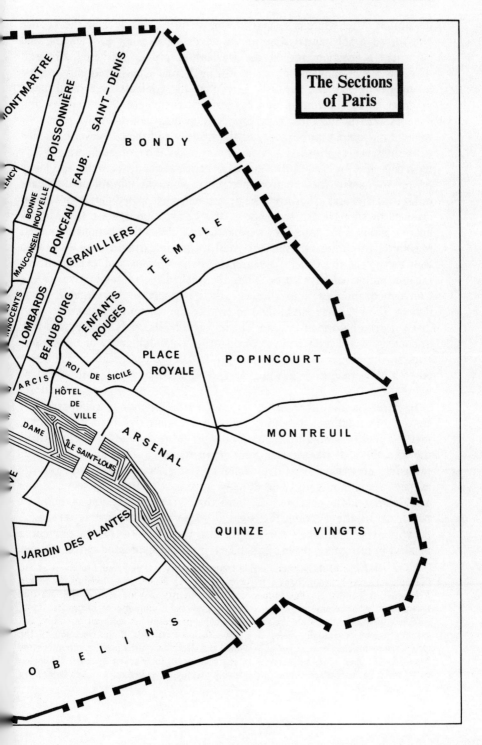

The Sections
of Paris

MONTMARTRE
POISSONNIÈRE
FAUB.
SAINT–DENIS
ENCY
BONNE NOUVELLE
MAUCONSEIL
PONCEAU
GRAVILLIERS
BONDY
TEMPLE
INNOCENTS
LOMBARDS
BEAUBOURG
ENFANTS ROUGES
POPINCOURT
ARCIS
ROI DE SICILE
PLACE ROYALE
HÔTEL DE VILLE
DAME
ÎLE SAINT-LOUIS
ARSENAL
MONTREUIL
VE
JARDIN DES PLANTES
QUINZE VINGTS
OBELINS

disruption. After winning several striking victories, the rebels in the Vendée had forced a substantial Republican force to surrender at Thouars, and elsewhere a reaction against the Revolution rapidly gathered strength. This 'sectional movement', as it is called, was almost certainly rooted in an attempt by the royalists to exploit the conflicts over recruitment in order to regain control of local government. Since, however, its first enemies were the Jacobins, it was supported by many constitutional monarchists and moderate republicans, and the wealthy and the conservative rallied to the defence of property against the radicals. The situation was in fact most complex, for local controversies cut across social distinctions, and many poorer townsmen tried to free themselves from the control of dominant minorities. Generally, however, the people who participated in this movement claimed to support the majority of the Convention against the Montagnards, and in some cities they were so successful that their actions amounted to counter-revolution. In Marseilles and Lyons, in particular, the well-to-do won control of the general assemblies of the sections and overthrew the Jacobin municipal authorities. They then defied the representatives of the Convention and began to eliminate their opponents. An illegal Revolutionary Tribunal was established to enforce the reaction at Marseilles, and in Lyons the notorious Jacobin Châlier, who had already ordered the rich to contribute five million livres to maintain a standing army of revolutionaries in the city, was thrown into prison after a conservative *coup d'état* on 30th May, an episode in which several hundreds of people died in violent fighting.

In Paris, on the other hand, the moderates' attempt to reimpose their control was a failure. Resenting the selective conscription of their young men by popular committees, some of those who did not normally attend the assemblies of the sections now began to do so. Had many appeared, the effect must have been overwhelming, for although there were, on the average, some thousands of adult male citizens in each of the sections, the assemblies seldom consisted of more than between fifty and a hundred persons.[1] In the Section Bonconseil, where the newcomers were temporarily successful, they announced that they had sworn 'to prevent a handful of intriguers, posing as patriots, from crushing good citizens under

[1] The *population* of the sections varied from about 3,500 (Pont-Neuf) to about 25,000 (Temple), 12,000 being perhaps a fair average. See G. Rudé, *The Crowd in the French Revolution*, Appendix II. The influence of the minority may be seen in the fact that Chaumette, who became *procureur* of the provisional Commune of December 1792, received thirty-one votes from the fifty-nine people present in his sectional assembly, and his election was eventually endorsed by less than a twentieth of the electorate of the city. Even major elections evoked only a small and declining poll: when Chambon became Mayor in October 1792, he received 15,474 votes from forty-seven sections, about 300 each; when Pache succeeded him in the spring of 1793, he polled only 11,881 votes from

a popular despotism'. Such success, however, was rare, probably because the movement was really that of a reactionary minority, which was not nearly so experienced and well-organised as the revolutionary one. The *sans-culottes* were soon able to send reliable militants from one section to another to help to vote the intruders down, and if necessary violence was used to drive them out of the meetings. The tension was nevertheless acute, and to Robespierre on 8th May it seemed that 'there are now only two parties in France, the people and the enemies of the people'.

By attempting to exploit this situation, the leaders of the majority in the Convention made their last mistake. Inevitably, they compromised themselves by encouraging the men who were hostile to the Revolution and restricting those who were most ready to defend it. In fact, the terrible weakness of the parliament had already been clearly revealed in April by the complete failure of the majority's attempt to indict Marat for the circular he had signed on 5th April. That circular was certainly seditious,[1] and on 13th April Marat was impeached by 226 votes to 93. His appearance before the Revolutionary Tribunal on 24th April, however, was a mere formality, and an immense crowd bore him back to the Convention in triumphal procession. Far from learning from this experience, the Brissotins and the Girondins only tried the harder to master Paris. They undoubtedly encouraged the sectional movement in the city by appealing directly to the interests of property-owners and by urging the bourgeoisie to attend their local assemblies in order to combat anarchy. They also tried to protect demonstrators, like those young men who paraded through Paris on 6th May and chanted 'Down with the anarchists! Marat to the guillotine! To the devil with Robespierre, Marat and Danton!' At the same time, moreover, they encouraged their own constituents in the provinces to resist the arbitrary authority of the Montagnard representatives on mission, and they urged them to do everything possible to support their deputies in Paris. Writing on 5th May, even Vergniaud exhorted the men of the Gironde to rise and be ready to come to his friends' defence, 'avenging liberty by exterminating tyrants'. Although they were probably unaware of it, those who behaved like this were opening the road to a reaction far more drastic than they themselves would ever have contemplated.

The position of the more prominent moderates in parliament was nevertheless intolerable. Daily denounced in the Convention and the clubs as

---

the city (as compared to 404 for Roland). It should also be said that the minority itself deplored this situation and constantly tried to persuade the apathetic majority to take more part in political life.

[1] If it called for a flood of petitions in favour of the expulsion of the *appellants*, it also urged Frenchmen to march on Paris, and its language was most inflammatory.

public enemies, they believed, not without reason, that their lives were in danger. Although on 12th May the assembly had at last been able to move into more spacious accommodation in the Tuileries, they were still scorned from the public galleries as well as being reviled in the press.[1] The growing threat of an insurrection in Paris brought matters to a head. On 18th May Guadet asserted that a plot to dissolve the Convention was in preparation, and he demanded that a shadow parliament should be convened at Bourges and that the Commune of Paris should be dissolved. By Barère's intervention, these proposals were rejected in favour of a searching enquiry into the activities of the sections, and for this purpose a Commission of Twelve was appointed on 20th May. The men who were elected to this dangerous office were not of any particular faction: only Boyer-Fonfrède, whose impartiality was generally recognised, was from the Gironde, and only he and Rabaut Saint-Étienne were men of any prominence. They nevertheless acted with vigour, interrogating officials from the Minister of the Interior downwards, and whenever possible inspecting the minute-books of the sections. On 24th May they reported that plans for an insurrection were being discovered, and they put forward proposals for preventing its development—including the compulsory closure of sectional assemblies by ten o'clock each night. When these were approved by the Convention, the Twelve proceeded to more drastic measures. Warrants went out for the arrest of several notable agitators, including the *enragé* Varlet, the 'apostle of liberty', and Hébert,[2] who was both the assistant *procureur* of the Commune and the editor of the most popular paper of the gutter-press, the journal *Père Duchesne*. The Commune promptly protested to the Convention, but its indignation only evoked from the President, Isnard, a reply which was to become notorious: 'I tell you in the name of the whole of France that if these ever-recurring insurrections should cause harm to the parliament of the nation, Paris will be annihilated, and men will search the banks of the Seine for signs of the city.'

All this belated activity simply promoted the insurrection it was intended to prevent. Infuriated by what they regarded as a violation of their sovereignty, sixteen sections sent a deputation to protest to the Convention on

[1] It was at this time that Camille Desmoulins published his sensationally scurrilous *Histoire des Brissotins*, in which Brissot's associates were portrayed as agents in English pay.

[2] Hébert, (Jacques René), b. Alençon 1757, led a precarious existence until he established a reputation in revolutionary Paris by ribald political satires and the journal *La Lanterne magique*. Founding the *Père Duchesne* in November 1790, he launched a virulent campaign against the monarchy early in 1792 and was elected to the Commune of 10th August. As editor and as deputy *procureur* of the Commune of December 1792 he was associated with the campaign against Christianity and the extreme terrorism of the autumn of 1793. Executed at Paris 24th March 1794.

26th May about the arrest of Hébert. The Twelve replied by ordering the arrest of Dobsen, the president of the Cité Section, who had refused to surrender his minutes for inspection. Next day a protest by the citizens of that section was followed by the irruption into the Convention of a considerable number of *sans-culottes*, and tumult continued until about midnight, when the Montagnards and the intruders out-numbered the remaining moderates. The Montagnard Vice-President, Hérault de Séchelles,[1] then took the chair, and a motion for the abolition of the Commission of Twelve and the liberation of its prisoners was passed without difficulty. Well might Hérault remark: 'The force of reason and the force of the people are one and the same thing.'

On 28th May Lanjuinais persuaded the Assembly to reinstate the Commission, which it did by the significantly low margin of 279 votes to 238; but the authority of the Twelve had been destroyed. That night, as Hébert and Varlet returned to the Commune in triumph, the Cité Section summoned representatives of the other sections to assemble at the former bishop's palace near Notre Dame—'to discuss important matters', as a preliminary announcement at the Jacobins had put it. Thirty-three sections answered the call, and by 29th May a small Central Revolutionary Committee was in permanent session, with Varlet and Dobsen among its most active members. Robespierre, who had already on 26th May given advance approval to the rising from the Jacobins, now spoke there again, theatrically emphasising his own exhaustion and announcing: 'It is not for me to tell the people how to save themselves. At this moment I have no further duty to perform.'[2] The Department of Paris, probably hoping to prevent the movement from going too far, sent its own delegates to sit in committee at the Jacobins on 30th May, and that night the Central Revolutionary Committee announced the city to be 'in a state of insurrection against an oppressive aristocratic faction'. At three o'clock in the morning of 31st May the city gates were closed and the tocsin rang. At about six o'clock, in accordance with the theory that all power must revert to the people when an emergency

---

[1] Hérault de Séchelles, (Marie-Jean), b. 1759 at Paris; a wealthy aristocrat, connoisseur and epicurean, by influence and ability became a royal attorney at eighteen and *avocat-général* to the Parlement of Paris at twenty-five. Supporting the popular movement, he was prominent in the attack on the Bastille, became a judge in the reformed law-courts in 1790 and deputy for the Seine in the Legislative Assembly and for Seine-et-Oise in the Convention. Appointed to the Committee of Public Safety at the end of May 1793, he was President of the Convention in the Revolution of 2nd June and was largely responsible for the Montagnard Constitution of that year. Suspected by his colleagues, he was compelled to retire from the Committee at the end of December 1793 and was executed with Danton in April 1794.

[2] '*Je suis incapable de prescrire au peuple les moyens de se sauver . . . il ne me reste d'autre devoir à remplir dans ce moment*'; A. Auland, *La Société des Jacobins*, Vol. V, p. 213.

157

makes insurrection imperative, an astonishing ceremony was enacted at the Hôtel de Ville. Delegates from the Revolutionary Committee entered the council chamber, suspended the Municipality and all its principal officers, and then formally reinstated them 'in the name of the sovereign people'. Once this was done, the delegates of the sections and those of the Department established themselves in the Hôtel de Ville, together with representatives of the Commune, and issued their orders. As Santerre was in the Vendée, it was decided to appoint Hanriot, a politically reliable man, as commander of the National Guard. An additional revolutionary militia of 20,000 men, who were to be paid at the rate of forty sous a day, was also to be maintained until the insurrection was over.

When the Convention assembled it was presented with a series of far-reaching demands. The members of the Commission of Twelve, as well as the twenty-two deputies named in April and the two Brissotin ministers, Clavière and Lebrun, were to be arrested; the rich were to be heavily taxed to provide poor relief and to subsidise food prices in general; the army and the civil administration were to be purged of the nobility; the franchise was to be restricted to *sans-culottes*; and a revolutionary army was to be created and furnished with arms.[1] Soon afterwards the hall was again invaded by the crowd, many of whom took their seats beside the Montagnards. At this point Vergniaud and some of his friends walked out in protest, hoping that others would follow. They had little support, however, for many moderates had stayed away from the assembly, and Vergniaud eventually returned to find Robespierre in the midst of a lengthy speech. 'Conclude, then!' he called. Robespierre replied: 'Yes, I will, and against you!'; and he then demanded that those whom the people had named as traitors should be accused by the Assembly.

Here, however, the insurrection was temporarily halted. So far, it being Friday, comparatively few working men had answered the call to arms, and some sections had even sent the Convention assurances of their support. The Montagnards, moreover, only wanted to break the parliamentary majority; they were uneasily aware that the political and social programme advanced by the *sans-culottes* went far beyond the wishes of most of France. The joint committee at the Hôtel de Ville had been quick to guarantee the security of property, but its demands seemed likely to imperil it again and to leave the Convention and the whole Jacobin movement at the mercy of the urban crowds. Strong in their faith in their own ability to interpret the Revolution, and fully aware of the importance of reconciling the radicalism of

---

[1] This should not be confused with any of the regular armies. Although the *sans-culottes* certainly desired to revolutionise these by purging them of all of noble birth, their immediate objective was the creation of a mobile and permanent Parisian force composed of *sans-culottes*.

15 Vergniaud

From a lithograph by F. S. Delpech

16 The Convention confronted by the armed forces of the Sections outside the Tuileries, 2nd June 1793

Both from engravings by P. G. Berthault after J. F. Swebach de Fontaine

17 The Death of Marat, 13th July 1793

Paris with more cautious provincial opinion, the Montagnards temporised, and the day ended in no more than a fresh dissolution of the Commission of Twelve.

After much recrimination among the leading demagogues of the Central Revolutionary Committee, a much more formidable movement was mounted two days later, on 2nd June. As this was a Sunday, ample manpower was available, and the Convention was soon surrounded by the most reliably radical battalions of the National Guard and some 20,000 armed *sans-culottes*, recruited *ad hoc* by the sections. In this situation the deputies were compelled to consider a new petition presented the previous day by a chemist, Hassenfratz, on behalf of the Commune and the Department of Paris. This demanded above all else the arrest of the 'conspirators'. Reports of the success of the reaction at Lyons helped to harden Montagnard opinion. As Saint-André put it: 'When the audacity of the aristocracy is at its height, we must fall back on the laws of war. Terrible as it is, this measure is imperative.' Even so, there was an impasse, for most of the Montagnards wanted to avoid any obvious capitulation to the crowd. In an attempt to preserve the appearance of parliamentary independence the Committee of Public Safety let Barère suggest that the accused men should offer to resign their seats. Such men as Barbaroux and Lanjuinais,[1] however, boldly refused to betray their constituents at the bidding of Paris. All but a few of the most militant deputies therefore welcomed a second proposal by Barère, that the Convention should march out of its hall and show itself to be free.

A dramatic scene ensued. In disorderly procession the deputies went across the courtyard of the Tuileries until they came face to face with Hanriot, the National Convention confronting the National Guard. As acting President, Hérault de Séchelles then read aloud a decree by which the Assembly banned any impeding of its doors. Hanriot, however, replied by ordering his gunners to prepare to open fire. The deputies had no alternative save to turn away and walk along the front of the armed forces of Paris. Although they made the full circuit of the precincts of the palace, they found themselves everywhere opposed by an unyielding mass of men, and they had eventually to retreat ignominiously to their chamber. There Couthon told them that as they had found the people good and generous, and indignant only against the conspirators, they should recognise that they were free in

---

[1] Lanjuinais (Jean Dénis), b. 1753, a lawyer of Rennes, deputy for Rennes in the National Assembly and for Île-et-Vilaine in the Convention; noted for his courageous opposition to the Mountain, he was proscribed in the Revolution of 2nd June but hid himself in his own house at Rennes until readmitted to the Convention in 1795. After being a member of the Council of Ancients he opposed the creation of the Consulate and the Empire, and subsequently presided over parliament in 1815 as a peer of France. Opposed reaction during the Restoration, d. 1827.

their deliberations. His motion for a decree of accusation against the deputies who had been denounced led to an order for the arrest of the ministers Clavière and Lebrun, and of twenty-nine deputies, ten of whom had been on the Commission of Twelve. From the Montagnard point of view the insurrection had failed in only one particular: some of the accused, forewarned, had already effected their escape, and several others soon eluded their guards. These fugitives left Paris and made a desperate attempt to move the provinces to rebellion against the 'monstrous power' of the Jacobins and the Commune.

Unlike the attacks upon the Bastille and the Tuileries in 1789 and 1792, this remarkable affair made comparatively little impression upon European opinion. It was nevertheless nothing but a third Revolution, and it was indeed commonly referred to at the time as the Revolution of 31st May. Revealing as it does the rapid progress which had been made in the technique of insurrection, it also affords a striking demonstration of the way in which, even in emergency, the organised power of the people of Paris was exercised with restraint and with respect for democratic forms. Had its objective been different it might well have become the Glorious Revolution of French history, a triumph of moral force over those whose authority had become no more than nominal. Even as it was, the insurrection ended that stalemate at the centre of affairs which had brought France to the edge of disaster. Although the Montagnards' position was to remain very precarious until late in the autumn, the events of 2nd June enabled them to begin to substitute direction for disunity and to turn defeat into victory. Moreover, the social significance of the day was considerable. The *sans-culottes*, whose demands had been evaded, were to be profoundly dissatisfied with the immediate results of their demonstration of power; but the conservative, property-owning and financial interests that had accumulated behind the moderate majority of the Convention had suffered a sharp rebuff. In the months to come the Montagnards had to rely upon popular support, and this they had to purchase by such drastic social and economic legislation that class-conflict was intensified and the future of France permanently affected.

It is, nevertheless, questionable whether this insurrection can legitimately be interpreted, as it has been by such eminent authorities as Professors Lefebvre and Soboul, as no more than a defensive measure, a natural response by the *sans-culottes* to social reaction and national danger. The day was, above all, a Montagnard victory, the significance of which has long been obscured by historians' readiness to believe that the rising was directed against a powerful and coherent conservative faction, the so-called 'Girondins'. In fact this idea originates in a myth. In order to justify their own usurpation of power, the Montagnards deliberately propagated the view that their victims, and anyone else who later dared to show any sympathy for them, were, and always had been, united in a great conspiracy against the Mountain. Although even they did not use the term 'Girondins' (except, of course, in referring to the deputies of the Department of the Gironde), they certainly exploited the fact that there were connections between some of the most prominent men who had opposed them in the Convention, and in doing so they made these men scapegoats for all the ills of France. In this, a succession of historians has followed them, identifying an imaginary party with everything they consider reactionary. In reality, however, the insurrection of 2nd June was directed against a majority of individualists, and it was on individualism, the aspiration and achievement of 1789, that men turned their backs that day. Since the Convention was not dispersed, it was possible for the Montagnards to invest their control of France, even when it became most dictatorial, with some semblance of parliamentary authority, and to assert that they stood for the sovereign power of the nation: but the nation was now more sharply defined than ever, and its authority was identified with that of a dominant and exclusive minority. If the Revolution was to be saved by force, it was also to be interpreted and imposed by force.

7

The Evolution of the Terror

The Revolution of 2nd June 1793 marks the beginning of the Terror, for Parliamentary democracy was set aside on the day that the Montagnard minority was put into power by the *sans-culottes* of Paris. The Terror, however, was a gradual growth. Determined as they were to save France and establish the Revolution, the Montagnards had no preconceived programme to put into effect. As their Jacobinism was essentially an attitude of mind, they had constantly to develop particular policies to meet the needs of the moment, preserving their unity by repudiating those whose opinions were either too moderate or too wild. The Committee of Public Safety, moreover, was still in June substantially what it had been in April, a comparatively moderate body which was strongly influenced by its principal member, Danton. Initially, therefore, the Montagnards' triumph over their opponents in parliament tended only to accentuate their own divisions. Real resolution and unity of purpose remained to be achieved: as Robespierre wrote in his private note-book, single-mindedness was the supreme need of the time.

The situation of the country was now indeed one of great gravity. Mainz, where Custine had left a force of 22,000 men when he retreated from the Rhineland, was besieged by the Prussians. On the all-important northern frontier the Austrians had been reinforced by a British and Hanoverian army, led by the Duke of York, as well as by 15,000 Dutch, and these allied forces had begun the systematic reduction of the quadrilateral of fortresses which blocked the road to Paris. Mons was already in their hands, Condé and Valenciennes were cut off and closely besieged, and Maubeuge awaited investment. At the same time the Vendéans were dominating western France: on 9th June they took Saumur, and it seemed likely that their Royal and Catholic army would turn eastwards against Tours and Paris. By the middle of June, moreover, the greater part of republican France was also in revolt against Paris, for most of the departmental directories and some of the municipalities repudiated the Revolution of 2nd June as a violation of the sovereignty of the nation by the Commune of Paris. Many of the evicted deputies stimulated this movement to restore the authority of parliament by escaping from the capital. Buzot, Barbaroux, Guadet, Louvet, Pétion and a dozen other notable fugitives gathered at Caen, and Normandy and Brittany rallied to them. Their cause, however, was soon compromised, for it naturally attracted the support of all who had been antagonised by the development of the Revolution. Avowed royalists, constitutional monarchists, non-juring Catholics, as well as those whose wealth and security seemed to be in danger, now had an apparently legitimate cause to follow, and the revolts which had already begun in Bordeaux, Lyons and Marseilles were carried forward with enthusiasm. Bordeaux ordered the enlistment of 1,200 men and sent delegates all over the south to organise resistance to Paris and to convene a new parliament at Bourges. Montpellier, Nîmes, Grenoble and Toulon adhered to the rebellion, and soon only the imperilled areas near the Vendée and between Paris and the frontier were still loyal to the new authorities in Paris.

Even in the capital itself, however, the Montagnards were not secure, for what they regarded as the 'conspiracy' had many supporters there. Vergniaud and some of the others who had been expelled from the Assembly stayed in Paris and deliberately defied their conquerors. In the Convention, such men as Ducos and Boyer-Fonfrède demanded that their colleagues should either be reinstated or put on public trial, and no fewer than seventy-five deputies signed a protest which was kept by Deperret, a deputy from Marseilles who was in close touch with his fugitive friend Barbaroux. As for the sections, on whose power the Montagnards had ultimately to rely, they were deeply divided and far from reliable. The most conservative of them shared the anger of the provinces, and three of these even began negotiations with the exiles at Caen. On the other hand, the more radical sections were deeply disappointed by the Montagnards' evasion of their own demands, and they were slow to respond to new calls for sacrifice. Although the Commune tried to enlist 18,000 men to meet the threat from Normandy, no more than two battalions of volunteers could be raised within the city itself.

For some six weeks the Dantonist Committee of Public Safety sought to meet these manifold dangers by concessions and compromise. It tried to find some basis for negotiation with the allied powers, and it tried to placate the anger of the provinces by damping down the popular insurrection in Paris. The insurgents who had surrounded the Convention on 2nd June were paid off, and in the process the Central Revolutionary Committee which had organised them was reduced to an administrative capacity. The establishment of a Revolutionary Army was approved in principle but neglected in practice, and the rest of the *sans-culottes'* programme was ignored. On the other hand considerable economic concessions were made to the peasantry. Villages which possessed common lands were authorised to distribute these equally amongst their inhabitants, and other villages were allowed to break up the estates of *émigrés* and lease them out among the poorer peasants in small lots. On 17th July, moreover, all remaining manorial dues were abolished outright and without any question of compensation. Middle-class support was similarly purchased by an increase in the salaries of officials and by a reduction in the level of taxation. Local authorities, too, were given every opportunity to retract their declarations of protest about 2nd June, and the problem of the future of the excluded deputies was shelved for as long as possible.

According to some historians these measures amounted to a deliberate attempt by the Montagnards to conciliate the bourgeoisie by repudiating the social and political ruthlessness which the *sans-culottes* wanted. Whether the Montagnards were consciously applying a policy or, as seems more probable, simply coping with the most immediate problems, they were certainly more concerned at this time with France than with Paris alone, and the Dantonists in particular were anxious to avoid spreading alarm by any appearance of violence. Even so, orderly intimidation had a place in their proceedings. The report which Saint-Just eventually presented to the Convention about the evicted deputies on 8th July was an appeal for domestic peace and for the exoneration of most of the accused; but it also demanded that the nine principal fugitives should be outlawed as 'conspirators' who were responsible for all the ills of the Republic. 'Liberty', as Saint-Just ominously said, 'will not be terrible for those who submit to the law.' Characteristically, however, the Montagnards placed their greatest trust in propaganda, and throughout the country local Jacobin societies reiterated their story of a conspiracy and praised the men who had saved the Convention from its snares.

Above all, the Montagnards made much of the fact that they had a new constitution to offer to the nation. Behind this lay a long story of wasted effort. The Convention, originally summoned to provide France with a Constitution to replace that of 1791, had appointed its first constitutional committee on 11th October 1792, and after months of labour Condorcet had presented the proposals of this committee on 15th April 1793. The Montagnards, however, had at once opposed these, alleging that they concealed a Brissotin project to break the republic down into a federation of local oligarchies. The committee had in fact included several of Brissot's associates,[1] and although Condorcet's proposals combined universal suffrage with apparently endless elections, his intricate and indirect system would have favoured the well-to-do and strengthened rural areas at the expense of the towns. The real reason for the Montagnards' opposition, however, was that acceptance of the Constitution would give credit to their opponents: the work of the Convention would be ended and the Revolution

---

[1] Brissot himself was initially a member of this committee. Couthon claimed in October 1792 that the composition of the Constitutional Committee had opened his eyes to the presence of a 'faction' in the Convention.

would be regarded as complete. For this same reason, the Montagnards hastened to produce a version of their own as soon as they had gained control of the Assembly. On 30th May five deputies, including Couthon, Hérault de Séchelles and Saint-Just, were added to the Committee of Public Safety to draft a new document, which they submitted to the Convention on 10th June. 'In a few days', announced Barère, 'we have reaped the enlightenment of all the ages.'

The Montagnard representatives, notably Hérault de Séchelles, had in fact cut Condorcet's plan to a quarter of its length and adapted it to appeal to the widest possible public. The new draft was extremely democratic. It retained Condorcet's universal manhood suffrage and developed his use of the referendum, but it added a system of annual parliaments and restored most of the excessive local freedom of 1791. For the first time, moreover, provision was made for direct elections, constituencies being composed of 50,000 citizens. The attractions of this plan were enhanced by an elaborate Declaration of Rights, which the Convention discussed at length. This reflected the development amongst the Montagnards of a new concern with social welfare as well as an increased awareness of the importance of authority.

Like the original Declaration of 1789, that of 1793 was to be proclaimed 'in the presence of the Supreme Being', a point significantly absent from the more Voltairean draft by Condorcet and his colleagues. The principles of 1789 were recapitulated, even property right remaining unconditional despite Robespierre's desire to establish the principle that its exercise ought to be limited by law. On the other hand, the aim of society was now declared to be 'the happiness of all', and the Declaration stated that society was bound to provide work for the able-bodied, relief for those in need and education for all. Liberty, moreover, now yielded pride of place to equality: one article asserted that insurrection was 'a sacred right' whenever government violated the rights of the people; but another drew a sharp distinction between the people on the one hand and the individual on the other, saying that 'any individual who usurps the sovereignty of the people shall be instantly put to death by free men'. Robespierre, at least, had no doubt that since the new constitution would enshrine the natural goodness of the sovereign people, opposition to it would be morally unforgivable. As he told the Jacobins on 10th June;

> We can now present to the universe a constitutional code infinitely superior to all moral and political institutions, a work . . . which presents the essential basis of public happiness, offering a sublime and majestic picture of French regeneration. This constitution . . . is the work of the Mountain . . . and becomes the centre to which the people can rally without giving itself new chains.

After being formally adopted by the Convention on 24th June, the plan was referred to the primary assemblies for ratification.

By such means as these the Montagnards succeeded in reconciling most of France to their rule. Time aided their efforts, for those who opposed them soon proved to be deeply divided. Although the departmental directories had protested loudly about the insurrection in Paris, the more radical communes suspected that this concern was simply conservative self-interest, and many republicans withdrew from the movement when the royalists' interest became obvious. Moreover, the peasants and townsmen soon proved even less willing to march against the Mountain than against the Austrians. At Bordeaux only some 400 men answered the Municipality's call to arms. When the royalist Wimpfen called for volunteers from the National Guard at Caen, only seventeen men stepped forward. Despite everything it seemed to most people that the Convention still spoke from the capital and that its long disunity was at an end. The fugitive deputies, too, were quite inadequate as leaders. Those at Caen did little more than entertain each other, entrusting the command of their total force of 4,000 men to a notable royalist, Count Puisaye, and the revolt in Normandy ended when this little army encountered the equally ineffective force sent out from Paris. At Pacy-sur-Eure on 13th July both sides ran from their opponents; but as the Normans fled the faster, the Parisians claimed the day and the countryside was easily pacified by the moderate conduct of Robert Lindet,[1] the Montagnard representative on mission.

The Montagnards were also able to restrict the various revolts to separate areas. As Normandy was severed from the Gironde by the terrifying royalism of the Vendée, so Bordeaux was cut off from the Rhône by the stability of Toulouse, and at the end of July General Carteaux occupied Avignon for the Convention and so isolated both Lyons and Marseilles. As by that time most of the departments had acknowledged the error of their ways, the rebellion was effectively confined to these few great cities which had little more in common than pride in their past and a deep desire to assert their independence of Paris. This, the logical consequence of decentralisation and popular sovereignty, was to the Montagnards 'federalism' the antithesis of the unity which must now be maintained in the name of

[1] Lindet (Jean Baptiste Robert), b. 1743 at Bernay, Normandy, brother of Robert Thomas L., who was deputy for the clergy of Evreux in the National Assembly and constitutional bishop of the Eure. Jean Baptiste, usually known as Robert, was a lawyer who became deputy for the Eure to the Legislative and Cambon's assistant on the Finance Committee. Re-elected to the Convention, he became a member of the Committee of Public Safety and was largely responsible for the organisation of the Central Food Commission. Surviving Thermidor, he was Minister of Finance in 1799 but refused to recognise Napoleon and resumed legal practice, dying undisturbed in Paris in 1825.

the sovereignty of the nation. A capital offence since the previous December, 'federalism' was the supreme heresy of 1793, and the Montagnards' success was due in no small measure to their skill in extending its stigma to all who opposed them.

Even reduced to its real proportions, however, the revolt remained formidable. Bordeaux and Marseilles were great commercial ports whose names had long been synonymous with the leadership of the Revolution. Toulon was an important arsenal as well as an essential naval base, and Lyons, the second city of France and a potential rival to Paris, was a vital strategic centre for the defence of the southern frontier against Sardinia. The revolt at Lyons was also of particular social and political significance, for the textile industry there was highly developed on capitalist lines. In this city, where the conflict between the rich and the poor was more obvious than elsewhere, a large class of wage-earners confronted a wealthy and remarkably self-centred commercial bourgeoisie. As the latter had no qualms about accepting the aid of avowed royalists, their revolt seemed likely to give the enemies of the Republic an invaluable advanced base for a final assault. Although further conciliation might have ended resistance to the Montagnards in other places, negotiation with Lyons seemed akin to treason once the émigré Count of Précy had taken command of its defence on 8th July.

By then it was indeed becoming evident to the Montagnards that compromise would no longer serve. At the end of June they were sharply reminded that even Paris, which Robespierre had recently described as 'the rallying point of the Republic', might not remain loyal to them indefinitely. The assignat being by now depreciated to 36 per cent of its nominal value, prices there were higher than ever, and their fluctuations aggravated the recurrent shortage of essential commodities. As public anger rose against the hoarders and speculators who were held responsible for all this, the 'wild men' of the Revolution suddenly assailed the Montagnards' sacred citadel, the Constitution. Even when Robespierre had first extolled this at the Jacobins on 10th June the unscrupulous Chabot had been bold in criticism: 'The Constitution', he had declared, 'fails to assure bread to those who have none. It fails to banish beggary from the Republic.' A fortnight later, on 25th June, the enragé Jacques Roux read a powerful petition of protest to the Convention in the same vein:

Have you outlawed speculation? No. Have you made hoarding a capital offence? No. Have you done anything to limit freedom of trade? No. Deputies of the Mountain, why have you not climbed from the third to the ninth floor of the houses of this revolutionary city? You would have been moved by the tears and sighs of an immense population without food and clothing, brought to such distress and misery by speculation

167

and hoarding, because the laws have been cruel to the poor, because they have been made by the rich and for the rich. . . . You must not be afraid to sacrifice political principles to the salvation of the people, which is the supreme law.[1]

The Montagnards reacted very sharply to this attack. In a vigorous speech at the Jacobin Club on 28th June, Robespierre defended 'the Jacobins, the Montagnards and the Cordeliers' as 'the old athletes of liberty', and he denounced Roux as an Austrian agent and a priest who had dared to don the mantle of patriotism in order to insult the majesty of the National Convention. Thus began the discrediting of Roux and the *enragés*. Those Jacobins who had inclined to support them hurried to recant, and a systematic campaign of denunciation against Roux led the Cordeliers and even his own Gravilliers Section to disown him. But although the Montagnards weathered this particular squall without undue difficulty, the danger remained: in the long run they would have to unite France and drive out its invaders if they were to retain control of the Revolution without yielding to pressure from the streets.

As it happened, in mid-July bad news from the fighting fronts tilted the balance against Danton and the policy of moderation. Although the Vendéans had turned west, not east, and had been repulsed in their desperate endeavours to capture the port of Nantes, they still continued to inflict defeats upon the republican armies in the field. The allies, too, continued to creep forward. On 10th July, five days after the Vendéans had beaten Danton's friend, the gigantic Westermann, at Châtillon, the fortress of Condé surrendered to the Austrians. On that same day Danton and most of his supporters failed to secure re-election to the Committee of Public Safety. Ever since 30th May, when the Committee had been increased by the addition of the five men who drafted the Constitution, it had been an unwieldy coalition, and Danton's efforts to negotiate a separate peace with one or other of the allies had delayed the development of any real war effort. He had little to offer the enemy except the life of Marie-Antoinette, and the idea that she was being kept as a bargaining counter was enough to add some suspicion of royalism to the accusations of appeasement and even defeatism which were becoming current about him. As it was reconstituted on 10th July the Committee was reduced to nine members, and seven of these—Barère, Couthon, Hérault de Séchelles, Lindet, Prieur of the Marne,[2] Saint-André

[1] Cited by N. Hampson, *A Social History of the French Revolution* (London, 1963) p. 187.
[2] Prieur of the Marne (Pierre-Louis), b. 1756. Little is known of his life. A lawyer at Châlons in 1789, he was a radical deputy in the National Assembly, deputy for the Marne to the Convention, and the close associate of Lindet (See note p. 166 above) in organising food supplies as a member of the Committee of Public Safety. Surviving Thermidor, he was proscribed for Jacobinism in 1795, apparently resumed legal practice during the Empire, rallied to the emperor in 1815 and was exiled to Belgium, where he died in 1827.

and Saint-Just—were to be among the twelve men who would rule France for the next year. For the first time since the beginning of the Revolution, a real government was appearing, and it was already composed of men more interested in victory than in peace.

The great Committee was certainly born in emergency. Scarcely had its new members been elected than the army that had been besieged for six weeks in Mainz surrendered to the Prussians, and five days later, on 28th July, Valenciennes fell to Coburg's Austrians. In the same fortnight all the torment of the times was exemplified by the murder of Marat. As is well known, the 'Friend of the People' was stabbed to death as he sat at work in his medicinal bath. Charlotte Corday, his assassin, was a well-educated and well-balanced young woman, but she won admission to Marat's simple room by an unscrupulous appeal to his kindness and his patriotism, and then killed him without compunction as one whom she supposed to embody all that was evil in the Revolution. In fact, she only cleared the way for far more dangerous demagogues. Wild as Marat's words had been, deeply as he was implicated in the September massacres, he had at least been sincere in his sympathy for the poor and in his denunciations of all whom he suspected of betraying them. Those, like Hébert, who thrust the weaker but more honest *enragés* aside in the competition to succeed him, were lesser men, who almost wrecked the Revolution by exploiting public misery for their own advantage.

Although Charlotte Corday went to the guillotine on 17th July in the full assurance that she had done great service for freedom and for France, her crime had really been fatal to all moderation. The myth of a murderous conspiracy against all patriots had acquired a new reality: to the fevered imagination of the time Paris seemed full of ferocious assassins whose malevolence concealed itself in innocent respectability. Since Charlotte had come from Caen and carried a letter of introduction from Barbaroux to Deperret, the Montagnards at once assumed that the fugitive deputies and their friends in the Convention had planned the murder. Many of them, indeed, became convinced that all who still advocated restraint were hypocritical villains. As Saint-André told the Convention: 'Those who have endlessly prated to us of their principles, and of their respect for law and order and peace, have now lent themselves to the most horrible of crimes.' On 15th July the violent Billaud-Varenne presented a new report about the expelled deputies, which asserted that as 'moral proof' was sufficient evidence of conspiracy, all those still under arrest were as guilty as those who had fled to join the rebels. When the Convention eventually accepted a decision on 28th July, eighteen men were named as traitors and eleven others were declared to be suspects. On the same day the Committee of Public Safety was given general powers to issue warrants of arrest.

A new intensity was now apparent in the development of the Revolution.

Two days after Danton had lost his place on the Committee, the Convention declared Lyons to be in a state of rebellion. Soon afterwards, the reactionaries at Lyons had Châlier, the local Jacobin leader, executed.[1] In Paris, Charlotte Corday also went to the scaffold. Even the nascent authority of the Committee was challenged from both sides of the Convention simultaneously. The more cautious deputies on the Right were concerned about the stability of the army. They alleged that Bouchotte, the Minister of War, was removing able commanders in order to make way for such unqualified *sans-culottes* as Rossignol, the 'patriotic' Parisian goldsmith who had just replaced General Biron in command in the Vendée. These deputies were still more alarmed when on 22nd July an order was issued for the arrest of Custine, who had succeeded Dumouriez as commander of the Army of the North. Their attacks on Bouchotte were, however, exploited by the Dantonists until they aroused the anger of the *sans-culottes*, and Billaud-Varenne and his still more violent associate, Collot d'Herbois, then took the opportunity on 26th July to force through an ill-considered decree against hoarding. To withhold essential commodities from the open market, to destroy such goods, or even to allow them to perish, became an offence punishable by death. Merchants were required to make and maintain public declarations of their stock, local authorities were empowered to search out and confiscate undeclared supplies, and private persons were encouraged to expose offenders by the promise of one-third of the proceeds of any seizure that followed their denunciations. In itself so savage that it was practically unworkable, this was an obvious indication of the threat to the Committee from the Left.

It was now that Robespierre, who had taken an active part in the defence of Bouchotte, was invited by the members of the Committee to join them in their work, and this he did on 27th July. His presence had in fact become imperative to the survival of the Committee, for he alone, by his immense influence in the Jacobin Club, the Convention and the Commune, could link the Committee both with the middle-class Jacobins of France and with the *sans-culottes* of Paris. Robespierre did not dominate his new colleagues; but his prestige, his widely-ranging interests, and above all his ability to formulate the general principles of the Jacobin faith, made him their principal spokesman. He had, moreover, much to give to the Committee. Able, experienced and astute, an ardent democrat and the personification of disinterested patriotism since 1789, he shared to the full that complete resolution which

---

[1] After this the popular societies had three Montagnard martyrs: Marat, Châlier and Lepelletier, a deputy who had been assassinated by a royalist fanatic on the eve of the king's execution. Busts of these three eventually appeared in some of the clubs as a new holy trinity of Equality. Marat himself became the object of a new popular cult: the grotto in the gardens of the Tuileries where he was buried became a place of pilgrimage and a casket containing his heart was suspended from the vaulting of the Cordeliers Club.

was the outstanding characteristic of the new government. Now, as on the eve of the insurrections of 10th August 1792 and 31st May 1793, he believed that the state must be saved by any means and at any cost. Now, as then, he believed that this meant that the general will of the sovereign people must prevail over every other interest, and he had no doubt that the Committee, whose powers were confirmed each month by a properly purged Convention, was in itself the embodiment of this general will. Deeply as he sympathised with poverty, sure as he was that the people, particularly the *sans-culottes*, must be sustained and stimulated to anger until the hostility of the bourgeois was broken, he was still more convinced that the triumph of the Revolution and the eventual regeneration of mankind depended upon the survival and success of the Committee.

In August, even while the general situation grew gradually worse, the new government began to make its presence felt. The Austrians moved forward to invest the subsidiary fortress of Lequesnoy, the Duke of York went off to try to take Dunkirk, the Spaniards advanced across the Pyrenees into Perpignan, and the Piedmontese re-entered Savoy: but the crisis was encountered with much more determination and ruthlessness than before. On the day after Valenciennes fell, two members of the Committee, Saint-André and Prieur of the Marne, went to investigate the position on the northern frontier at first hand. They found Austrian patrols ranging abroad almost at will, and their first action was to arrange the despatch of strong reinforcements from the Army of the Rhine. On 1st August, moreover, the powerful army which had been besieged in Mainz and which was barred by its terms of surrender from further fighting against the allies, was ordered to march against the rebels in the Vendée. That area was to be cleared of women and children and then systematically devastated. At the same time the Queen was taken from the Temple to await trial in the Conciergerie, and General Kellermann was authorised to use part of the Army of the Rhine to crush the revolt in Lyons. So far as it could the Committee also met social unrest with similar resolution. While Robespierre again attacked the *enragés* as new-born patriots whose agitation was subsidised by the enemies of the people, agents of the Committee scoured the countryside for grain for Paris. Substantial grants were made to the Commune for the purchase of foodstuffs, and the Convention approved a plan by which surplus corn was to be bought up and stored by local authorities.

Propaganda, too, was again brought into play. On 10th August a spectacular festival was staged in Paris to celebrate the first anniversary of the attack on the Tuileries and to announce the fact that the people had accepted the new constitution by 1,801,918 votes to 11,610. Although in reality these represented less than a quarter of the qualified electorate, more than a million livres were spent in elaborate preparations for the day, and its dawn was hailed by the singing of a Hymn of Liberty on the Place de la Bastille. There now stood there a Fountain of Regeneration, a colossal female figure from whose breasts sprang jets of water, and the crowds of spectators were soon privileged to see Hérault de Séchelles, the President of the Convention, fill a bowl with this precious liquid and pour it upon the ground in token of Frenchmen's devotion to the laws of nature. Delegates from the primary assemblies of France then formed a procession with the deputies and other officials and heroes of the Revolution, and all went along the boulevards until they reached the Altar of the Country in the Field of Federation, once the Champ de Mars. There the Constitution was formally promulgated, and on the following day it was ceremonially presented to the Convention and deposited in its ark of cedar-wood.

As it happened, the very success of all this pageantry almost brought the Committee to grief, for it gave the moderates a moment of opportunity. If, as many deputies apparently believed, the Convention's sole function was to provide France with a Constitution, it followed that the Revolution was now over; some therefore offered their resignations, while others simply sought safety by unauthorised retirement. There was also talk of a general amnesty—which would of course mean the rehabilitation of all those deputies who had been imprisoned or excluded from the Convention since 2nd June. Then, on 11th August, Danton's friend Delacroix carried a motion to initiate the election of a new Legislative Assembly. That night Robespierre roused the Jacobins to angry protest, ascribing all this to treason and declaring that nothing could save the Republic if this proposition were to be put into effect. The result was that they and the delegates of the primary assemblies successfully persuaded the Convention to agree to prolong its own existence. The Constitution of 1793 remained, and was to remain, inoperative.

As always, however, the Committee had to fight on two fronts. Despite all its efforts, bread grew scarcer in Paris. A prolonged drought brought the mills to a halt and reduced the daily delivery of flour to the city to less than a third of the normal. Prices continued to rise sharply, while the value of the *assignat* sank in August as low as 22 per cent. Present hardship, and the prospect of starvation, again sharpened the *sans-culottes'* instinctive reaction to the perpetual news of military defeat and domestic treason, and the rising tide of their anger forced the Committee to accept still more drastic measures. Inspired by the mythology of Valmy and Jemappes, hysterically convinced that every enemy could be overcome if the people of France would rise against them as the Parisians had risen against the Tuileries, the sections demanded that the Convention should proclaim a *levée en masse*: all patriotic Frenchmen must be stimulated to join in a tremendous national insurrection against the foreigners and the royalists. The Jacobins and the

Commune were converted to this cause, which was powerfully promoted by the *fédérés* who had come to Paris for 10th August, and although Robespierre at first foresaw only futile disorder, the Committee eventually yielded. On 23rd August Barère proposed the famous decree by which the whole population of France was summoned to the service of the Army until the soil of France was freed from its enemies.[1] In the words of the decree: 'The young men shall go to battle; the married men shall forge arms and transport provisions; the women shall make clothes and tents, and serve in the hospitals; the children shall turn old linen into bandages, and the old men shall betake themselves to the public squares to rouse the courage of the combatants, and to preach the unity of the Republic and hatred of kings.'

Unrealistic as this might seem, the decree introduced the principle of the total mobilisation of men and materials. Further articles were more practical. The Committee of Public Safety was charged with the task of creating armaments factories, and a first class of conscripts, unmarried men aged between eighteen and twenty-five, was ordered to report for duty—the time-honoured abuse of providing substitutes being expressly disallowed. Since in practice this initial call-up provided France with nearly half a million men, the real problem was that of ensuring that they could be adequately fed and armed and trained for war. In anticipation of this need, the Committee had already secured the services of two new members, Prieur of the Côte d'Or[2] and Lazare Carnot,[3] both of whom were determined republican deputies and experienced professional soldiers. They had done much to give coherent form to the *sans-culottes'* desperate scheme, and they now began the mighty task of organising the first modern war. The *fédérés*, meanwhile, began to go home: they had been ordered to supervise the operation of the *levée* under the direction of deputies to be sent out for the purpose, but they were really expected to act as government agents and inspire the whole nation with revolutionary enthusiasm.

[1] ' . . . *tous les Français sont en réquisition permanente pour le service des armées.*'

[2] Prieur of the Côte d'Or (Claude Antoine Duvernois), b. 1763, a military engineer, deputy for the Côte d'Or to the Legislative Assembly and the Convention, member of the Committee of Public Safety and, as Carnot's principal assistant, concentrated on administration and supply. After Thermidor he gradually retired from public affairs. Died 1832.

[3] Carnot (Lazare Nicolas Marguerite), b. 1753 in Burgundy, son of a lawyer; an able mathematician, he served in the Royal Engineers and became captain 1784. Elected deputy for Pas de Calais to Legislative Assembly and the Convention, he was a poor speaker but an able and hard-working officer, known from his service on the Committee of Public Safety as 'the organiser of victory'. Surviving Thermidor, he became a Director, but had to flee to Switzerland after the coup d'état of Fructidor (4th September 1797). Returning after Brumaire, he served Napoleon briefly as Minister of War, then opposed him in the Tribunate and retired in 1807. Rallying to the defence of the Empire in 1815, he was exiled in 1816, wandered in Poland and Prussia and died at Magdeburg 1823.

The *sans-culottes*, however, were far from being satisfied by this single success. Seeing in all misfortunes the hidden hand of some enemy, they saw in the Convention only timidity and torpor. The measures they had demanded in May had not been taken, and what laws there were did not seem to be enforced. Though hoarding was now a capital crime, patriots still went hungry while the rich waxed fat; though the arrest of suspected persons had been approved in principle on 11th August, nothing had yet been done to imprison them. Custine went to the guillotine on 27th August, but the Brissotins and Marie-Antoinette still survived unscathed. The deputies, it seemed, must be made to purge the army and the administration of men of noble birth, to control both prices and wages, and to curb the accumulation of fortunes. Above all, they must be taught to terrify traitors and speculators and to strike out savagely against all who would not help to save the Revolution.

As angry activity swept the sections towards yet another insurrection, a new group of agitators, headed by Hébert, appeared in the place of the *enragés*. Hébert himself, the deputy *procureur* of the Commune, had hitherto supported the Montagnards against both the Brissotins and the *enragés*, and his associates were already well-entrenched in the staff of the War Office and in the Commune, which had been reconstituted after new elections in July. Some of the men of 31st May were nevertheless aggrieved because high offices were not opened to them after the insurrection, and when in mid-August Hébert failed to secure appointment as Minister of the Interior, he turned against his allies, accused the Committee of tyranny, and tried to secure power by identifying himself with popular discontent. His paper, the *Père Duchesne*, which purported to print—so far as they were printable—the comments of a tough old townsman on current politics, preached unmitigated violence. Annexing the *enragés'* proposals for general price controls, for the stern repression of suspects and for the creation of a revolutionary army, Hébert added the cry of *la guerre à l'outrance*—war to the knife against each and every enemy. This new extremism soon gained ground in the Jacobins, and on 28th August the Society approved Hébert's proposal that it should join the Commune and the popular societies in presenting a petition to the Convention. The familiar pattern of Parisian revolt seemed about to be repeated.

In the Convention the popular movement was well represented by Billaud-Varenne, the man who had joined Collot d'Herbois in securing the draconian decree against hoarding. On 29th August he opened his assault upon the Committee of Public Safety by demanding the appointment of a new commission to see that the laws were implacably enforced. Robespierre and Danton successfully opposed this as an impolitic plan which could only paralyse the Committee, but Danton nonetheless proposed that three new members should be appointed. Although this proposal, which amounted to

18 Collot d'Herbois

From a contemporary engraving

19 Billaud-Varenne

From a contemporary engraving

20 The wounded Robespierre in the waiting-room of the Committee of Public
Safety, 28th July 1794

Both from engravings by Jean Duplessi-Bertaux
21   The closure of the Jacobin Club, 1794

offering places on the Committee to Billaud and Collot and perhaps Danton himself, was also shelved, Danton continued to try to revive his dying popularity. The next night he told the Jacobins that the Convention would join the people in initiating another revolution. At this Royer, the foremost of the remaining *fédérés*, announced the slogan of the hour: 'We must make Terror the order of the day! Only this can animate the people and force them to save themselves!' Robespierre tried desperately to quieten things down, but events conspired against him: just as the shortage of bread became most critical, there came the news that the royalists of Toulon had surrendered their fortress and the Mediterranean fleet to the British. On 2nd September the Jacobins resolved to act next day, and although in fact they temporised a little longer, they soon had no choice but to join Hébert and the other officers of the Commune in trying to stand at the head of a storm of public anger.

The *journées* on 4th and 5th September, which Hébert was long thought to have organised, really began spontaneously. On 4th September a crowd of working men assembled before the Hôtel de Ville, or Common House as it was now called, to demand higher wages and better supplies of bread. Chaumette,[1] the *procureur* of the Commune, hurriedly obtained an assurance from the Convention that the price of all essential goods would be regulated within a week. This, however, only made matters worse. 'We don't want promises', cried the crowd, 'we want bread, and we want it now!' Chaumette promptly proceeded to divert the anger of the crowd. 'I, too, have been poor', he declared, 'and I know what poverty means. This is open war between the rich and the poor! They want to crush us—very well, we must strike first, we must crush them ourselves!' The Commune, he continued, must tell the Convention to establish a revolutionary army immediately, so that it could 'go out into the countryside and ensure that requisitioned grain is really collected and delivered, and that rich egoists are thwarted and handed over to the vengeance of the law'. Hébert, to whom what would now be called economic unrest was as useful as militant patriotism, then seized the chance to propose that there should be a massed march to the Convention next day.

As it happened, 5th September was not to be a day of outright revolution, but it was one of great consequence. Undismayed by the darkness of an eclipse, considerable crowds collected during the morning at the Hôtel de

[1] Chaumette (Pierre Gaspard, called 'Anaxagoras'), b. Nevers 1763, son of a cobbler. A medical student, he became a member of the Cordeliers Club and served on the Commune of 10th August for the Théâtre Français Section. As *procureur-général* for the Commune after December 1792 he was an active opponent of the Brissotins and took energetic measures to develop social welfare in Paris. Noted for his campaign against Christianity in the autumn of 1793, he was executed 13th April 1794 as a potential successor to Hébert as a leader of the *sans-culotte* movement.

Ville, and soon after noon they followed Pache (the mayor) and Chaumette to the Convention, the benches of which were rapidly filled to overflowing by an intermingled mass of deputies and *sans-culottes*. Their purpose was clearly expressed both by their placards, which proclaimed 'War on tyrants!', 'War on aristocrats!', 'War on hoarders!', and by the petition which Chaumette presented in their name. This announced that the tyrants of Europe and the traitors within France were persisting in their atrocious scheme to starve the people into submission, and that they must all be fought and slain without mercy. The people, according to Chaumette, demanded only one thing: 'Food, and to have it, force for the law!' A revolutionary army must therefore be established straight away, and wherever its columns went, a guillotine should go also to kill off conspirators and to compel greedy and avaricious countrymen to disgorge the products of the soil.

While Saint-André and Robespierre, who was presiding over the assembly, tried to contain the situation until the Committee of Public Safety could decide what to do, a separate delegation arrived with further demands from the Jacobins. This second address, which matched the former in ferocity, reiterated the call for a revolutionary army, but it was more concerned with the destruction of traitors than with hoarding alone. Demanding the prompt provision of public education and some simple form of civil code, the Club called also for a ruthless purge of the army and the administration; twelve new revolutionary courts ought to be set up in Paris, and traitors like Marie-Antoinette and the Brissotins should be tried at once. The time had come, the Convention was told, 'to impose equality by signal acts of justice upon conspirators. Terror must be made the order of the day!'

The members of the Montagnard Committee of Public Safety were now in practically the same position as the Brissotins had been before them. Having no means of opposing the power of Paris, they knew that the more extreme section of the Convention was quite ready to sweep them aside and assume power in the sacred name of the people. Collot d'Herbois was away on mission at this time, but Billaud-Varenne had at once reiterated his demand for the replacement of the Committee by a new commission, and amidst the tumult the Convention enthusiastically accepted a whole series of radical proposals without any reference to the Committee at all. If some of these, like Danton's motion for the expenditure of 100 million livres on the manufacture of armaments, were obviously in the national interest, others were particularly favourable to the *sans-culottes*. Although the general assemblies in the sections were now to meet only twice a week, citizens were to be paid for attending them.[1] Payment was also promised

[1] Both parts of this measure were intended to prevent the more leisured and well-to-do people from controlling the assemblies while the others were at work. Both eventually served to increase governmental control of the sections.

to those serving on the *comités de surveillance* in the sections, and a motion approving the purge of the membership of these committees was in practice given much more general application. Other motions provided for the creation of the revolutionary army, for the arrest of all suspected persons and for the acceleration of the work of the Revolutionary Tribunal.

The Committee of Public Safety, meanwhile, sat in anxious debate. Since, unlike the Brissotins, the Montagnards had always deliberately identified themselves with the opinion of Paris, they could not hope for support from the provinces. If they were to survive at all, they now had to accept at least some part of the popular programme. When Barère at last appeared to speak for the Committee he therefore began by praising the policy of Terror. More specifically, he presented proposals for the immediate organisation in Paris of a paid revolutionary army of 6,000 men and 1,200 artillerymen. Although this sufficed to placate the people and to end the session, the Committee next day bowed still further before the storm: accepting the inevitability of an alliance with the extremists, it invited the Convention to appoint Billaud-Varenne and Collot d'Herbois to its table as additional members.[1]

In this way the Committee succeeded in avoiding annexation by the Hébertists. The policy of the Republic, however, was apparently being determined by pressure from below. The arrest on 6th September of an agent whom Danton had employed in negotiations with England marked the complete success of the Hébertist campaign for *la guerre à l'outrance*. Before the end of the month France had broken off relations with all countries save Switzerland and the United States, which were regarded as the only free republics in existence.[2] The *sans-culottes*, moreover, proceeded at once with a wholesale purge of the popular authorities and assemblies of Paris and with a general round-up of suspected persons. Anxiety lest their actions should lead to new prison massacres was a considerable contributory cause of the promulgation on 17th September of the terrible Law of Suspects. This ordered the immediate arrest of all persons who could be suspected of political disloyalty, and eventually some 300,000 people were imprisoned as a result of it. Political disloyalty was so broadly defined that almost anyone might be

[1] The invitation was also extended to Granet, a representative of the more moderate deputies. Granet however refused to serve, and Danton himself also declined nomination by the Convention. Although he had in effect protected the Committee on the previous day, this refusal inevitably made him a centre of attraction for all moderate opposition to its subsequent proceedings.

[2] On the 13th April 1793 Danton had persuaded the Convention to modify its famous decree of 19th November 1792 and to repudiate interference in the internal affairs of other countries. After Danton's exclusion from the Committee of Public Safety in July 1793, however, this conciliatory attitude had again given way to bellicosity.

considered a suspect,[1] but at least a definition was attempted and a beginning was made in the long process of bringing the *comités de surveillance* under central control.

Popular pressure on the Convention also eventually compelled it to accept sweeping measures of economic regulation, an objective which had been lost sight of in the excitement of 5th September. On 11th September a national maximum price was imposed on all grain, flour and forage, and on 29th the long desired *maximum général* was at last decreed: each district authority was to fix the price of all essential commodities by adding one-third to their cost in 1790, and each municipality was to limit wage increases to 50 per cent above the levels of the same year. The enforcement of this law was to prove very difficult, and the restraint of wages was to mean much more than the *sans-culottes* had expected when they demanded a limitation of fortunes. The *maximum*, however, was seen as an attempt to control the economy. With other measures, it restored confidence in the *assignat*, which gradually recovered until in December it again stood at 50 per cent of its nominal value.

This measure was certainly forced upon an Assembly which was reluctant to accept it, but it need not therefore be supposed that the militants of Paris were wholly responsible for the advent of the Terror. Concentration upon seeing the Revolution 'from below' can too easily suggest that all the momentum came from the *sans-culottes*, who had ever to hustle a hostile bourgeoisie into decisive action. Even the direction of the economy had been accepted by the Convention in principle on 4th September, and in approving the *maximum* on 29th many deputies were strongly influenced by their belief in the existence of a great conspiracy to ruin the republic. Supposing that their enemies were combining to create artificial shortages, they believed that this coalition would have to be broken up before trade could function freely for the benefit of all, and it was natural for them to decide to treat all offenders against the law as politically suspect persons. More generally, too, it would seem that the Hébertist rising quickened rather than caused the coming of the Terror. The deputies whose influence was now predominant, and particularly the members of the Committee of Public Safety, were Jacobins as well as Montagnards. Some of them were quite as ready as

---

[1] Suspects were defined as those people who had in any way encouraged tyranny or federalism or shown themselves enemies of freedom; those who could not show satisfactory means of livelihood and prove the proper performance of their civic duties; those who had been refused certificates of good citizenship by their sections; those public officials who had been removed from office by the Convention or any of its agents; those nobles, or relatives of nobles, who had not given constant proof of their ardour for the Revolution; and all those who had emigrated since the Revolution began, even though they had returned to France in accordance with the laws of 1792.

Hébert to penalise and proscribe their opponents, and others certainly preferred a regulated repression to any sort of spontaneous popular action, no matter how patriotic it might be. Two days before the *journée*, on 3rd September, a drastic law had imposed a forced loan on the rich,[1] and on 5th September, before the crowd burst in upon it, the Convention had already reorganised the Revolutionary Tribunal and increased its personnel so that two separate courts, each of equal competence, could be in session simultaneously. Moreover, the Law of Suspects itself was prepared in order to give proper effect to the decree which Danton had proposed on 12th August for the arrest of all suspected persons. The *journée* and the initiative of the *sans-culottes* in making arrests only hurried the Convention along a course to which it was already committed.

Amidst the many perils and the widespread ignorance and apathy which confronted the revolutionary minority in France, some men were naturally quicker to have recourse to violence than others. Nearly all would nevertheless have agreed that some sharp shock of ruthlessness was necessary if the Republic was to be saved in the autumn of 1793. Differences of opinion about the extent and the duration of this form of treatment were quite soon to divide the more moderate men from their colleagues and to cause them and their champion, Danton, to be known and suspected as 'Indulgents'. For most, if not all, of the period of the Terror, however, the more important distinction was that between those, in parliament and outside it, who believed in the direct exercise of revolutionary authority by the people, and those who were determined to keep things under some degree of control. This distinction was apparent on 5th September itself, when the deputy Drouet (the man who had arrested the Royal Family at Varennes in 1791) exhorted the members of the Convention to renounce all humanity and to behave like the brigands and murderers men called them. He was at once shouted down, and amidst general approval Thuriot took the tribune to refute him. 'Citizens,' Thuriot declared, 'it is not for crime that revolutions are made, but for the triumph of virtue. Let us not say that it is for France that we work; it is for humanity. In achieving our task we shall cover ourselves with eternal glory. Far from us to be the idea that France thirsts for blood, she thirsts only for justice!' To all in authority, save for a minority of extremists, the Terror was always the antithesis of anarchy. It had, above all else, to be sanctioned by law and controlled by government.

Despite first appearances, therefore, government inevitably grew much stronger as a result of the events of September. By conciliating the *sans-culottes*, the Committee of Public Safety acquired an ally on whose power

---

[1] All taxpayers having, by their own declaration, incomes of more than 1,000 livres were to contribute to the loan on a steeply rising scale, all income above 9,000 livres being appropriated outright.

and patriotism the Revolution for the time being depended; by accepting the Terror, it made its own gradual assumption of dictatorial authority seem both necessary and desirable. The presence of Billaud-Varenne and Collot d'Herbois on the Committee gave it new contacts with the sections and societies of Paris, and the strength of the combination was evident in the swift elimination of the *enragés*, whom Hébert had already superseded. Jacques Roux was arrested for a second time on 5th September, and Varlet followed him to prison on the 18th for having dared to question the restriction of the sections to two meetings in each week. The Committee, moreover, profited greatly from the attacks which Hébert and the Jacobins made on its only real rival, the Committee of General Security. This body, which was responsible for the suppression of counter-revolution, was generally regarded as slack and corrupt, and Hébert's jealousy of its members' influence led to a general demand for a purge of all the Convention's committees. The Convention first agreed to re-form the Committee of General Security, and then on 13th September it accepted Danton's proposal that members of this and all other committees should be nominated by the Committee of Public Safety alone.[1] Thus the one committee which commanded general confidence was in effect made master of the others. Even the reformed Committee of General Security, which remained nominally the equal of that of Public Safety, became its resentful junior partner.

At the same time the Committee of Public Safety steadily increased its control of the people who acted as its agents. On 13th September the Convention invited all popular societies to report on any officials of the various ministries whose conduct seemed unpatriotic, the reports to be sent to the Committee of Public Safety. Later, on 13th November, these societies were similarly invited to indicate the men who were best suited for office in the public service. In the same way the Law of Suspects required the local *comités de surveillance* to send detailed reports of their proceedings to the Committee of General Security. Although the new government had to feel its way forward and secure the sanction of the Convention for each step in its struggle to impose order upon the administrative chaos that existed throughout France, its growing power soon made its position unchallengeable.

On 25th September a clash in the Convention made this quite clear. General Houchard, Custine's second successor as commander of the Army of the North, had on 6th–7th September won the Republic's first major engagement since 1792 by defeating the Hanoverians at Hondeschoote, and so forcing the Duke of York to raise the siege of Dunkirk. He had, however, failed to follow up his victory, which had petered out in bloody fighting while

---

[1] Since Danton's critics see ulterior motive in his every action, it may be said here that he had long been an advocate of effective executive power. The Finance Committee, which Cambon represented, still retained independent authority.

the main English army escaped unhurt. Although Houchard himself was very much a man of the people, uncouth and battle-scarred, he was dismissed by the Committee on the advice of the representatives on mission, and he was then accused of treason and sacrificed to clear the Committee of any suspicion of incompetence. His arrest caused a crisis in the Convention, for many deputies still distrusted political interference in military matters, and other malcontents, particularly those who had just lost places on the Committee of General Security, were more than ready to support them. Thuriot, the last Dantonist in the Committee of Public Safety, resigned his position on 20th September, and on 25th he led an attack on the increasing influence of the *sans-culottes* and on the whole policy of regulation and repression. 'We must check this torrent which is sweeping us back to barbarism', he cried. The Committee, however, met the assault as a united body: Barère, Saint-André, Prieur of the Marne and Billaud-Varenne all defended its conduct, and Robespierre, in a fighting speech, condemned the folly of attempting to distinguish between weakness and treason. 'I tell you', he declared, 'that in the last two years a hundred thousand men have died through treason and through vacillation: softness to traitors will destroy us all!' His speech made it clear that criticism of the Committee would be regarded as unpatriotic: 'Whoever seeks to debase, divide or paralyse the Convention is an enemy of the country, whether he sits in this hall or whether he is a foreigner. Whether he acts from stupidity or from perversity, he is of the party of tyrants who make war upon us. . . .' After this, the deputies hastened to reaffirm their unanimous confidence in their Committee.

This was not merely a matter of fear, though the Law of Suspects was in the background. As Robespierre reminded the deputies, the Committee's tasks were immense; as they could see, he and his colleagues were united in their determination to succeed. The resignation of Thuriot had in fact established the Committee in its final form, and Danton himself left Paris soon afterwards to take his newly-married second wife home to Arcis-sur-Aube. With the one exception of Hérault de Séchelles, who was soon to incur distrust, the twelve members who now made up the Committee were to direct the Revolution until its most critical days were accomplished. Despite the victory at Hondeschoote, their position was unenviable. In the Rhineland the enemy had at last succeeded in forcing the Wissembourg lines, and in the north the fall of Lequesnoy on 11th September allowed the Austrians to invest Maubeuge, the last bastion of the frontier. Like the government of any modern state in a time of total war, the Committee had to try to direct all the efforts and resources of the nation towards the destruction of the enemy; but as their war was revolutionary, they had also to combat conservative resistance and to discipline those who held that revolution meant

181

ever-increasing freedom. All this, moreover, had to be attempted in the most adverse conditions, for the old instruments of government had been destroyed and the new ones had hardly begun to function. As the Committee fought to effect the *levée en masse*, to regulate the economy and to rally the nation, they were confronted everywhere by local independence, with all its attendant evils of misdirected initiative and complacent inertia.

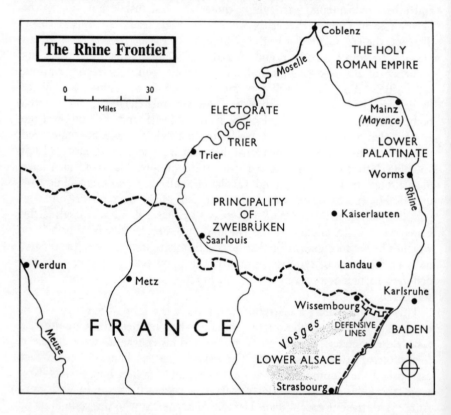

The Committee of necessity governed informally, having apparently neither chairman nor secretary, agenda nor minutes. Indeed, since its members tried to ensure that at least one of their number went in person wherever the Republic's need was greatest, the twelve were never all present at once in their famous Green Room in the Tuileries. Some, particularly Saint-André and Prieur of the Marne, were away in the provinces for long periods, and others, like Saint-Just and Couthon, were away frequently. The number of those in Paris never fell below six, but only Robespierre and Barère were always there. Moreover, as the work was incessant, the Com-

THE EVOLUTION OF THE TERROR

mittee was practically in permanent session, and members came to its table as occasion allowed. There they would deal, individually or together, with the endless flow of reports which reached them from all parts of France, and from there their orders went out, according to the importance of the subject, above the signatures of one or more of those who happened to be present. More general deliberation, the determination of policy and the preparation of major measures, usually took place after nightfall, when the ending of debates at the Convention and the Jacobin Club at last allowed every available member to take his share in the discussion and in the responsibility. Attempts have been made ever since 1794 to distinguish between the members of the Committee, so that some may be condemned as terrorists and others praised as administrators, but these have been inconclusive. Since all was done in secret and in the name of the Committee, it has never been possible to determine the extent of any particular individual's influence. The order and frequency of signatures on documents simply show that some division of labour developed as members dealt with matters of which they had special knowledge or in which they were strongly interested. Carnot and Saint-André, for example, respectively attended principally to military and naval affairs. It seems, too, that Robespierre and Barère had the widest interests and were particularly concerned with public morale. Saint-Just was most obviously a fanatic and Collot d'Herbois most obviously a man of blood, but the twelve shared a common resolution and took common responsibility for all that they did during their period of power.

The amount of work which these men accomplished is staggering. Nothing was too great or too small for their attention, and the records which Aulard compiled of their activities fill nearly thirty substantial volumes. To supply the armies with weapons alone they summoned scientists to their aid, requisitioned the services of metal workers, and initiated a nation-wide search for saltpetre and metals which could be made into cannon, bayonets and muskets. Prieur of the Côte d'Or, who was particularly concerned with this munitions drive, promised the manufacture of 1,000 muskets a day, a figure which exceeded the whole production of Europe, and in time nearly 300 forges were at work in the public places of Paris.[1] Although the Committee encountered its share of labour troubles, and kept wage claims down by decreeing that anyone obstructing the manufacture of arms should be punished by two years in irons, the spirit which these twelve men inspired and represented is well illustrated by an episode reported from a remote village in the Pyrenees. There, in response to the appeal of a commissioner for

[1] The target was never achieved, but between 3rd November 1793 when the first six muskets were formally presented to the Convention, and July 1794 when the Committee's power was broken, production rose to about 500 a day.

183

articles of iron, an old village woman came forward with a great cast-iron cooking pot. This the commissioner refused to accept, seeing that it was perhaps her most valuable possession; she, however, raised the pot above her head, smashed it down against the cobbles, and then thrust the shards forward for the benefit of the nation.

While such work was going forward, those who were held to be enemies of the people paid the price of opposition. So far the Revolutionary Tribunal had only functioned slowly, its judges giving careful attention to formalities and allowing the accused every opportunity of showing a proper regard for the Revolution. Consequently only sixty-three of the 233 persons who appeared before the court before 21st September had been condemned to death, and some trials, like that of the twenty-five people who were accused of conspiring with La Rouerie in Brittany, had lasted for long periods.[1] The intensification of the Terror in September soon altered this situation. When the size of the Tribunal was increased, its lenient President, Montané, was replaced by Robespierre's more 'patriotic' friend Hermann, and the Law of Suspects kept even the assiduous Public Prosecutor, Fouquier-Tinville,[2] fully employed in preparing indictments.[3] Where only twenty-nine persons had been condemned between 6th August and 1st October, fifty-one died in October, fifty-eight in November and sixty-eight in December; in all, 395 people came before the court in these three months, and 177 of them were condemned to death.

These totals included the victims of a series of important state trials: the condemnation of Marie-Antoinette in mid-October was followed by that of the Brissotins at the end of the month, and in November such men and women as Philippe-Égalité, Madame Roland, Bailly, Barnave and the unfortunate Houchard were sent to the scaffold. These trials were brought on by Hébertist pressure, which was on occasion reinforced by that of the

---

[1] Twelve of those concerned in this, the first collective trial to come before the court, were condemned to death. The technical savagery of the law is more evident in the case of the thirteen people who were accused of the 'assassination' of Léonard Bourdon, a deputy who had been manhandled whilst on mission in Orléans. Nine were executed, although Bourdon himself was present in the court during the trial.

[2] Fouquier-Tinville (Antoine Quentin), b. 1746 of prosperous farming stock near Saint-Quentin, he followed a successful legal career and became attorney to the Châtelet in 1774. Abandoned practice 1783 for unknown reasons, apparently ruined. Secured position of prosecutor to the Tribunal of 17th August by application to Desmoulins, a distant relative, and thereafter became prosecutor to the Criminal Court of Paris and to the Revolutionary Tribunal from its creation in March 1793. Arrested on 14th Thermidor (1st August 1794), he was tried 28th March–6th May 1795 and executed 7th May.

[3] At the end of August, there were 1,417 prisoners in the Paris prisons. The figure increased to 2,398 by the beginning of October, and to 4,525 by 21st December.

Jacobin Club; but like the Terror itself, they were implicit in the position of the Montagnards. All demonstrated the power of the governing Committees, and each served some particular Montagnard purpose. As the execution of the Queen was a renewed repudiation of royalism and of negotiations for peace, so the execution of Égalité cleansed the Mountain from the taint of Orléanism. Above all, the trial of 'J. P. Brissot and his accomplices' was an outstanding piece of propaganda, designed and publicised in order to provide a final justification for the Montagnard seizure of power on 2nd June. This affair was in reality the first of the *fournées*, those 'mixed bakings' in which a miscellaneous assortment of people were tried collectively on a common charge. Twenty-one deputies, including Brissot, Vergniaud, Lasource and Gensonné, were accused of conspiring against the unity and indivisibility of the Republic, the implication being that the Montagnards had saved France from their machinations by supplanting them. In fact, however, only nine of those in court had been purged from the Convention on 2nd June, the others having *subsequently* challenged the validity of that *coup d'état* by a variety of individual acts. Although the prosecution laboured for six days to prove that the whole course of the Revolution had long been distorted by the conspiracy, it soon became apparent that if the accused were to be allowed to defend themselves they would present the story in a very different light and would make mincemeat of the charge of collusion. They were therefore silenced. The Jacobins and Fouquier-Tinville protested to the Convention about the formalities which were impeding the work of the Tribunal; Robespierre, amending a still more drastic proposition, obtained a decree authorising the President to close any trial if, after three days' hearing, the jury felt themselves sufficiently enlightened. Next day, on 30th October, sentence was passed, and on 31st October all the victims were guillotined in half an hour. Thus the trial fulfilled its purpose, and the mythical 'Girondin party' was finally imposed upon history.[1]

Outside Paris the Terror developed more slowly, for extensive repression

---

[1] The twenty-one who were tried were those of the forty-six deputies indicted on 3rd October who happened to be available in the prisons of Paris. One other, Philippe-Égalité, who would have brought the total up to the figure of twenty-two, which was so popular when these villains were being denounced in the spring, was kept back for separate trial. In the event, only twenty were actually guillotined, since Valazé committed suicide when the verdict was announced. Of the other prominent opponents of the Montagnards before 2nd June, Guadet, Salle and Barbaroux were eventually caught and guillotined, and Condorcet, Roland, Clavière, Pétion and Buzot committed suicide. The majority of the seventy-five deputies who signed the most famous protest against the events of 2nd June were arrested after indictment on 3rd October, but these remained in prison under Robespierre's protection until the Terror was over. Robespierre's attitude is sufficiently apparent in his own words: 'There is no need to multiply the numbers of the guilty.'

could not begin until armed resistance had been broken.[1] Even so, the Committee of Public Safety soon became alarmed by the conduct of some of the representatives on mission, whose independence long allowed them to interpret the Terror as they felt inclined. In one district, where all was quiet, the elected authorities might continue in office almost undisturbed; in another, one of the people's deputies might appear, to urge on the war-effort and to reorganise the administration, weeding out the unreliable and replacing them by patriots as the local Jacobin Society advised. Elsewhere again, this process might be accompanied by extensive requisitioning and savage taxation, both enforced by such crippling fines or prison sentences that the whole amounted to class warfare conducted by the authority of the state. In this respect, as in his attack upon religion, the conduct of Fouché[2] in the Nièvre is notorious. Still worse, perhaps, many deputies were compelled to delegate their authority freely, so that the power of the Convention frequently fell into the hands of obscure men and petty tyrants. Thus the Committee of Public Safety had the almost impossible task of trying to stimulate those representatives who were slack, while at the same time restraining those who might raise up new enemies by being too fanatical. This, moreover, had to be done from a distance, and at a time when no man, no matter how highly he was regarded, could afford to seem less ardent than his neighbour. Not surprisingly, the Committee sought perpetually for more direct control of both policy and administration.

Effective control of the economy was equally imperative. Although the introduction of the *maximum* on 12th October increased public confidence, its operation raised immense practical problems. As soon as goods were put on sale at the controlled prices, they disappeared from the shops. Prices, which were determined by the districts, were far from uniform throughout France, but the absence of any allowance for the cost of transport or for profits quickly halted distribution. Local authorities were therefore driven to act independently, requisitioning corn wherever they could, and often following the example of the Commune of Paris by introducing some sort of rationing

[1] See Chapter VIII below.

[2] Fouché (Joseph, later Duke of Otranto), b. near Nantes 1759, son of a merchant captain. Educated by the Oratorians, he became one of their teachers in minor orders and was in 1789 the principal of their college at Nantes. Renouncing his order, he became prominent in the Jacobin Club at Nantes and was elected deputy for Loire Inférieure to the Convention. An active Terrorist campaigner against Christianity, he participated with Collot d'Herbois in the repression of Lyons and was a principal in the conspiracy which overthrew Robespierre. After living in poverty and obscurity 1795–98, he went on missions to Italy and Holland before becoming Minister of Police to the Directory and to Napoleon from 1799 onwards, an office in which he became indispensable and all-powerful. After helping to arrange the Restoration of 1815 he retired from France, became a naturalised Austrian, and died at Trieste in 1820.

system. Fearful confusion ensued as representatives on mission and agents for the armies scoured the countryside for food and forage, in direct competition with each other and with commissioners appointed by the districts and the communes, the latter sometimes being supported by armed bodies of *sans-culottes*. The Commune of Paris, in particular, competed for supplies with both the Army of the North and the Army of Italy. Although hundreds of horses were at one time dying daily from starvation in the force assembled to relieve Maubeuge, the Committee was forced to decree that supplies for Paris should have priority over those for the army. Here again, direction on a national scale was obviously required.

More control came to the Committee gradually. An attempt by Billaud-Varenne on 4th October to restrict the independence of representatives on mission was premature, but on 10th October Saint-Just won much wider political and economic powers for his colleagues by the decree which declared the government of France to be revolutionary until the peace. This did much more than simply postpone the operation of the Constitution of 1793. It authorised the Committee to supervise the Executive Council, the generals and the local authorities, and to correspond directly with the sub-divisions of the departments, the districts. Further, it empowered the Committee to take stock of all grain production and to requisition whatever any area had above its own needs. Control of the Revolutionary Army of Paris was also reserved to it alone. An important result of this decree was that the Committee established a Central Food Commission, for the direction of which Robert Lindet was recalled from Calvados. This body soon became a power in the land, rivalling the War Office in the size of the staff it employed. Having practically unlimited pre-emptive powers, it began to re-distribute food and military supplies according to the needs of the various armies and of the zones into which it divided France, and at the same time it initiated even wider long-term plans for a uniform scale of prices and for the development of industry and agriculture. Although it was only in the manufacture of arms that state production replaced private enterprise, regulation of the economy was soon as extensive as the bureaucracy of the day and the power of coercion could make it. The return of the authority of the state is strikingly illustrated by the fact that when the problem of transport was tackled early in 1794, road-work, the hated *corvée* of the *ancien régime*, again became a compulsory form of patriotic duty.

The Committee of Public Safety was nevertheless dissatisfied, for it required complete political authority as well as economic power. As Saint-Just had said on 10th October, 'Prosperity can not be hoped for while the last enemy of liberty still breathes'. He had then asserted that the Committee's efforts to stamp out disloyalty and to promote positive revolutionary action were constantly frustrated by the resistance of the very authorities through whom it had to work. The revolutionary government had in fact inherited an established system of central and local administration from the time of the constitutional monarchy, and feeble as this was, its officials were still strong enough to retard the operation of laws which they themselves disliked. As Billaud-Varenne put it in a powerful report to the Convention on 18th November, the revolutionaries had decapitated royalism but left its trunk intact. On 4th December,[1] therefore, a new decree provided for a complete re-organisation of government. This measure, which is often called the 'Constitution of Terror', first provided for the publication and distribution of copies of the laws, and then placed all the agencies of government firmly under the control of the Committee of Public Safety, matters of police being separately reserved for the Committee of General Security. All commissioners, generals and heads of tribunals were required to report at ten-day intervals to the Executive Council, the ministers of which were similarly required to report both individually and collectively to the Committee of Public Safety. At the same time the representatives on mission were finally placed under the Committee's direction: their powers were explicitly limited, and they, too, were ordered to present regular reports. These provisions in effect concentrated all central authority in the hands of the two governing Committees and reduced the ministers to the position of puppets.

The alteration of local government was still more drastic, being intended to eliminate or curtail the power of all intermediate bodies and to increase that of a multiplicity of small authorities, each of which would be in direct contact with the people and subject to control from Paris. To this end, the directories of the departments, which were regarded as irredeemably conservative, were restricted to routine work, while the more radical authorities of the districts were entrusted with the enforcement of all revolutionary legislation, matters of police again being reserved for the local revolutionary committees (the *comités de surveillance*) and the Committee of General Security. Moreover, the principal officials of the districts and the communes, the elected *procureurs*, now became, or were replaced by, nominated 'national agents', whose first duty was that of purging the local councils and administrations of unreliable personnel. All these authorities were again required to send their reports to Paris every ten days, and the formation of any sort of union amongst them, or the maintenance of any revolutionary army other than that established by the Convention in Paris, was expressly forbidden.[2]

---

[1] I.e. '14th Frimaire'. The new chronology adopted by the revolutionaries is considered in the next chapter.

[2] The unfortunate national agents of the Commune were in fact required to present reports at ten-day intervals to both the governing committees.

This decree was not, of course, fully implemented. If it had been, the reading and writing of reports would have brought all other activity to a halt. Nor was the law immediately obeyed by all concerned, for the representatives on mission and the Committee of General Security could only gradually be pushed towards their allotted positions. The law nevertheless imposed a new and powerful form of authoritarianism upon France. The Committee of Public Safety held unprecedented power in Paris, and throughout the country the *comités de surveillance* and the popular societies were masters of men's lives and fortunes. The revolutionaries undoubtedly regarded this rigorous regulation as an expedient which would be ended as soon as the Republic was established, and it indeed happened that much of the new centralisation was abolished soon after the Committee of Public Safety was overthrown six months later. The re-assertion of the power of the state at the end of 1793 is nonetheless remarkable. As the decentralisation of 1789–91 had been beyond all reason, some restoration of the authority of government was certainly necessary. As certainly, the increasingly complex needs of a rapidly developing nation, as well as the mounting administrative demands of a national war, made it essential that the authority of government should become considerably more far-reaching and effective than it had ever been before. The decree of 4th December is therefore quite as significant as the Declaration of Rights itself: after emancipating the sovereign power of the nation from the moral sanctions of the old order, the Revolution was now subjugating local to central government, and so destroying the last of the 'intermediate bodies' which the aristocracy had once successfully upheld against the monarchy. Wherever the order foreshadowed by the law of 4th December took root, the individual would stand alone against the state.

Nor is this all, for the 'Constitution of Terror' was something more than a measure of control in war-time. According to the thought behind it, the state, which represented the community, was necessarily opposed to the individual. In his speech of 10th October, Saint-Just had argued that the people had really only one enemy, its own government; authority ought therefore to be dispersed until it became identified with the revolutionary movement. The people of a free society, in other words, ought to be able to regulate their own affairs without the direction of any superior authority. This vision of an ideal democracy had as its terrible counterpart the conviction that if in fact such freedom could not be immediately established, this was the fault of those who refused to identify themselves with the revolutionary movement, but tried instead to thwart it or destroy it. The first task of true friends of freedom must therefore be the elimination of these enemies. With them, in Saint-Just's words, there could be no compromise; as they were 'outside the sovereign' they must be ruled by iron and by right of conquest, for 'liberty must conquer at all costs'. All virtue was thus identified with

189

what was in reality a militant minority, and all safety was seen in its supremacy. So that the complete triumph of this supposedly freedom-loving minority might be assured, the Committee of Public Safety exercised dictatorial power as the embodiment of the sovereign will of the people, and the electoral principle was openly and deliberately abandoned. France was thus subjected to the rule of a single party, which was enforced by in-numerable security committees with extensive powers of arrest. Only men like Saint-Just, who believed that it would one day be possible to kill the last enemy of liberty, could believe that all this would be but temporary. Saint-Just, however, also believed that 'the repression of all evil will bring forth the good'.

8

The Republic of Virtue

According to what is sometimes called the 'thesis of circumstance', the Terror was forced upon France by the war, which made dictatorial government essential as a means of national defence. This interpretation, which was first authoritatively advanced by Aulard, has subsequently been considerably modified by his successors at the Sorbonne. Mathiez, who was much more conscious of the economic aspects of the Terror, regarded the Montagnards as men who were prepared to sacrifice the interests of their own class in order to extend the benefits of the Revolution to the 'little men' of France. He believed that they tried to control the economy in order to promote social revolution, as well as for the sake of victory. More recently still, Soboul has shown that the Montagnards usually acted in response to spontaneous pressure from the *sans-culottes* of Paris; the latter, he suggests, came to regard them as *endormeurs*, men who were less reactionary than the Brissotins but who were still conscious of their middle-class superiority and implacably opposed to direct popular democracy or any permanent regulation of prices. For all these historians, however, the 'thesis of circumstance' is ultimately fundamental: as opposed to those who have seen the Terror as the inevitable outcome of a dangerous ideology, they accept the view that the war explains and justifies it. The bloodshed and violence of 1793–94 is thus ascribed to something external to the Revolution itself, and the old order, now identified with the foreign tyrants and their 'aristocratic' allies, remains the ultimate enemy.

The Terror, in the widest sense of the word, may however also be seen as something which was always implicit in the Revolution. Violence, common enough in the time of the monarchy, became endemic when the royal government disintegrated. The danger of anarchy, which affected the *sans-culottes* as much as the middle-class, tended always to produce emergency forms of government. As we have seen, the taking of the Bastille in July 1789 was followed by the appearance of lynch law in Paris and by a rapid movement towards the creation of political controls and extraordinary tribunals. In September 1792 the same sequence was evident. Violence in speech and writing, too, increased constantly, intensifying the passionate hatred of the aristocratic enemy, who perpetually reappeared in some new

191

guise. Moreover, although ideology seems to have developed with the Revolution, being more its consequence than its cause, men of all shades of opinion talked in uncompromising terms; they tended, in the tradition of the *ancien régime*, to approach political and economic problems from the position of supposedly sovereign authority and unquestionable rights. Official authoritarianism and unofficial violence undoubtedly increased sharply as the military crisis of 1793 developed, but the needs of national defence were neither their original nor their only cause.

Military danger to the Republic in fact receded even as the revolutionary government began to acquire real power. By the end of September 1793 the French armies had driven the Spaniards out of Roussillon and the Piedmontese out of Savoy. On 9th October, the day before Saint-Just first won extensive authority for the Committee of Public Safety, Lyons finally fell to the Montagnard forces which had been besieging and bombarding it since August. The Count of Précy himself escaped, but the troops he tried to lead to safety were completely cut to pieces. A week later, on 16th October, Tallien and other Montagnard commissioners quietly entered Bordeaux, the municipality of which had been in the hands of their friends since mid-September. On that same day, which was also that of the execution of Marie-Antoinette, forces from the combined Armies of the North and the Ardennes beat the Austrians at the battle of Wattignies and compelled Coburg to abandon the siege of Maubeuge. Although it was not in itself decisive, this victory pointed to future triumphs. Ever increasing in numbers, the French army was skilfully concentrated by its new commander, the young Jourdan, and in the presence of Carnot himself the men showed that their morale was now fully equal to the strain of forced marches and fierce fighting. By mid-November these northern armies were able to go into winter quarters.

During these same months the republican armies also broke all effective resistance to the Revolution within France. In the west the Vendéans were caught between converging columns at Cholet on 17th October, and were badly beaten. One of their leaders, Charette, then returned to the Marais, but the main body moved north of the Loire, and for a month a great mass of men, women and children roamed and ravaged in aimless disorder. News then came that Britain had promised to aid them and required them to seize control of some northern port. Two weeks later, on 24th November, the peasant host surged down to the sea at Granville, only to be repulsed by the townsmen. Unaided by the British, who knew nothing of their plans and did not despatch any expeditionary force until December, the Vendéans fell back inland. On 13th–14th December they were caught and slaughtered by Kléber's forces in the streets of Mans, and on 23rd December the remnants of their army were overwhelmed at Savenay on the estuary of the Loire.

Although men like La Rochejacquelin[1] and Stofflet survived to continue guerilla warfare south of the river, alongside Charret, and although this 'Chouannerie' spread to Brittany and outlived the Revolution, the great military revolt was broken.

On other fronts the Revolution was equally successful. Hoche and Pichegru, the new commanders of the Armies of the Moselle and the Rhine, had to fight desperately to repel the Austro-Prussian penetration into Alsace, and at the end of November a sustained French attack on Kaiserlauten failed in spite of great sacrifices. In December, however, the weight of numbers and disregard of casualties had their effect: after winning a decisive engagement on 26th December, the French relieved Landau and re-entered Wissembourg. These republican victories coincided with, and were symbolised by, the recapture of Toulon, which had been held since August by the British and a large but polyglot force of Piedmontese and Spaniards. On 15th December the besiegers began their final bombardment of Fort Éguillette, the importance of which had been indicated by Bonaparte, then an artillery commander, and on 19th December Admiral Hood gave the order for evacuation. As the British sailed away with some 15,000 royalist refugees and the remnants of the French Mediterranean fleet, the republicans reoccupied the city. Thus by the end of 1793 the Convention's armies had mastered every major military threat and occupied all French territory except a narrow strip of the northern frontier.

At the same time the Terror reached its peak in the provinces. The repression, which at its worst was accompanied by appalling atrocities, was naturally most severe where resistance to the Revolution had been most obstinate, but it also varied considerably according to the character of the representatives on mission in the different areas. At Marseilles, the first of the 'federalist' cities to be reoccupied, a popular movement had prevented the merchants who controlled the Municipality from calling in the British fleet, and General Carteaux's troops had entered the city without resistance in August. Even in October, when Barras[2] and Fréron superseded more moderate representatives from

---

[1] La Rochejacquelin (Henri de), b. near Châtillon 1772, became the nominal commander of the Vendéan army after its defeat at Cholet. Unable to prevent the disasters which followed from courses he disapproved, he nevertheless upheld the cause courageously until he was shot in March 1794.

[2] Barras (Paul Jean François Nicolas, Vicomte de), b. 1755 in Var, lived indolent life between intervals of military service, elected deputy for Var to the Convention, for which he acted as a representative enforcing the Terror at Toulon 1793–94. Organised defence of the Convention against the Commune at Thermidor and arrested the Robespierrists at the Hôtel de Ville. Leader of the Thermidorian reaction, suppressed rising of 13th Vendémiaire (5th October 1795) with help of Napoleon, became a Director 1795–99 and aided Napoleon to command of Army of Italy. Notorious for luxurious living, he was distrusted by

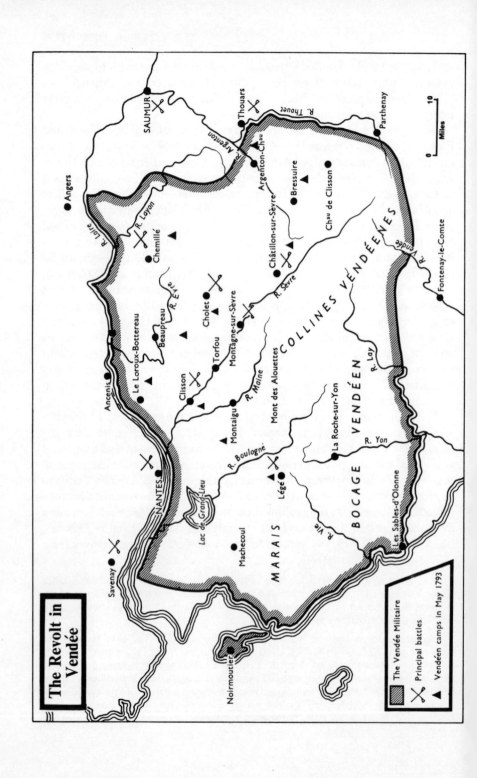

The Revolt in Vendée

SAUMUR
Angers
Thouars
R. Argenton
R. Thouet
Parthenay
Argenton-Ch^au
Bressuire
Ch^au de Clisson
Châtillon-sur-Sèvre
R. Layon
Chemillé
R. Sèvre
Fontenay-le-Comte
R. Vendée
R. Èvre
COLLINES VENDÉENES
Cholet
Beaupréau
Montagne-sur-Sèvre
Torfou
Le Loroux-Bottereau
R. Lay
Ancenis
R. Maine
Clisson
Montaigu
R. Yon
Mont des Alouettes
La Roche-sur-Yon
R. Boulogne
BOCAGE VENDÉEN
R. Loire
NANTES
Lac de Grand-Lieu
Légé
R. Vie
Savenay
Machecoul
Les Sables-d'Olonne
MARAIS
Noirmoutier

0   10
Miles

The Vendée Militaire
Principal battles
Vendéen camps in May 1793

the Convention, the development of Marseilles as a base for the attack on Toulon seemed more important than the punishment of the townsmen. In 1793, therefore, only about 160 people, mostly members of the old Municipality, were put to death. Meanwhile Tallien and his colleagues had made a great show of establishing the Terror at Bordeaux. The prisons there were soon filled with suspects, but since this city had also been taken fairly easily the repression was relatively mild. When Tallien, who was far more ferocious in words than in deeds, was recalled to Paris in March 1794, his guillotine had only claimed 123 victims.[1] While the continued public execution of political offenders in these two cities may seem monstrous, the initial penalty for what was regarded as rebellion can be considered comparatively light.

The full impact of the Terror outside Paris was first apparent at Lyons. The rising there had begun in class-conflict, it had obviously passed under royalist control, and it had held forces eventually amounting to 35,000 men at bay for more than two months. Retribution was correspondingly severe, and it was intended to symbolise the triumph of the people and to paralyse resistance everywhere else. On 12th October, three days after the fall of the city, the Committee of Public Safety presented the Convention with an extravagant order for its total destruction. All the houses of the rich were to be demolished, and the very name of Lyons was to be blotted from the records. Amidst the ruins of the 'liberated city', now to be known as *Ville Affranchie*, there was to stand a column commemorating the crimes of the royalists, and bearing the inscription: 'Lyons made war upon Liberty, Lyons is no more.' On that same day Robespierre wrote to his friend and colleague, Couthon, who had brought the siege to a conclusion, to warn him and the other deputies with him at Lyons that humanity would only encourage new conspiracies: the orders of the Convention were to be effected with 'inexorable severity'. Couthon promptly asked to be transferred to Toulon. Not himself a man of violence, he simply established a military commission to deal with captured rebels, and ceremonially marked a few great houses down for destruction.

Couthon was soon replaced by Collot d'Herbois and Fouché, both of whom were ready to rejoice in the death of traitors and the impoverishment of the rich.[2] To enforce the Revolution in the whole Department of the Rhône,

Napoleon, who sent him first from Paris and then from France. Returning in 1815, he died at Paris in 1829.

[1] Tallien, who was master of Bordeaux at the age of 26, was influenced to mercy by the 18-year-old girl who became first his mistress and then his wife, Theresa Cabarrus. Her first husband, the elderly Count of Fontenay, to whom she had been married at the age of 14, was released from prison on agreeing to apply for a divorce.

[2] Collot, indeed, considered that only some 60,000 of the working people of Lyons need be saved at all, and that these should be re-settled in more patriotic places; the remaining 'individuals', of whom he thought there were about 80,000, should be shown no mercy.

195

they set up a temporary commission of twenty members. This, in the notorious Instruction of 16th November, stated as its first principle: 'A revolutionary agent may do anything. He has nothing to fear, except failure to reach the level of republican legality. He who anticipates this, or even seems to have passed its goal, may not yet have reached it.' All who were even remotely implicated in the rebellion were to be put to death, and the wealth of the rich was to be put at the disposal of the Republic. 'There is no need here', said the Instruction, 'of mathematical exactness or timid scruples in the levying of public taxes.' On 25th November a strong contingent of the Revolutionary Army of Paris arrived under its commander, Ronsin, and on 27th a new Tribunal of Seven, soon to be known from the name of its principal member as the *Commission Parein*, was established. On 4th December, nearly two months after the fighting had ended and on the very day that the Convention gave the Committee of Public Safety sufficient authority to control the Terror, a form of mass murder known as the *mitraillades* began in Lyons. Sixty people, condemned by Parein's commission, were marched to an open space and forced to stand between ditches already dug as graves. Three cannon were then fired upon them, and those who survived were killed off with the sword. Next day 200 more died in the same way, and other batches of sixty-seven and twenty-three succeeded these on December 18th and 23rd. Thereafter the firing squad and the guillotine sufficed for the work, and Collot d'Herbois returned to Paris. Fouché, however, remained, and if the demolition of houses did not get far, 1,665 more victims were put to death before the Terror ended.

The death rate at Lyons was exceeded elsewhere, though in conditions that were more closely related to the immediate passions and problems of war. When Toulon fell, *fusillades* (i.e. mass slaughter by firing squads) began at once. As Barras wrote to the Convention: 'Everyone found in Toulon who had been employed in the navy, the rebel army, or in naval or military administration, was shot.' Only when this unrecorded killing had accounted for some 800 lives was a military commission established, and this eventually ordered a total of 309 more executions. In the west of France, where the slaughter was greatest of all, the authorities were not dealing with a single city, but were trying to conquer a countryside. As the civil war there had been singularly cruel on both sides, the repression was ferocious. Each defeat of the Vendéan army was followed by the shooting of hundreds of fugitives. Thousands more, who surrendered or were taken captive, crammed the prisons and spread diseases in the towns. Since none could be released lest the civil war should be renewed, and since all were already outlawed as rebels taken under arms, the firing squads were again employed. At the end of December 1793 and the beginning of January 1794 at least 1,500 people were shot without trial near Angers alone.

The repression in the west, moreover, was continued as a military operation. In accordance with the decree of 1st August for the devastation of the Vendée (by which should be understood the fighting area, the *Vendée militaire*) twelve bodies of troops were formed from the Army of the West, and from January until the spring of 1794 these 'infernal columns' traversed the area, killing and destroying all that lay in their paths. Under these conditions the conduct of Carrier, the representative of the people at Nantes, who had at least 2,000 people drowned in the Loire on various occasions between November and January, at first passed almost unnoticed. During the whole period of the Terror, recorded condemnations by the revolutionary courts in the Departments of Loire Inférieure, Maine et Loire and Vendée amounted to more than 7,000, a figure almost half the total number of deaths in the whole of France. In the words of Donald Greer, the best authority on the subject, 'it was precisely in the departments of the most atrocious civil war in French history that revolutionary justice took the heaviest toll'.[1]

Coming in each of these areas as the aftermath of military victory, this phase of the Terror was clearly coincident with the resurgence of the Republic as a whole. In December 1793, when the revolutionary courts alone put over 3,300 persons to death, France had at least secured itself from foreign attack. Although the revolutionaries were at this time more than ever convinced that the country was riddled with conspiracy, this much was clear, and on 30th December Paris witnessed another of David's spectacular pageants, now arranged 'in honour of the capture of Toulon and of the other victories of the republican armies'. Once again an immense procession symbolised the fraternal unity of the people and their various authorities. This time, however, the column was led by cavalry, trumpeters and engineers, and at its end came Victory herself. Standing in a splendid triumphal car, she was surrounded by fourteen selected soldiers, each one of whom represented one of the fourteen victorious armies of France.

Not surprisingly, this changing situation was accompanied by the rapid development of a movement for a relaxation of the Terror. Danton, who had hurried back to Paris from Arcis-sur-Aube in mid-November, began this campaign by a speech on 22nd November in which he demanded 'economy in human blood'. His immediate objectives were, as we shall see, somewhat dubious, but his inclination for some less exclusive and less exacting form of republicanism was real enough. Many of the deputies who rallied round him, the so-called 'Indulgents', were concerned with their own fortunes, but his call for clemency soon won wide support. Under his aegis, Camille Desmoulins launched a new journal *le Vieux Cordelier*: the first two numbers had

---

[1] D. Greer, *The Incidence of the Terror* (Havard U.P., 1935), p. 40 *ff*. He estimates that 100,000 men were killed on the rebel side in the war and the repression together.

attacked the Hébertists, but the third appeared on 15th December as a brilliant attack upon the whole Terror and even upon the revolutionary government itself. In what purported to be a translation of Tacitus, Camille portrayed a society dominated by denunciation and driven frantic by fear. The application of this to France was obvious, and if Camille's own solutions to the problems of the day were childishly naive, his journalism was devastatingly effective. 'I shall die in the belief', he wrote, 'that to make France free, republican and prosperous, a little ink would have sufficed, and only one guillotine.'

Whilst this daring attack upon the Law of Suspects was having a sensational success in Paris, two delegations appeared before the Convention. First a number of women came to beg for the release of their menfolk, whom they said had been unjustly imprisoned. Then on the same day, 20th December, a deputation of citizens from Lyons appeared to plead for re-admission of their city into the Republic. The Convention's agents, they asserted, had gone far beyond their instructions in inflicting a savage and inhuman punishment upon Lyons; the Convention itself must intervene and allow 'the reign of love to succeed to that of Terror'. In response to the first of these appeals, Robespierre himself supported the creation of a 'committee of clemency', which was to examine the lists of those who had been arrested and release those who were found to be innocent. Encouraged, perhaps, by this, Camille Desmoulins grew still bolder: on 24th December, a fourth issue of the *Vieux Cordelier* appealed for the immediate release of 'two hundred thousand citizens who are called suspects', and Robespierre's name was used in a way that implied that he stood behind the movement for moderation.

In this, Desmoulins had over-reached himself. Robespierre had indeed known and approved of the first two numbers of the *Vieux Cordelier* before their publication, but he had known nothing of the later issues. From the point of view of the Committee of Public Safety, for the general policy of which Robespierre was probably particularly responsible, the whole situation was far more delicate than it appeared to Desmoulins. The Committee was indeed inclined to repudiate any sort of independent terrorism, but the Terror itself was undoubtedly government policy. All in authority were agreed that the known enemies of the Revolution had to be eliminated, that suspected enemies must be kept under guard, and that potential enemies must be deterred from conspiracy by the sight of the guillotine at work.

The complexity of the position at this time can only be fully appreciated if it is seen in relation to some of the other developments that had occurred in the autumn. As we know, Robespierre and most, though not all, of the members of the Committee had long been anxious to check the Hébertist type of Terror, which tended to excite social conflict and multiply opposition by its own excesses. Some of the representatives on mission had not only repressed rebellion ruthlessly, but had also raised revolutionary armies, terrorised all traders indiscriminately as an 'aristocracy of merchants', and filled all offices with reliable *sans-culottes*. The Committee was not of course unduly squeamish about the rights of the rich: Saint-Just, on mission in Alsace in October, had imposed a forced loan of nine million livres on 193 citizens of Strasbourg, and had later allocated two millions of the proceeds to the relief of needy patriots in the city. Like the *sans-culottes*, the Jacobins regarded the possession of great wealth as an indication of a lack of civic virtue. As always, however, the Committee's main concern was to maintain its own authority and ensure that the nation was united against the enemy. The conduct of men like Carrier and Fouché, so far as it was known at all, might have to be tolerated while the influence of the *sans-culottes* was at its height in Paris, but it could never be permanently accepted.

In the autumn of 1793 this general problem of controlling the Terror and checking the tendency to class-conflict was aggravated by the fact that some extreme terrorists had encouraged a general wave of hostility to Christianity itself. Such a development was implicit in the Revolution, which had from its beginning been nothing less than a new religion. Of this, the trees of liberty, the innumerable festivals, the civic oaths and the altars of the fatherland had been but the outward forms. Initially the clergy had participated in the new ceremonies, and many of them had believed that the reform of the Church and the freedom of the people would begin a new era of practical Christian conduct. From 1789 to 1793, however, the two religions had moved further and further apart. While the schism in the Church over the Civil Consti-tution of the Clergy had led eventually to violent and indiscriminate anti-clericalism, the gradual introduction of secular marriage, divorce, education and poor relief had deprived the constitutional clergy of much of their social importance. When the king had been executed and when religious war had been preached in the Vendée, it became hard for the revolutionary to distin-guish one priest from another. Nor could the constitutional *curé* obey his bishop without isolating himself from the *sans-culottes* who held their assemblies in his church and expected him to join them in patriotic ardour and revolutionary zeal.

Still more important, the religion of the Revolution was ultimately alien to that of the Church. The ideal which inspired both the *sans-culottes* and the Jacobins was not, indeed, an ignoble one: in the society which the best of them were striving to achieve, all men would co-operate as equals in volun-tary and fraternal associations, and all forms of selfishness and immorality would give way to the public interest and republican sobriety. In practice, however, their associations were highly selective ones, in which unity was maintained by repeated purges and public confessions of political faith and conduct, and their vision was a combination of nationalism and social morality. Their societies had no place for priests who dressed differently from the people and who lived apart from them in suspicious celibacy, and their vision had no real place for God. The educated revolutionaries believed in Man, who was good and who might be made perfect by education and good government. The less literate had an even more passionate faith in the possibilities of brotherly co-operation. All alike held the welfare of the people to be the final criterion of virtue.

Although in 1793 the nation-wide search for the materials of war again encouraged popular iconoclasts, the open attack on Christianity sprang more from bourgeois influence than from public frenzy. Soon after the Festival of Unity on 10th August, in which the clergy had no share, the Convention introduced the new Republican Calendar. This it declared, in its ingenuous Voltairian way, to be a 'measure of time freed from all the errors which credulity and superstitious routine have handed down to us from centuries of ignorance'. By the decree of 5th October, the year was 'rationally' divided into twelve months of thirty days each, with five complementary days, soon to be called the *sans-culottides*, left over; each month was similarly divided into three periods of ten days each, every tenth day, or *décadi*, being a day of rest. By a further decree, for which the poetic Fabre d'Eglantine was responsible, each month was given a 'natural' name appropriate to its season, and every day of the year was distinguished by the title of something natural or agricultural. By this reckoning, the 4th December, the day of the great law on revolutionary government, became the 14th day of Frimaire, the month of frost; on paper at least, it was also the day of the fir-tree. This new nomenclature dissociated religion from daily life, while the chronology was incompatible with the observance of Sundays. The festivals of the Church also disappeared, and on 5th November provision was made for an alternative series of civic celebrations.

In the provinces, meanwhile, certain representatives on mission had begun a more violent assault upon Christian worship. In September, after a momentous meeting between Fouché, who was at that time in the Nièvre, and Chaumette, the *procureur* of the Commune in Paris, the former announced that the object of his mission was 'to substitute for superstitious and hypocritical cults . . . that of the Republic and Natural Morality'. In addition to stripping churches of their ornaments, he banned all religious ceremonies outside them, ordered the destruction of calvaries and crosses and had notices posted at the gates of cemeteries to announce that 'Death is an Eternal Sleep'. He also initiated a campaign to compel the clergy to marry or to adopt a child or support an elderly person, the alternative being resignation. A similar course was followed by such men as Dumont in the Somme and Lequino at Rochefort.

In October this movement gained ground rapidly in Paris, and by the end of the first week in November the Archbishop of Paris, Gobel, had been intimidated into going to the Convention to abjure his priesthood and to put on the *bonnet rouge*. On 10th November, again in the presence of the Convention, a great 'Festival of Reason' was staged in Notre Dame, with an actress from the opera presiding in the dress of Liberty. When the *sans-culottes* were sufficiently excited, the Commune on 23rd November ordered that all the churches in the city should be closed. Thereafter the movement spread rapidly throughout France, being generally accompanied by the plundering of churches and by masquerades in mockery of Christian rites. By the spring of 1794 it would seem that most of the churches in the land had either been closed down or converted into Temples of Reason.

To the Committee of Public Safety all this was dangerously impolitic. Most of the members of the Committee were, indeed, as anti-clerical and as rationalist as anyone, and several of them had to countenance attacks on religion when they were on mission in the provinces. Couthon, before he knew his colleagues' mind, positively encouraged the movement in the Puy-de-Dôme, and Collot d'Herbois was as extremist in this as in other matters. As a government, however, the Committee was compelled to oppose violent demonstrations against the religious beliefs of most Frenchmen, for like the economic levelling and the excessive repression with which it was often associated, religious terrorism seemed certain to discredit the Revolution and to harden hostility to it. 'It seems to us', as Robespierre put it in a letter from the Committee to André Dumont on 27th October, 'that you have of late struck too hard against the objects of Catholic worship. . . . We must be careful not to give the hypocritical counter-revolutionaries, who seek to excite civil war, any excuse for saying that their accusations have been justified. They must not be allowed any opportunity to allege that freedom of worship is violated or that we make war on religion itself.' Expediency alone, therefore, would probably have made the religious question the occasion of a trial of strength between the Committee and the Hébertists. As it happened, however, the matter was also one of profound personal concern to Robespierre.

In one of the debates in the Jacobin Society early in the previous year, when Robespierre was apparently being thrust aside by the more war-like Brissotins, he had almost accidentally referred to Providence, 'which watches over us far better than our own wisdom'. Guadet had promptly seized upon this point and suggested that Robespierre was resurrecting the despotism of superstition. In a spontaneous reply, Robespierre had renounced all sympathy for the priesthood, but he had also proclaimed his heart-felt belief in the existence of God, the Eternal Creator of men and nature, the Providence 'which is an essential influence on the destinies of nations and which seems to me to watch over the French Revolution with very particular care'. This

201

consistent conviction distinguishes Robespierre not only from what J. M. Thompson called 'the easy-going intelligentsia' of the Legislative Assembly, but also from the great majority of deputies in the Convention and from many otherwise ardent Jacobins. As opposed to those who identified God with Reason and the Church with superstition, Robespierre had a deep appreciation of the religious faith which underlay the Revolution, and it was this which made him its truest prophet. To him, the attack upon Christianity was not only politically dangerous: it was a blasphemous affront to the Supreme Being and to the Revolution itself.

To a man in this frame of mind there could be but one explanation of the extremism which seemed likely to ruin the Republic in the autumn and winter of 1793. Social confusion, religious anarchy, unrestricted violence and an irresponsibly aggressive attitude towards foreign neutrals—all were evidence of a conspiracy, fomented and financed from abroad. The presence in Paris of a considerable number of influential foreigners, which had once seemed to show the universal appeal of the Revolution, now appeared extremely suspicious to Robespierre. On 10th October he told the Convention: 'I distrust all these foreigners, who wear the mask of patriotism and pretend to be more republican and energetic than we are ourselves. They are the agents of foreign powers.'

About two days later, Fabre d'Eglantine, a man who was close to Danton, came forward with a story that seemed to confirm all Robespierre's worst fears. At a special joint meeting of the Committees of Public Safety and General Security, Fabre asserted that a number of extreme revolutionaries were involved in a great foreign plot to discredit and destroy the republic. More specifically, he denounced at least seven well-known men—Chabot and Julien of Toulouse, who had been purged from the Committee of General Security in September; Desfieux, Dubuisson, the Belgian Proli and the Portuguese Pereira, all of whom were later labelled Hébertists; and Hérault de Séchelles, the most aristocratic member of the Committee of Public Safety itself. From this time onwards, the so-called 'Foreign Plot' had a profound effect upon the whole political situation. The Committees began investigations at once, and as information and denunciations accumulated it seemed that no-one was wholly free from some taint of treason or corruption. The Committee of Public Safety, moreover, had now acquired a very powerful weapon to use against any opponent, and the more the Hébertists pressed their attacks upon the Church, the more guilty they made themselves appear.

As something organised and financed by enemy powers—and particularly, of course, by the arch-enemy, William Pitt—the Foreign Plot seems to have been mainly mythical. Its investigation, however, revealed a real evil: beneath the surface of the Revolution, corruption and racketeering were rife.

There were certainly in Paris several big financiers of foreign extraction, like the Moravian Jews Siegmund Gotleb and Emmanuel Dobruska, who had not surprisingly changed their names to that of the brothers Frey (i.e. free). Such men as these were undoubtedly hand-in-glove with a considerable number of municipal and government officials as well as politicians from the level of the clubs to that of the Convention. Chabot, for example, was said to have married into the Frey family so that his wife's dowry might account for the great increase in his personal fortune. Working together at a time when all was insecure and everything was in demand for the war effort, these people could rig the markets, secure government contracts and defraud the public very much as they chose. The scale which these activities had long since attained is illustrated by the well-known case of the prominent Jacobin d'Espagnac, who secured an army contract for which he was paid over five million livres a month although he spent only a tenth of that amount.

There seems every reason to suppose that these financiers and politicians, as well as rich royalists like the Baron de Batz, had a strong common interest in keeping popular agitation at fever pitch and encouraging the attack on religion as a convenient cover for graft. In 1793, moreover, the technique of threatening revolutionary legislation in order to play the markets profitably, or to secure substantial protection money from prospective victims, became well-developed, and the profiteers were encouraged to pursue very big game indeed. In August the Convention was induced to order the liquidation of the East India Company, and a group of five deputies—Chabot, Julien of Toulouse, Delaunay of Angers, Basire and Fabre d'Eglantine—so arranged things that the decree was falsified and they netted half a million livres for themselves. This, the 'India Scandal', was the reality behind the Foreign Plot which Fabre denounced in October, double-crossing his associates in order to cover his own tracks. In this he was so successful that even when Chabot grew alarmed and also denounced the affair in mid-November, the charge against Fabre was not believed, and only the other four were arrested.

For Robespierre, certainly, all these things flowed together. His hopes of reassuring neutral countries like Switzerland were compromised by the expansionist propaganda of men like the Prussian Cloots, while people like the Portuguese Pereira, whom Fabre had denounced, were ardent agitators against Christianity. Pereira and his associates, moreover, were prominent in the organisation of a central committee of the 'popular societies of the sections'. Through these associations the sans-culottes were trying to evade the restriction imposed in September on the meetings of their general assemblies, and the 'central committee' was a new threat to the Committee of Public Safety's control of Paris.

When Chabot and his associates had been arrested, Robespierre felt strong

203

enough to move against these various enemies on the Left. Speaking on 17th November on the situation of the Republic, he attacked 'both the cruel moderation and the systematic exaggeration of false patriots . . . in the pay of foreign courts'. Four days later, in a great speech to the Jacobins, he openly attacked atheists and announced the government's intention to maintain religious freedom. Priests who abused their office to disturb public order would be punished, but so would those who persecuted peaceful ministers unnecessarily. 'Priests', he said, 'have been denounced for saying the Mass; they will say it longer if an attempt is made to stop them. He who would prevent them is more fanatical than they.' Speaking, as he said, as a member of the Convention, a body charged with 'protecting not only the rights but also the character of the French people', he condemned those who were trying to elevate atheism to the status of a religion. 'Atheism', he averred, 'is aristocratic; the idea of a great Being who watches over oppressed innocence and punishes triumphant crime is altogether popular. . . . I repeat: we have no other fanaticism to fear than that of immoral men, paid by foreign courts to re-awaken fanaticism and to give our Revolution an appearance of immorality.'

This speech, which undoubtedly reflected the opinion of the majority, was of decisive effect. At Robespierre's demand, the Society expelled Pereira, Proli, Desfieux and Dubuisson. It also began a *scrutin épuratoire*, a process in which all members gave a public account of their opinions and conduct in order to justify their orthodoxy to their fellows, and this went on for weeks. Two days after the speech, the 'central committee' of the popular societies was condemned as dangerous to liberty. The Commune, too, was soon pushed into recognising religious freedom, which the Convention itself reaffirmed in a solemn decree on 8th December. Although the churches which had been closed were not reopened, although the movement against Christianity continued to spread across France, a turning-point in the Revolution had been reached. Just when the administrative demands of the war were drawing the *sans-culottes* steadily under the control of the governing Committees, the Hébertists who had tried to profit from the popular exaltation were effectively discredited. With Robespierre's approval, Camille Desmoulins attacked them in the first two issues of the *Vieux Cordelier*. After Fabre had added new denunciations, some of the most advanced amongst them, including Vincent, who was influential at the War Office, and Ronsin, the commander of the Revolutionary Army, were arrested. For the first time the Revolution's long swing to the Left was checked.

In achieving this striking political success, Robespierre and his colleagues were assisted by Danton, who, as we have seen, had returned to Paris on 20th November to demand 'economy in human blood'. This intervention from the Right, however, was manifestly not disinterested. Fabre and his friends now clearly required Danton's protection to save them from arrest, and Danton himself may well have hoped that a tide was rising which would carry him to power.

Indeed, if Robespierre could have been led to press the attack on the Hébertists far enough, a revolt by Collot d'Herbois, who was quite as violent as they were, might well have split the Committee of Public Safety apart. Seen in this light, the Dantonists' campaign for clemency in December 1793 appears only as an attempt to inveigle Robespierre into an alliance with them in order to overthrow the Committee, and Robespierre had every reason to reject it.

Even if Robespierre had not resented Desmoulins' attempt to force his hand, he could have had little confidence in those who now sought a share in power. If Danton was not yet implicated by the investigations into the Foreign Plot, many of his friends were suspect, and the men like Delacroix and Philippeaux who supported him in the Convention showed few signs of either ability or responsibility. It is, in any case, inconceivable that Robespierre could have compromised with people who were attacking not merely the abuses of the Terror but the very machinery and authority of government. When the Dantonists were pressing most strongly for clemency, the Law of 4th December, which gave the two governing Committees power to discipline their own agents, was barely a fortnight old. The representatives on mission, now nominally wholly subordinate to the Committee of Public Safety, were still independent in fact, and there were a considerable number of them scattered about France,[1] acting as they thought best, learning of the new law by correspondence, and on occasion writing to Paris to question its validity. Though Robespierre waited for the right moment before committing himself, it seems most unlikely that any thought of a real relaxation of the Terror was ever in his mind.

The situation was clarified by the return of Collot d'Herbois from his bloody work in Lyons. On 20th December, when the petition to the Convention from the citizens of Lyons was referred to the Committee of Public Safety, Collot was with his colleagues in the Green Room to receive it. The Committee rejected the cry of the Lyonnais. On 21st December Collot himself disposed of the matter in the Convention, reminding the deputies of the sins of the city. That evening, at the Jacobins, he roundly denounced the arrest of Ronsin and identified himself with the extremists. 'Citizens', he cried, 'patriotism must always be at the same height! If it drops for an instant, it is no longer patriotism.'

[1] More than 100 deputies had been sent out on one or more of three *general* missions between March and October, 1793, and many of these had remained in the provinces. Fifty-one deputies were sent out in December 1793 to put the Law of 14th Frimaire into effect.

To remain united, to remain a government, the Committee had to disassociate itself from the demand for moderation. On 26th December the 'committee for clemency', which had been established to review the lists of suspects, was abolished at the demand of Billaud-Varenne, and after further agitation in the Cordeliers in January 1794, Vincent and Ronsin were released from prison on 2nd February. Moreover, when Camille Desmoulins again attacked the Hébertists in the fifth issue of the *Vieux Cordelier*, he was attacked in the Jacobins by Collot, and Robespierre himself described his paper as 'the joy of the aristocracy', and demanded that it should be burned in front of the Society.[1] In re-asserting its neutrality, however, the Committee did not discriminate between the Right and the Left. Hérault de Séchelles, who had presided over the Convention on 2nd June and drawn up most of the Constitution of 1793, was a cultivated man of aristocratic birth and considerable fortune, but he had connections with the Hébertists; as Fabre d'Eglantine had accused him, and as he was wrongly suspected of betraying the Committee's secrets to the enemy, his colleagues forced him to resign on the last day of 1793. When Fabre's own part in the India Scandal finally came to light a few days later, he was in turn denounced, and on 12th January he was arrested despite Danton's attempt to protect him.[2]

About this time Robespierre tried in two major speeches to lift politics above personalities. In the first of these, on 25th December 1793 (5th Nivôse), he began by defining the aim of revolutionary government, which, as he rightly said, was something as new as the Revolution itself. This aim was the consolidation of the Republic, and Robespierre held that until this was achieved the government could legitimately exercise extraordinary authority, for the Revolution was by definition the war of liberty against its enemies. Constitutional government and individual freedom, he explained, were appropriate to a time of peace, but while the revolutionary government was still struggling to establish the Republic, 'public liberty', the liberty of society, was of much greater importance. 'Under constitutional rule', he said, 'it is almost enough to protect individuals against the abuse of public power; under revolutionary rule, the public power is obliged to defend itself against all the factions that attack it.' Having established this, Robespierre repudiated both those who wished to push revolutionary action to extreme lengths and those who wished to moderate it; both courses were abuses, and both were liable to ruin the Republic. 'What, then', he asked, 'must be

[1] It was on this occasion that the mischievous Camille goaded his old friend Robespierre to anger by crying out: 'Well said, Robespierre, but I reply with Rousseau—"burning is no argument".' Robespierre secured the readmission of Camille to the Club a few days later.

[2] On 13th January Billaud-Varenne rejected Danton's intervention with the ominous words: 'Woe to him who has sat beside Fabre d'Eglantine and still remains his dupe.'

done? We must track down the guilty who would lead us into evil ways, we must protect patriotism even when it goes astray, we must enlighten patriots and strive unceasingly to awaken the people to a full realisation of their rights and their high destiny.'

In its immediate context, this speech was a warning to both the factions that threatened the supremacy of the Committee of Public Safety. More than ever, the Revolution was, for the time being, to be identified with the authority of the government, and both insufficient and excessive zeal were classed as forms of counter-revolution. There was no question here of ending the Terror: as Robespierre put it, 'the revolutionary government owes its enemies nothing but death'. His speech, indeed, ended with a proposal for expediting the work of the Revolutionary Tribunal.[1] Neither for Robespierre nor for the Committee, however, was repression alone to be sufficient: in the second of his two speeches, he tried to state the aim of government still more clearly and to develop further the point that the repression of evil must be accompanied by the encouragement of virtue.

This he did on 5th February, 1794 (17th Pluviôse), in the *Report on the Principles of Public Morality*, a speech which has well been called one of the most notable utterances in the history of democracy.[2] Although we today may doubt his conviction that all evils would disappear as soon as freedom allowed men's natural goodness to develop, the ideal which inspired him was undoubtedly a noble one. 'We desire', he said,

an order of things where all base and cruel passions are enchained by the laws, all beneficent and generous feelings awakened by them; where ambition is the desire to deserve glory and to be useful to one's country; where distinctions arise only from equality itself; where the citizen is subject to the magistrate, the magistrate to the people, the people to justice; where the country secures the welfare of each individual, and each individual proudly enjoys the prosperity and glory of his country; where all minds are enlarged by the constant interchange of republican sentiments and by the need of earning the respect of a great people; where industry is an adornment to the liberty that ennobles it, and commerce is the source of public wealth, not simply of monstrous riches for a few families.

We wish to substitute in our country morality for egotism, probity for a mere sense of honour, principle for habit, duty for etiquette, the rule of reason for the tyranny of custom, contempt

---

[1] This proposal eventually gave rise to the Law of 22nd Prairial. See below, p. 218.

[2] By R. R. Palmer. See *Twelve Who Ruled* (Princeton U.P., 1958), p. 275. With occasional slight variations, the translation given there is followed here.

for vice for contempt for misfortune, pride for insolence, large-mindedness for vanity, the love of glory for the love of money, good men for good company, merit for intrigue, talent for conceit, truth for show, the charm of happiness for the tedium of pleasure, the grandeur of man for the triviality of grand society, a people magnanimous, powerful and happy for a people lovable, frivolous and wretched—that is to say, all the virtues and miracles of the Republic for all the vices and puerilities of the monarchy.

We wish in a word to fulfil the course of nature, to accomplish the destiny of mankind, to make good the promises of philosophy, to absolve Providence from the long reign of tyranny and crime. May France, once illustrious among peoples of slaves, eclipse the glory of all free peoples that have existed, become the model to the nations, the terror of oppressors, the consolation of the oppressed, the ornament of the universe; and in sealing our work with our blood, may we ourselves see at least the dawn of universal felicity gleam before us! That is our ambition. That is our aim.

This high objective Robespierre regarded as inseparable from democratic self-government. He believed that in the Revolution the French people had become 'the first people in the history of the world to establish a real democracy by inviting all men to share equality and the full rights of citizenship'. This, however, had still to be consolidated, and in the transitional period the revolutionary government had both to crush the enemies of democracy and to encourage others in that sense of public responsibility and that spirit of self-sacrifice on which Robespierre believed democracy to depend. This was what he meant by virtue, which was at once the object and the counter-part of the Terror. If, as he said, 'the basis of popular government in time of peace is virtue, the basis of popular government in time of war is both virtue and intimidation: virtue without which intimidation is disastrous, intimidation without which virtue is impotent'.

Taken together, these two speeches of 25th December and 5th February show that the 'thesis of circumstance' is not in itself sufficient to account for the continuation of the Terror after the invaders had been driven out of France in 1793. What Aulard described as the determination 'to assure victory' does not explain its nature. On each occasion Robespierre presented his report in the name of the Committee of Public Safety, and even if some of its members were more occupied with administration than with policy, the policy was common to them all. They seem, indeed, to have assumed that the war would continue indefinitely. The government was becoming geared to it, and, regardless of victory, any hint of compromise was politically dangerous. As Barère said on 1st February, those who spoke of peace were 'the aristocrats, the moderates, the rich, the conspirators, the pretended patriots'. Political opposition was now the more immediate problem, and the Committee was evidently at least as much concerned with its ultimate political objectives as with military success alone.

Robespierre's second statement of policy was soon followed by what seems to have been an initial step towards its implementation, the 'Laws of Ventôse'. Despite price controls, the people of Paris were still suffering great hardship in the winter of 1793–94. Most provisions were in short supply, the bread was of very poor quality, and by the middle of February meat was almost unobtainable. Disorders inevitably increased again, and on 21st February matters were made worse by the introduction of the second general *maximum*, which Robert Lindet's Food Commission had been preparing for the last three months. By allowing for the cost of transport and for legitimate profits, the Commission had tried to treat the honest trader fairly. As Barère said, 'We must cure commerce, not kill it.' A compromise with commerce, however, seemed to be a departure from the principle of keeping prices down to a level which ordinary people could afford, and the result was that the cost of living increased sharply even before details of the new price-lists were published.

As popular agitation rose, Saint-Just came forward with what he really seems to have regarded as a revolutionary solution to the problem of poverty. On 26th February (8th Ventôse) he proposed a decree by which the property of known enemies of the Republic was to be confiscated. By a further decree on 3rd March (13th Ventôse) the communes of France were ordered to prepare lists of those in need, and the Committee of Public Safety was instructed to prepare a report on the means by which the unfortunate might be assisted with the confiscated property. Although the decrees did not say so explicitly, Saint-Just at this time certainly expected that, after innocent prisoners had been released, the property of all those who were considered guilty would be redistributed to the poor. As he put it, no one could have any civil rights who had not helped to make France free, and the Convention ought to abolish the pauperism which dishonoured a free society.

These laws were never put into practice. The 'indigent patriots' were understandably reluctant to appear, for the Law of Suspects encompassed those without visible means of support, and the task of sorting out the thousands of suspects who had already been imprisoned was so great that it was perpetually postponed. Moreover, although the Committee of Public Safety had accepted Saint-Just's scheme, time soon showed that the majority of its members were content to leave the laws on paper, simply relieving poverty by grants as occasion arose. Few of them had in fact been present when the proposals were approved, and although Saint-Just probably consulted Robespierre and Couthon, who were both ill at the time, the plan seems to have been more his than theirs.[1] Its significance has therefore always been controversial: where Mathiez saw an attempt by the Robespierrists to initiate a far-reaching social revolution, other historians have seen little more than a political manoeuvre which was intended to appease the people and to steal a march on such agitators as Hébert. The truth may be that Saint-Just, seeing this advantage and being genuinely sympathetic towards poverty, was nevertheless principally interested, like Robespierre, in punishing political crime and rewarding political virtue. Certainly his plan appeared on 26th February only as an appendage to a prolonged denunciation of disloyalty.

Whatever their purpose, the Laws of Ventôse did not check agitation in Paris, for while they accorded well with the general outlook of the *sans-culottes*, they obviously provided no remedy for the immediate sufferings of the poor and hungry. Moreover, the Hébertists were not interested in any particular measures, but only in the possibility of securing power. For a time, their faction again looked dangerous. Ronsin and Vincent, newly released from prison, were anxious to avenge themselves. Hébert, the publicist of the group, might influence the Commune, and Momoro, a prominent Cordelier, might bring in the Department of Paris. Moreover, although Carrier, the man responsible for the drownings at Nantes, had been recalled after an agent of the Committee[2] had reported his conduct to Robespierre and Barère, he was welcomed back to the Jacobins by Collot d'Herbois on 21st February, and he was soon in the forefront of the agitation at the Cordeliers. From attacking the Dantonists, these men turned to almost open denunciation of Robespierre, and on 4th March (14th Ventôse) Carrier and Hébert called for insurrection at the Cordeliers Club, where the Declaration of Rights was symbolically veiled in black. Their call, however, was unanswered: only a handful of enthusiasts from the immediate vicinity of the Club went to the Commune, where they were coldly received.

This fiasco can be partly accounted for in terms of the evident self-interest and incapacity of the men concerned. The affair was quite unorganised, and although Hébert had long expressed the *sans-culottes'* craving for social security—for work for all, for public assistance to the elderly and the infirm, and above all for public education—the faction had really nothing to offer except a policy of unrestricted violence. By this time, moreover, much of the political force of the democratic movement in Paris

[1] Robespierre was taken ill soon after his speech on 5th February, and did not return to the Convention until 11th March. Couthon, who had returned to Paris from Lyons, was also ill for most of the same period.

[2] I.e. Marc Antoine Jullien, known as Jullien of Paris to distinguish him from his father, who was also a deputy, Jullien of Drome. Marc Antoine subsequently succeeded Ysabeau as proconsul at Bordeaux, and it was he who hunted down the fugitive deputies who had taken refuge at St.-Émilion.

THE REPUBLIC OF VIRTUE

had been absorbed by the war effort. While many of the rank and file were in the army or in some form of government employment, the active minority in the sections was devoting its energies to a multitude of administrative tasks, like that of providing help for soldiers' families. The government's control of the sections, too, had increased considerably since the previous September. The *comités de surveillance*, the most powerful bodies in the sections, were now directly responsible to the Committee of General Security, which had succeeded in isolating them from the Commune.[1] The failure of the Hébertists nevertheless illustrates the essential seriousness of the *sans-culotte* movement. Although economic hardship was undoubtedly severe at this time, the Revolution itself was not in danger, and in the absence of any great peril the people of Paris were not prepared to re-assert their sovereign authority.

Ineffective as it was, the attempted insurrection had important consequences. Its immediate effect was to cause the Committee of Public Safety to bring intimidation back to the forefront of its policy. On 9th March, when the return of Robespierre and Couthon made a fuller meeting of the Committee possible, the nine members who were present decided to strike down the Hébertists. In the Convention next day, Saint-Just attacked 'the conspiracy which the foreigners have inspired to destroy representative government by corruption, and to starve Paris'. He made no attempt to specify any particular charges, but simply denounced opposition to the people's government as a crime in itself. 'Every party', he announced,

> is criminal, for it is a form of isolation from the people and the popular societies, a form of independence from the government. Every faction is criminal because it tends to divide the citizens; every faction is criminal because it neutralises the power of public virtue; . . . The sovereignty of the people demands that the people be unified; it is therefore opposed to factions, and all faction is a criminal attack upon sovereignty.

There could hardly be a clearer statement than this of the 'terrible postulate of unanimity' which was characteristic of the whole of the Revolution; nor, perhaps, is there any better illustration of the Jacobin attitude, which identified all criticism with disloyalty to the fundamental principles of their new order.

---

[1] An attempt by Chaumette to convene a meeting of delegates of these committees at the City Hall in December 1793 was expressly vetoed by the Committee of Public Safety. Chaumette asserted that the committees were 'an emanation of the Commune' and feared that Paris was in danger of 'sectionising itself'. The Committee warned him against 'trying to popularise the authority of the Commune at the expense of that of the Convention'. Deville, *La Commune de l'an II* (Paris 1946).

In the course of the next few days, Hébert, Momoro, Ronsin and Vincent were arrested, as were sixteen others, including Proli, Pereira, Desfieux, Dubuisson and Anarcharsis Cloots, the Prussian-born 'Orator of Mankind'. Carrier, however, was not molested, his safety being perhaps the price paid by the Committee to keep Collot d'Herbois content. The accused appeared on the benches of the Revolutionary Tribunal on 21st March. Their trial was a collective one, in which the politicians were mixed up with suspicious-looking foreigners and ordinary offenders, and it was soon disposed of. On the afternoon of 24th March, Hébert and seventeen others died on the guillotine.[1]

The execution of the Hébertists implied that of the Dantonists also. If they were left alive after their opponents had been killed their position would be relatively stronger, and it would appear that the Committee had acted at their command. The unity of the Committee itself was also at stake, for Billaud-Varenne and Collot d'Herbois could not have been expected to accept the suppression of the extremists unless the moderates were also destroyed. Even before the Hébertists were put on trial, Fabre d'Eglantine and those who had conspired with him in the India Company fraud were indicted by the Convention, and on the night of 30th March (9th Germinal) the Committees of Public Safety and General Security together ordered the arrest of Danton, Desmoulins, Delacroix and Philippeaux.

According to Billaud-Varenne, who was the first to sign the order, Robespierre was most reluctant to add his name to what was, in reality, the death-warrant of Danton, the hero of 1792.[2] Politically, however, Robespierre had no choice. He had already made several speeches warning the moderates that their turn was coming, and Danton was the obvious opposition leader. Moreover, to those who were determined to develop a state based on morality, Danton's robust contempt for virtue was offensive, and he was associated with men whose manifest corruption and venality was itself regarded as a form of counter-revolution. Robespierre, however, did not only sign the order for Danton's arrest: he also briefed Saint-Just with a series of political and puritanical charges against him, many of which were too pettifogging to be used, and on 31st March he personally intervened to silence the Convention's indignation at the breach in parliamentary immunity involved in the arrest of Danton during the previous night. 'Whoever trembles now', he said, 'is himself guilty, for innocence need never fear public enquiry (*surveillance*).'

[1] One of the other two who were tried with them was a police spy, and Citizeness Quétieneau, the only woman in the amalgam, succeeded in escaping execution on the plea of pregnancy.

[2] It should be recorded that Robert Lindet and one member of the Committee of General Security refused to sign the order.

After the Convention had been silenced by Saint-Just's accusations and by his assurance that no further purges would be necessary, Danton and his friends were indicted. At the Revolutionary Tribunal they too were inter-mingled with discredited Frenchmen and dubious foreign financiers: the batch of fourteen included Fabre and his associates, the brothers Frey, the contractor d'Espagnac, the giant soldier Westermann and Hérault de Séchelles. The *coup*, however, was not complete, for Danton dominated the trial, his great voice ringing round the room and attracting a crowd even in the street outside. Bringing all his powers of mind and all his rough humanity into play, he so impressed the public and the jury that on the third day of the trial Fouquier-Tinville and Hermann were compelled to appeal to the Convention, reporting that a terrible storm was raging in the courtroom. In reply, the Committee introduced a decree by which prisoners who insul-ted the justice of the nation were to be deprived of their right to speak. A mysterious letter (possibly one which showed that Danton had tried to protect Marie-Antoinette) was circulated amongst the jury, and on the next morning the accused were hastily condemned. They died that same afternoon, on 5th April (16th Germinal).[1]

These terrible blows to both Right and Left were accompanied by several measures of consolidation. The War Office had been influenced by the Hébertists, the Foreign Office by the Dantonists: on 1st April, the whole Executive Council was abolished outright, and the various minis-tries were replaced by twice as many commissions, each of which had to report each day to the Committee of Public Safety. In this way the executive and the legislative powers, which had once been rigorously separated for the sake of freedom, were again completely united. The Commune, too, was brought under still closer control. On 13th April, Chaumette, once the *procureur* and lately the National Agent of Paris, went to the scaffold as an accomplice of Hébert, along with the unfortunate Archbishop Gobel and the widows of both Hébert and Desmoulins. Payan, who replaced Chau-mette, and Lescot-Fleuriot, who became Mayor of Paris in place of Pache, were both Robespierre's supporters, and a new process of purification soon reduced the Commune to subservience. From April until the Terror ended in July, the governing Committees were in a position of unassailable authority.

Henceforth, everyone was afraid and no one knew whom to trust. For the first time the deputies in the assembly and those on mission in the provinces felt their lives to be in danger, and the majority of them did their best to efface themselves. The people too were disillusioned and bewildered. The

---

[1] According to oral tradition, heard by the author but not to his knowledge supported by literary evidence, a red sunset encardined the whole execution scene.

apparent treason of Hébert, their supposed champion, caused general confusion, and his death deprived the most ardent revolutionaries both of their contact with the Commune and of their most popular political journal. Nor did the execution of the Dantonists restore the Committee's popularity, for Danton too had once been adored; the crowd which witnessed his death seems to have been sure of the Tribunal's impartiality, but it dared not show either sorrow or joy. The government, moreover, seemed in its new security to have become blind to the economic and political aspirations of the *sans-culottes*. On 27th March the Revolutionary Army was disbanded; on 1st April, the inspectors of hoarding were dismissed. The new policy of encouraging trade did indeed improve the provisioning of Paris, but at the end of March the publication of the price-lists of the new *maximum* increased the cost of living still more, and after the death of Hébert the general relaxation of controls began the return of inflation: by the end of July, the *assignat* had again fallen to 36 per cent. Popular democracy, too, was soon completely stifled. '*Père Duchesne*' had no successor, the surviving papers being generally subsidised and filled with official information. Many of the 'popular societies of the sections', in which free discussion had sought to escape from official business, were closed down in the early summer, and even the Jacobin Society itself was compelled to give most of its time to the consideration of administrative reports.[1]

Impressed by the general apathy, Saint-Just noted down the observation: 'The Revolution has got frozen up. Every principle has been weakened.' The Committee, and more particularly Robespierre, Saint-Just and Couthon, whose association and ascendancy were now well-marked, were only the more convinced of the necessity for combining repression with the moral regeneration of France. This they were now free to attempt. For them, the stagnation of the Revolution was but a new form of a familiar evil: the corrupt and the self-seeking, who had always oppressed the people and prevented them from attaining their full moral stature, had now cunningly established themselves within the revolutionary administration. The remedy seemed equally simple: the government must scrutinise the conduct of its own agents, dealing drastically with every abuse of power, and it must spare no effort to spread enlightenment. This was the theme of the speech which Saint-Just made in his *Report of Public Morale* on 15th April, ten days after the death of Danton. 'You must make people understand', he told the Convention, 'that revolutionary government does not mean war or conquest, but the transition from evil to good, from corruption to probity.' At the same

[1] Paul Deville, in *La Commune de l'an II* (Paris, 1946), p. 168, points out that seven sections whose delegates at the Commune had been drastically reduced by the purge that followed the fall of Hébert, simply asked the Committee of Public Safety to fill the vacancies by the nomination of patriots 'whom it thinks most suitable'.

THE REPUBLIC OF VIRTUE

time, 'to uproot the last remnants of faction', he proposed the law which became known as the Law of 27th Germinal (16th April). This ordered all prisoners accused of conspiracy in any part of France to be transferred to the Revolutionary Tribunal at Paris, and it also particularly charged the Committee of Public Safety with the task of supervising 'the authorities and public agents co-operating with the administration'. To call these agents to account, and to prosecute them as the law required for 'any perversion of the powers entrusted to them', the Committee established its own police department, the *bureau de police générale*.

This policy is not to be hastily condemned. In the last few months, evidence of corruption and of the abuse of power had been plentiful, and the advent of strong central direction was no bad thing. In the west, the operations of Turreau's 'infernal columns' was halted, and Prieur of the Marne attempted to reach an agreement with the Vendéans. On 27th March, Fouché was recalled from Lyons; a month later the revolutionary commission there was dissolved, and a more moderate régime began. The general tightening of control was also apparent in the recall of many other representatives on mission in April, and in the abolition on 8th May of most of the revolutionary tribunals and commissions in the provinces. The government, however, was not now being indulgent. Tallien was brought back from Bordeaux to answer charges of moderation and loose-living. His successor, Ysabeau, also seemed insufficiently severe, and he was superseded by Julien of Paris, a nineteen-year-old protégé of Robespierre's, who intensified the Terror in the city and hunted the fugitive 'Girondins' from their hiding-place at Saint Émilion. Some significant exceptions were also made to the law of 8th May. Joseph LeBon, whose rule at Arras had long been marked by steady but ordered bloodshed, was allowed at this time to establish a tribunal at Cambrai, where nearly 150 people were condemned to death. It was in May, too, that the notorious Commission of Orange was established: when Maignet, who had governed Marseilles humanely, encountered the conditions that prevailed in Avignon, he asked his friend Couthon to secure special powers for him, and the popular tribunal which Couthon devised passed 332 death sentences in two months. Even this, however, was a regulated Terror. Only in rare instances did uncontrolled abuses by representatives continue into the early summer of 1794.

The prosecution of the war effort throughout the country also clearly required a strong patriotic impulse from Paris. For Robespierre and Saint-Just, however, the promotion of *vertu* meant much more than this. Twelve months before, on 10th May 1793, Robespierre had declared that the object of society was the preservation of Man's rights 'and the perfecting of his nature'. Now, after about three weeks' retirement from the Convention, he returned on 7th May to speak on 'the relationship between religious and

215

moral ideas and republican principles'. Losing all his usual nervousness of manner, he posed the principal problem of the modern world: 'Everything is changed in the physical order: where is there any similar change in the moral and political order? The world has been half revolutionised: how can the other half be accomplished?' Robespierre believed that Revolutionary France, which was 200 years ahead of the rest of the world, could show the way. The art of government, which had hitherto been that of cheating and corrupting the governed, must be changed into that of enlightening them and *making them better*. 'Immorality', said Robespierre, 'is the basis of despotism: the essence of Republicanism is virtue. The Revolution is the transition from the régime of crime to the régime of justice.' At the same time, the nation must constantly dedicate itself to the worship and service of the Divinity which was guiding the Revolution. Atheism was arid and sterile, but 'if the existence of God and the immortality of the soul were no more than dreams, they would still be the finest creations of the spirit of man.'

A new form of worship, however, was necessary, for Christianity had become a religion of priests. 'The true priest of the Supreme Being', declared Robespierre, 'is Nature; his temple is the universe; his worship is virtue; his festivals are the rejoicings of a great people assembled under his gaze to renew the bonds of universal brotherhood and to give him the homage of appreciation and pure hearts.' He therefore proposed a decree which should establish this new civic religion without infringing freedom of worship. Article I declared: 'The French people recognise the existence of the Supreme Being, and the immortality of the soul.' The second article recognised that the proper worship of the Supreme Being consisted in the practice of human duties, and the third defined the most important of these duties: 'to hate treachery and tyranny, to punish tyrants and traitors, to succour the unfortunate, respect the weak and defend the oppressed, to do all the good one can to one's neighbour and to treat no one unjustly.'

The first of the forty festivals for which the decree provided, that in honour of the Supreme Being, took place at the time of Pentecost, on 8th June. The weather was perfect, the occasion the greatest day in Robespierre's life. Unanimously elected President of the Convention four days beforehand, he had a prominent part to play in the spectacular pageantry which David had devised for Paris. When the Convention went from its Chamber into the Tuileries Gardens, where the people of the forty-eight sections were already assembled, Robespierre led the way, impeccably dressed in blue and carrying, like all the deputies, a small bouquet of flowers bound with tricolour ribbon. In the gardens, he appealed to the people to crush the wicked league of kings even more by greatness of character than by force of arms, and he solemnly set fire to an effigy of Atheism—which revealed, as it burned, a statue of Wisdom. A vast procession, half civic and half military, then

216

marched to the Champ de Mars, now renamed the Champ de Réunion, and there, beneath an artificial 'Mountain', the whole multitude took part in patriotic demonstrations and public worship of the Supreme Being. Much of this was of course contrived. In reality, the new religion took no root in France; after the towns and villages had celebrated the first fête, the unpopularity of an official cult and an artificial calendar was soon apparent. Robespierre, however, was certainly sincere, and on this occasion at least the symbolism only embellished an act of national dedication. On 8th June, Paris forgot its fears and manifested once again the French people's determination to uphold their Revolution against all the world.

Both before and after this festival the Committee was occupied with still more far-reaching schemes for public enlightenment. David was instructed to design a national dress, 'appropriate to republican manners and the character of the Revolution'. Poets and writers, musicians and artists were summoned to glorify the Revolution, the literary men being required 'to give history that firm and stern character which befits the annals of a great people' and 'to inject republican morality into works intended for public instruction'. Plans were also prepared for the reform of language: an address presented to the Convention on 4th June deplored both diversity of speech and coarseness in expression, and the Convention authorised the recruitment of teachers to take 'the language in which the Declaration of Rights is written' into Alsace, Brittany and other outlying parts of France. Some of these measures were indeed remarkably progressive. On 11th May Barère introduced an extensive scheme for social welfare, by which state assistance and free medical aid was to be made available to all the aged and the infirm, as well as to nursing mothers and widows with children. A three-year period of free and compulsory primary education having already been decreed by the Convention in December, the Committee now proposed to establish a teacher-training college. All, however, was closely related to the revolutionary government's determination to strengthen the state and to develop the character of the citizens. The college students were to become teachers inspired by the new faith; the purpose of education was 'to teach republican laws and morality'. In founding a military college for the selected sons of worthy parents, the Committee explicitly stated that its object was 'to rear truly republican defenders of the *Patrie* and to revolutionise youth as we have already revolutionised the armies.'

The military training centre, the 'School of Mars', was in fact established in July, and for a short while 3,000 enthusiastic young cadets lived under canvas according to the austere rules prescribed by the Committee. As things happened, all the other projects remained almost entirely on paper, like the Laws of Ventôse and even the new national religion. The direction in which the revolutionary government was moving, however, is plain enough.

Although its plans were socially beneficent and morally commendable, its régime was to be one of systematic indoctrination. In practice, if not in theory, the 'enlightened' minority was already maintaining its position by force; there was every likelihood that it would increasingly use its power to impose uniformity and to subordinate everything to the service of the state. Both representative and popular democracy were rapidly yielding to the authoritarianism of those who believed themselves to be an *élite*.

Something of the gulf which separated the Committee's vision of the future from the unhappy reality of the moment is apparent in the happenings of 23rd and 24th May. On the first of these days, an assassin named Admiral fired at Collot d'Herbois, and it appeared that his real intention had been to kill Robespierre. The next day, a twenty-year-old girl, Cécile Renault, called on Robespierre at his lodgings; when detained, she said she wished 'to see what a tyrant looked like', and two knives were found concealed upon her. The Committee regarded these events only as irrefutable proof of the continuing reality of a royalist plot, and Robespierre himself saw his escape as proof of heavenly favour. As he told the Jacobins: 'the tyrants' crime and the assassin's steel have made me more formidable than ever to the enemies of the people; my mind turns more than ever to the unmasking of traitors.' Soon afterwards, the Terror was intensified, and, in what looks very like an act of personal vengeance, the girl and the man and fifty-two other persons were sent to the scaffold on 17th June. All these had to wear the red garments and black hats the law prescribed for parricides, and when one of them, the servant girl of the mistress of the royalist Baron de Batz, appeared on the scaffold, some people in the crowd cried out: 'No children!'

What is sometimes called the Great Terror began on 10th June, when the notorious law of 22nd Prairial was passed. This was introduced by Couthon, who explained that in the circumstances it was 'no longer a question of making a few examples, but of exterminating the implacable satellites of tyranny'. The law first stated as an axiom: 'The Revolutionary Tribunal exists to punish the enemies of the people.' It then defined 'enemies of the people' in such comprehensive terms that almost all those already detained under the Law of Suspects were included in them. The vagueness of these definitions may be gauged by the eighth, which included 'those who have sought to mislead opinion and to prevent the instruction of the people, to deprave customs and to corrupt the public conscience, to impair the energy and the purity of revolutionary and republican principles, or to check their progress, whether by counter-revolutionary or insidious writings, or by any other machination.' For all offences within the cognisance of the Tribunal, the penalty was to be death, and for conviction moral proof was to be as valid as material evidence; judgment would be determined by 'the conscience of the jurors, enlightened by their love of the *Patrie*, and concerned only to secure the triumph of the Republic and the ruin of its enemies'. There would therefore be no private or preliminary examination of prisoners, nor would witnesses be called unless they could help by exposing accomplices. Legal aid for the accused was expressly disallowed, for 'the law provides patriotic jurymen to defend slandered patriots; it does not grant defence to conspirators'.

The origins of this decree are obscure, for the men who eventually overthrew Robespierre did their best to suggest that only he and his intimates were responsible for it. It seems, however, that the general principles of the law, if such they can be called, were particularly developed by Robespierre and Couthon from those which the latter had already applied to the Commission of Orange. Although the Committee of Public Safety had probably approved the substance of the decree, it was apparently not properly consulted about the final draft. The Convention itself was considerably alarmed by a clause which seemed to invalidate parliamentary immunity, for the indictment of deputies was still legally a matter for the assembly alone. Whatever was intended, and it is likely enough that Robespierre indeed meant to dispose of some deputies whom he regarded as vicious or dangerous, he had to leave the presidential chair to override the opposition of such men as Tallien and to make his own assurances to the assembly a question of confidence.[1] The law itself can only be regarded as monstrous. If, as seems likely, it was intended to enable the Tribunal to cope with the influx of prisoners now being sent to Paris from the provinces, it defeated its own purpose by its enormous extension of the definition of political crime. If, as some historians suggest, it was designed to stimulate the nation on the eve of a new military offensive, it also came significantly soon after the two attempts on the lives of members of the Committees. Fear, in the final phase of the Terror, was certainly not shut out by the walls of the Tuileries.[2]

Trials having been reduced to the appearance of prisoners before one of its courts, the work of the Tribunal was vastly accelerated. In the fifteen months from its establishment in March, 1793, until 10th June 1794, the Tribunal had condemned 1,251 persons to death and acquitted or imposed lesser penalties upon considerably more. Under the revised procedure of Prairial,

[1] The clause was that which modified 'all those provisions of previous laws which are at variance with the present law'. It was rescinded on 10th June but re-established on the 12th.

[2] The question of intention is important here in relation to any estimate of Robespierre, for the law of 22nd Prairial apparently conflicts with both his generally well-balanced outlook and his known reluctance to put particular people to death unnecessarily. It is sometimes suggested that the law only legalised the existing practice of the Tribunal: this, however, does not account for the great increase in the execution rate after it was passed. The combined effects of this law and that of 27th Germinal may, of course, have been far more terrible than anyone anticipated.

219

there were 1,376 executions in the next six and a half weeks alone, and although there were still acquittals, these were only a fifth of the total. If these figures are integrated with those of the Terror as a whole, their significance is of course diminished. Donald Greer has shown that the total number of executions at Paris from March 1793 until August 1794 amounts only to 16 per cent of that for the whole of France, as compared with 19 per cent for the south-eastern region and 52 per cent for western France. He had also shown that the purpose of the Terror as a whole was political, that its heaviest toll was exacted in the areas where civil war or foreign pressure was most dangerous, and that 93 per cent of those who died were condemned for some form of treasonable activity or seditious opinion (whereas only 1 per cent died for offences against the economic regulations).[1]

It does not, however, follow from this, as some other historians imply, that the executions in Paris in June and July 1794 were nothing more than a measure of national defence against rebels and traitors. As Greer has proved, the Terror in France reached its climax in December 1793, and January 1794. Six months later the situation was very different. Although many of the victims of the guillotine in the last days of the Terror were people who had been arrested long before, there was no immediate military necessity for their deaths. The appalling and ever-increasing rate of executions and the general nature of the charges, as well as the reiterated statements of the principal Terrorists, all show conclusively that the Great Terror was intended to intimidate all those who dared to deny the government complete control of their lives. The instrument of emergency had become a means of political oppression.

The Great Terror must also be regarded as proof of the ultimate failure of the Committee of Public Safety to govern France. Since it could neither trust nor control its own agents, it had sought to centralise all repression in Paris. The result was chaos. By June, there were some 8,000 people in the prisons of Paris, of whom there were nearly 1,000 at the Luxembourg alone. Although the Tribunal was working at an unprecedented pace even before the Law of 22nd Prairial was passed, the prison population increased daily, and in the Conciergerie new arrivals slept beside their baggage in the courtyards until space could be made for them in the cells. To clear the ground, collective trials became commonplace. On the pretext of 'prison conspiracies' there were three major 'journées' in June, and seven more in July. At one of these alone, on 7th July, sixty prisoners from the Luxembourg were simultaneously condemned. The old Grand' Chambre of the parlement was now almost unrecognisable, for the benches of the accused stretched from floor to ceiling across the whole centre of the court, and Fouquier-Tinville had

[1] D. Greer, The Incidence of the Terror (Havard U.P., 1935), passim.

220

hardly room to move. In these conditions, justice was reduced to the administrative process on which Fouquier-Tinville prided himself, that of preparing endless indictments, finding the prisoners whom they named, presenting them to the Tribunal for exposure and ensuring that a steady stream of properly loaded tumbrils rolled away across the cobbles.

This carnage, of course, struck at all classes and at all kinds of men and women. According to Greer, 84 per cent of the victims of the Terror as a whole were of the Third Estate, this figure comprising 25 per cent bourgeois, 28 per cent peasantry and 31 per cent *sans-culottes*; and the records show that the proportion of ordinary citizens was rising rapidly in the last few months. Rat-catchers and washerwomen, noblemen, brewers and bankers were all one to a régime which 'cut down its enemies regardless of social caste'. The cumulative effect of all this can scarcely be doubted, for the government itself found it advisable to remove the guillotine from the city centre to the Place Antoine, and then to remove it again to the far-off barrière du Trône. Impassibility now became the hall-mark of patriotism: in those days, wrote the deputy Baudot, 'it was necessary to show a sort of joy unless you wished to run the risk of perishing yourself. At least, it was necessary to have an air of contentment, a calm and open air. . . . '

This bloodshed did not anticipate victory: it coincided with it and even followed it. In the summer of 1794, the armies of France were practically 750,000 strong, and they were well-armed and under firm central direction. Nowhere could the allies stand before them. In April, the French entered Sardinia; in May, they poured into Catalonia; by July, they had occupied most of the Palatinate. It was, however, on the vital northern frontier that the most striking victories were won, and these again occurred in May and June. When campaigning began, the allied forces attempted to encircle the French between Tournai and Menin. Pichegru's Army of the North, however, outmarched them, and fell in great force upon their most advanced army, that commanded by the Duke of York. At the battle of Tourcoing, fought on 18th May, the Duke's retreat was turned into a rout. Pichegru's men subsequently cleared the frontier between the Scheldt and the sea, taking Ypres on 19th June and then advancing towards Oudenarde and Brussels. To their right, meanwhile, the Armies of the Ardennes and the Moselle had been consolidated under the command of Jourdan and substantially reinforced; at the seventh attempt they forced the crossing of the Sambre, and at once invested Charleroi. Hardly had the town surrendered than Coburg's Austrians arrived in strength on the plateau behind it, and on 26th June, only a fortnight after the Law of 22nd Prairial had been enacted, battle was joined at Fleurus. This ended in a decisive victory for France. Condé, Mons and Valenciennes, which the Austrians had so painfully acquired, were now easily recaptured, and by 10th July the French were in Brussels, where

221

Jourdan and Pichegru met. The latter, pursuing the British and Dutch, afterwards entered Antwerp, and Jourdan's army, soon immortalised as that of the Sambre and Meuse, followed the Austrians eastwards and took Liège on 27th July. Fleurus had made the French complete masters of Belgium.

Even before this, France had also secured an equally important strategic victory in the naval campaign. The fleet at Brest, built up through the herculean efforts of Jeanbon Saint-André, put to sea on 16th May with specific orders to protect the great convoy of merchant ships that had sailed from the Chesapeake to break the British blockade. On the morning of 28th May the twenty-six ships of France sighted Lord Howe's line of twenty-five, and for the next four days the two fleets manoeuvred at long range. Villaret-Joyeuse, the Admiral of France, rightly drew the British away from the course of the convoy. As rightly, Howe sought to destroy the enemy fleet. On 1st June, the 'Glorious First', the British broke the French line in six places, firing fearful broadsides through the length of their opponents' ships and eventually capturing six of them and sinking one. The French flagship, the *Montagne*, which had Saint-André himself aboard, took a crippled fleet back to Brest; but the fighting had been so fierce that Howe had also to return home and on 13th June the merchantmen reached France without sighting the small squadron the British had left to intercept them. Famine, which had again threatened France in the months before the harvest, was thus averted.

These various victories set the French squarely on the road that was eventually to lead them to the conquest of Europe. Already 'evacuation agencies' had been established to strip occupied areas of all that France required, and neither the Committee of Public Safety nor any of its successors could contemplate calling the armies home. Nor did military success cause the Committee to relax its rule. To the 'administrators', Lindet, Prieur of the Côte d'Or and Carnot, organisation and central control were now more necessary than ever; to Billaud-Varenne and Collot d'Herbois it was still essential to crush religious 'fanaticism', uproot royalism and cut back the pretensions of wealth; and to Robespierre, Saint-Just and Couthon, the Republic of Virtue had still to be attained. All therefore tended to ignore or minimise the success they had achieved. Saint-Just, who had personally supervised the crossing of the Sambre and spurred on the soldiers at Fleurus, warned Barère not to extol the victories too much.

The triumph of French arms was nevertheless obvious enough to complete the disaffection of the nation. Those who had tolerated the Terror while it seemed necessary for national defence now needed only an opportunity to repudiate the rule of the Jacobins and to expel the *sans-culottes* from the *comités de surveillance*. To the bourgeoisie, all economic regulations now seemed superfluous; to the *sans-culottes* of Paris, on the other hand, revolutionary government was becoming synonymous with oppression: their leaders had been guillotined, their societies stifled. Although prices were rising, the Robespierre Commune winked at the *maximum* and invoked the *Loi Chapelier* to suppress strikes and silence all demands for higher wages. Wearied of control, recoiling from bloodshed, the people everywhere hoped for peace, and yearned, as they had since the Revolution began, for the existence of a Constitution. Of themselves, however, they could achieve little, for the grip of the government was strong. Between late April and late June thirty-nine 'popular societies' were closed down in the sections of Paris, and in July their successors, the open-air 'Community Dinners' (*repas fraternels*), were also being condemned. Even the celebrations of 14th July were drastically curtailed for fear of demonstrations.

Poised over this abyss, the revolutionary government disintegrated. The real effect of victory was to make it possible for the members of the Committee of Public Safety to quarrel violently, and to quarrel openly. Their unity, indeed, had always been forced upon them. Billaud-Varenne and Collot d'Herbois, who were only made members to placate the *sans-culottes* in September, 1793, had always been Hébertist; they had only reluctantly accepted the execution of Hébert, and their eagerness to execute Danton had divided them still further from their colleagues. Since then, moreover, Robespierre and his two closest associates, Saint-Just and Couthon, had become separated from the others through their determined pursuit of the Republic of Virtue.

Historians now rightly stress the collective responsibility of the Committee for all that its members said and did, and discount as deliberate distortion the later stories which suggest that only Robespierre and his intimates were responsible for the Terror. But apart from the very competent and cautious Barère, Robespierre and his two friends were the principal spokesmen of the Committee, and each was closely associated with at least one highly unpopular measure. Saint-Just's Laws of Ventôse had aroused general anxiety among property owners; Carnot and Prieur had apparently opposed them strongly in the Committee, and Saint-Just himself was annoyed by his colleagues' reluctance to enforce them.[1] Similarly, the worship of the Supreme Being was essentially Robespierre's vision. To many, this seemed ridiculous; to some, particularly Collot and Billaud, it appeared the prelude to a return to clericalism and Catholicism; and all these, and others again, disliked the pre-eminence that had been afforded to Robespierre at the Festival on 8th June. Finally, the Law of 22nd Prairial, apparently particularly the work of Couthon and Robespierre, was generally disliked, especially when its full effects

---

[1] Six commissions should have been established in March to sift the lists of suspected persons as a preliminary to redistributing their property, but only on 13th May had the first two of these been created.

became apparent. Except in the face of the enemy, the unity of the Committee had long been artificial, and if victory brought no relief from work and strain, it at least freed these authoritative and suspicious men to fall out amongst themselves. Saint-Just and Carnot were soon at loggerheads about a campaign against Holland, and sides were formed for some sort of showdown.

At this point, the antagonism that had long existed between the Committee of Public Safety and the Committee of General Security acquired importance. Several of the members of the latter, particularly Vadier, were violently hostile to religion and deeply suspicious of Robespierre's new cult. The Committee of General Security, moreover, had become bitterly resentful of the growing ascendancy of its partner. Although the Committee of General Security was the older of the two, and had once had equal status, the Committee of Public Safety had for some time acted independently and encroached on the other's preserves. When the Hébertists and the Dantonists were indicted, it was Saint-Just who spoke to the Convention. The Law of Prairial was apparently prepared by the Committee of Public Safety alone, and the *bureau de police générale*, which the Committee of Public Safety had established in Germinal to investigate complaints against officials, seemed likely to increase its own police powers very considerably.

These hostilities were again particularly concentrated on Saint-Just and Robespierre, since it was they who were most concerned with indictment and with the work of the *bureau*, and in the middle of June the Committee of General Security found a convenient weapon with which to strike at them. In the followers of Catherine Théot, a harmless old woman who believed herself about to bring forth a new messiah, Vadier discovered a 'conspiracy' that gave him an ideal opportunity to attack all religions, and even to suggest that Robespierre himself would eventually be discovered to be Catherine's deity. On his report, the Convention enthusiastically ordered the arrest of the 'conspirators', and Robespierre was faced with the prospect of public ridicule and even 'exposure' at the Revolutionary Tribunal. At an exceptionally stormy meeting of both Committees on 26th June, he managed to stop these proceedings, but he was deeply offended both by the attack and by the disloyalty of his colleagues. For the next month he absented himself almost entirely from the Committee of Public Safety and from the Convention.

For this retirement, Robespierre has been held unwise. His enemies in the Convention made head against him in secret intrigue, and his colleagues on the Committee now had reason to think of him as unfaithful and dangerous. He was, indeed, probably waiting, as he had so often waited before, for the right moment to move against his opponents. The fact that on 11th July he attacked Dubois-Crancé and Fouché at the Jacobin Society and had them expelled as terrorists suggests that he was still sensitive to the general trend of public opinion. This attack, however, was a challenge to Collot d'Herbois on the Committee, as well as to every deputy in the Convention who had been recalled from the provinces for violent conduct, and events soon showed that Robespierre was too intransigent to win allies, and too idealistic to repudiate his own past. On 22nd July (4th Thermidor), Barère, who was working to break the deadlock, at last persuaded the members of both Committees to agree upon a basis for compromise: the commissions necessary to implement the Laws of Ventôse would be established, but (it seems) the worship of the Supreme Being would be quietly abandoned. Next day Robespierre came by invitation to a second general meeting. He seemed to accept the programme, and Saint-Just agreed to incorporate this in a report which should show that the revolutionary government was still united. In fact, however, this attempt to paper over the cracks was a complete failure: Collot d'Herbois, who was at this time President of the Convention, in all probability abetted those who were conspiring in the assembly, and Robespierre, without even taking Saint-Just or Couthon into his confidence, went off to prepare a personal appeal to the Convention.

In the event, it was Robespierre who declared war on his colleagues. In the speech which he delivered in the Convention on 26th July (8th Thermidor), he denounced a new conspiracy, the ramifications of which ran to the heart of the government itself: now, new 'indulgents' were protecting aristocrats and sending patriots to the scaffold; now, new 'atheists' were trying to discredit the Revolution by making the Revolutionary Tribunal and the guillotine odious. The Assembly, Robespierre concluded, must punish the traitors; it must purge the Committee of General Security, and subordinate it to the Committee of Public Safety; it must also purge that Committee too and re-establish a united government 'under the supreme authority of the Convention, the centre and arbiter of all'. This speech, which was Robespierre's last, was by all accounts exceedingly eloquent and effective; but it was not enough. Although he disowned the abuses of the Terror, he had no new policy to propose. He asked for still stronger government, he called again for *vertu* and another final purge, but he could not, or would not, contemplate any abandonment of the Terror itself. Nor, even in this great crisis, was he prepared to commit himself completely and be openly ruthless. Although both moderates and extremists were threatened, although Billaud-Varenne, Collot d'Herbois, Carnot and Barère were evidently as much in danger as Vadier and as Fouché and Tallien and others, Robespierre would not present any definite list of names. All felt themselves to be in danger, and at the instigation of Cambon, whose financial policy had been criticised, the speech was referred to the very Committees that Robespierre had denounced.

That evening, the Incorruptible won his last victory: repeating his speech to a divided and turbulent audience at the Jacobins, he had Collot d'Herbois and Billaud-Varenne driven from the Society amid cries of 'To the guillotine with the conspirators!' Throughout the night and the following morning, however, Tallien and Fouché were completing their plans, and when the Convention met on 27th July (9th Thermidor), the stage was set. As Saint-Just, who had decided to stand by Robespierre, began to read a modified version of his report, he was interrupted by Tallien, who accused him of speaking without the sanction of the Committees. Billaud-Varenne at once charged Robespierre with conspiring against the Convention, and when Robespierre rushed forward to reply he was assailed by a pre-arranged commotion and cries of 'Down with the tyrant!' While prolonged hubbub, and the hostility of Collot as President of the Assembly, prevented Robespierre from making himself heard, a motion was passed for the arrest of Hanriot, the commander of the National Guard, and eventually two obscure Montagnards moved the arrest of Robespierre himself. The motion was carried unanimously, and at their own wish Saint-Just and Couthon, as well as the young Lebas and Robespierre's brother Augustin, were included in it. All five were removed to the quarters of the Committee of General Security, the Hôtel de Brienne in the Tuileries courtyard.

The fate of both Robespierre and the Convention now depended upon Paris, and for hours the outcome was uncertain. The Commune, which was completely controlled by Robespierre's friends, reacted to the news of his arrest by summoning the sections to concentrate their forces upon the Place de Grève, and Hanriot, who was partially drunk, went galloping across Paris with a rescue party of gendarmes. At the Hôtel de Brienne he was easily overpowered, while Robespierre and the others were sent off to different prisons in Paris. The Commune, however, had ordered the prison governors to refuse to admit them, and all five deputies were eventually liberated and taken triumphantly to the City Hall. Moreover, Coffinhal, Vice-President of the Revolutionary Tribunal and a man notorious for his great strength and brutality, took a strong column of men and guns to the Tuileries and released Hanriot, who for a few short moments had the whole situation in his hand. As the Convention learnt of the release of Robespierre, it believed that the Commune's artillerymen in the courtyard outside were about to open fire. 'If ever I expected to die, it was in that moment', wrote one of the deputies later. The Assembly, however, rose to the occasion. It proclaimed the Robespierrists, and all who should assist them, to be outlaws, and it appointed Barras and twelve other deputies to organise its own defence. Hanriot did no more than withdraw his men and return to the City Hall.

Inaction was indeed the hallmark of the whole of that critical night, for only thirteen of the forty-eight sections of Paris answered the Commune's

226

call to arms. This was due in part to the *sans-culottes*' distrust of the Robespierrist Commune, which had decided on 23rd July, only four days before, to publish the new wage rates that had been impending ever since general price control was imposed in September 1793. These rates, which took no heed of the recent increase in prices, threatened most workmen with a substantial loss of earnings, and it is significant that their demonstrations of protest coincided with the beginning of the political conflict, which was indeed at first reported as being 'a revolt occasioned by the *maximum*'. The general disillusionment and weariness with bloodshed, as well as the conscription or execution of so many of the leaders of the streets, also played their part in preventing any general rising for the Robespierrists.

It may, however, be most significant of all that as the night wore on the influence of authority carried increasing weight. The majority of the sections, receiving conflicting orders from the Commune and from the Convention at an early hour, either did nothing or asked for new instructions. When the Robespierrists were outlawed, when the governing Committees called for hourly reports from the sectional revolutionary committees, and when firm orders came from Barras in the name of the Convention, the sections gradually rallied to the established revolutionary government. In the same way, even Robespierre and the deputies with him at the City Hall seem to have been paralysed by the thought of resisting the Convention. Although at 7 p.m. on 27th July there were 3,400 men, and seventeen companies of artillery, on the Place de Grève, these were left without orders, and as the news of the outlawry spread, the sections which had sent them began to order their return. By 1.15 on the following morning, only 200 soldiers from the Section Finistère remained, and by 1.30 these too had left, scornfully rejecting a promise of payment to remain.[1] Almost immediately afterwards the columns from the Convention arrived, and as they did so Augustin Robespierre leapt from a window to fall injured at their feet. Within the hall they found that the crippled Couthon had fallen helplessly down the stairs, that Lebas had shot himself and that Robespierre had shattered his jaw, probably in attempting suicide; only Saint-Just stood calmly awaiting capture.[2]

This shambles was not intended to be an ending of the Terror. The men who had overthrown Robespierre had far bloodier hands than he, and they struck their captives hard. On 28th July, after identification by the Revolutionary Tribunal, Robespierre and his brother, Saint-Just, Couthon,

[1] '*Nous ne sommes (pas) des soldats d'argent.*'

[2] Hanriot was found later half-dead beneath a window from which he had fallen into a tiny interior courtyard. Coffinhal escaped, and was at large for a week until his strength gave out. He was executed on the Place de Grève amid cries of '*Coffinhal, Coffinhal, tu n'as pas la parole*'—a reference to his own words when silencing prisoners at the Revolutionary Tribunal.

Hanriot and seventeen others were hurried to the guillotine, which was brought back to the centre of Paris for the purpose. In the next two days, moreover, they were followed by no fewer than eighty-three members of the Commune. The Committee of Public Safety had nevertheless destroyed itself in destroying the Robespierrists, for the Convention seized its chance first to weaken the Committee, and then to dismantle the whole apparatus of the Terror. This was not only a matter of opportunity. The Robespierrists alone had had the vision to perceive, and the ability to explain, that security and victory were not ends in themselves, and that revolutionary government might still be necessary if men were to gain material welfare and achieve higher moral stature. 'Happiness', as Saint-Just had put it, 'is a new idea in Europe'. The very brightness of this vision apparently blinded them to the impossibility of its attainment and to the fearful and ever-increasing cost of the use of force for social and moral purposes. With them the Republic of Virtue died, and the fiercest light of the Revolution was extinguished.

Epilogue:
Power Prevails

After Thermidor, France began to retreat from the Terror. Finding themselves praised as the saviours of society, the shady and unscrupulous men who had destroyed Robespierre hurriedly made themselves into moderates. The release of suspects and the repeal of the Law of Prairial opened the way for the proscription of all but the most supple terrorists, and after protracted trials first Carrier and then Fouquier-Tinville himself were sent to the guillotine. Robespierre's old colleagues did their best to disown him, manufacturing yet another myth in order to make him solely responsible for all the evils of the past. The more they maligned him as a monster, however, the uglier their own association with him appeared, and within a year Billaud-Varenne, Collot d'Herbois and even Barère had been despatched to French Guiana, the 'dry guillotine' of the reaction.[1] On the other hand, the deputies who had survived proscription in 1793 eventually came back to the Convention, and these naturally hastened to rehabilitate their own reputations. Praising themselves as the men who had dared to defy the tyrant Robespierre at the first moment of his triumph, they seized upon the Montagnard legend of Brissot's federalist faction, converted this into that of a courageous liberal opposition to the Terror, and gloried in the name of 'Girondins'. It is no coincidence that the second anniversary of 31st May 1793 was marked by the suppression of the Revolutionary Tribunal.

In all this the Convention was swept along by a general wave of hostility towards the men who had controlled France in the previous year. Soon after Thermidor the *sans-culottes* were excluded from the general assemblies of the sections of Paris by more prosperous men, and throughout France they were evicted from the committees and administrative offices they had held during the Terror. The Jacobins, too, were hustled in the streets of Paris by gangs of young toughs known as the Gilded Youth, the *jeunesse dorée*. The incidence of violence varied greatly from place to place, but the early months of 1795 were in some areas stained by an unofficial 'White Terror'. At Lyons there were wholesale murders of revolutionaries, and a new form of violence racked south-eastern France as organised groups of royalists revenged themselves upon their enemies and plundered peaceful people as they chose.

[1] Barère in fact remained in France, having, as it was said, for once failed to sail with the wind.

Only the main features of this reaction can be indicated here. Seizing its chance, the Convention did its best to destroy the system of centralised government which the Committee of Public Safety had built up. The Committee itself survived for a year, but on the day after Robespierre's death the Convention ruled that one-quarter of its members must retire each month, and on 31st July six new men were elected to replace the four who had died and the two who were away on mission. Within a month the functions of the Committee had been drastically reduced and its authority had been redistributed among fifteen other committees of the Convention. Once these decisive steps had been taken, the rest of the machinery of revolutionary government was more gradually dismantled. The powers of the representatives on mission were restricted, the authority of the directories of the departments was restored, and the decimated Commune of Paris was so completely destroyed that the city simply ceased to be a self-governing municipality.

At the same time other measures helped to complete the rout of both the minority groups which had challenged parliamentary government in 1793. The general assemblies of the sections were forbidden to meet more than once in every ten days and the payment of forty sous for attendance at these meetings was abolished. The *comités de surveillance*, which had been the strongholds of the *sans-culottes'* power, were also reorganised and reduced in number. As for the Jacobin movement, which had for some time been more concerned with administration than with active politics, this was hamstrung by a ban upon all collective petitioning and upon the affiliation of public societies. In November 1794 a pre-arranged riot in the Rue St Honoré gave the men of Thermidor an excuse to close down the Club in Paris, and thereafter the Jacobins were reduced to disgruntled dissidence. By the autumn of 1795 the popular societies and the assemblies of the sections had both been suppressed and even the use of the word 'revolutionary' had become illegal.

This political reaction is usually condemned as excessive, and it would certainly seem that the after-effects of the Terror were most unfortunate for France. For a second time within six years the nation recoiled violently from extreme centralisation towards extreme localism, and for almost a century Frenchmen identified the very word Republic with a régime of bloodshed and anarchy. The reaction in religion, on the other hand, was superficially mild. The revolutionary calendar and the civic festivals were retained, but the worship of the Supreme Being was abandoned and in September 1794 the Convention accompanied a new announcement of religious freedom by the formal disestablishment of the Constitutional Church. This strict division of Church and state nevertheless widened the gulf which separated the Revolution from Catholicism. On the one hand it promoted a religious revival which benefited the royalist non-juror clergy so much that the Republic was eventually compelled to persecute them for political reasons, and on the other hand it encouraged other men to turn their backs on religion altogether. After Thermidor the pursuit of pleasure replaced the observance of virtue, at least among the people whose postures in Parisian society have attracted attention. 'The depravity of all ranks, if one can talk of ranks, is past belief', wrote an English visitor in 1796. 'Everyone plunges into the mud pool of vice as soon as he or she is strong enough to paddle in it without fear of parental or political control.'[1] Certainly the later years of the 1790's have become a period notorious for the extravagance, corruption and immorality which prevailed in high places.

Historians, who are curiously loath to admit that there might be some mean between regulated puritanism and unchecked moral licence, are nevertheless united in condemning the Thermidorian Convention's complete abandonment of the economic controls of 1793. Once the Committee of Public Safety's power was broken, the policy of fostering trade by easing restrictions gave way to the open encouragement of free competition, inflation being accepted. In October 1794 maximum prices were raised to a level two-thirds above those of June 1790, and in December controls were for all practical purposes abolished. The results were appalling. The *assignat*, which had already dropped to 36 per cent of its nominal value by Thermidor, had fallen to 20 per cent by December 1794 and to 7½ per cent by May 1795. In the course of a winter as severe as that of 1788–89 the government made matters a hundred times worse by issuing more and more *assignats* as currency. The cost of living soared, and things got so bad that taxation had eventually to be collected in kind. While speculators made fortunes and the peasantry paid off the debts on their land in worthless paper money, the people of the towns were only saved from outright starvation by local distributions of requisitioned grain. On occasion Paris was even reduced to eating rice, and even that could hardly be cooked for want of fuel.

In these circumstances the rate of wages, which the Convention had nominally revised to a higher level after Thermidor, became irrelevant, and bread-riots again became commonplace. On 1st April 1795 (the day of 12th Germinal) these led to an invasion of the Convention by the common people, and a few weeks later, on 20th May (the day of 1st Prairial) the *sans-culottes* of Paris rose for the last time in the Revolution. Despite the fact that they no longer had full control of the sections, some 20,000 of them surrounded the Convention and trained their cannon upon it in support of their demand for *Bread and the Constitution of 1793*. Great as was their

[1] Henry Swinburne (1743–1803). See C. Maxwell, *The English Traveller in France, 1698–1815* (London, 1932), p. 194.

strength, however, they had now no organisation or middle-class support. Fobbed off with promises, they retired before the even stronger forces of the National Guard of western Paris, and the Convention called in the regular army to besiege the Faubourg Saint-Antoine and compel its people to surrender. A very thorough repression ensued: more than forty deputies were arrested, of whom six were condemned to death by a military commission, and between 3,000 and 4,000 ordinary people were imprisoned. Paris, moreover, remained under military control.[1]

By the middle of 1795 the reaction had gathered such momentum that it seemed as if even moderate republicanism would be abandoned in favour of a return to constitutional monarchy. The hopes of the royalists, however, were dashed by fate and by the blind folly of the Royal Family. On 8th June Louis XVII, the young son of Louis XVI and Marie Antoinette, died in his captivity in the Temple prison, a most unhappy victim of hardship and deliberate neglect. Within the month the *émigré* Count of Provence, now Louis XVIII, had announced his own accession to the throne by a manifesto which made it quite clear that the *ancien régime* would not accept the slightest compromise with the Revolution. The monarchy, the aristocracy, the Church and the parlements were to be reinstated in all their authority and ancient privileges, while all those who had acquired nationalised land or held any office since May 1789 were to be dispossessed. It only remained for the crown to associate itself once again with futile foreign intervention and perpetual civil war, and this it did by persuading Britain to land an expeditionary force of *émigrés* at Quiberon Bay. These unfortunate men were quickly crushed by Hoche, some 700 of them being shot. The only result of their ill-starred expedition was the renewal of the savage guerrilla war in the west, which made a restoration more unthinkable than ever. At the same time the royalist plots provided an excuse for the establishment of military rule in Lyons.

Thus within twelve months of Robespierre's death the much-purged parliament had become dependent upon the readiness of the army to support it against either the people or the royalists. In this situation the Convention set a term to its own existence by issuing the Constitution of the Year III (1795). This was avowedly intended to establish the supremacy of men of property. Restriction of the franchise and a reversion to the system of indirect election now effectively reduced the electorate to about 30,000 owners of considerable wealth. Even this however was not enough to save the Republic, for a really conservative Assembly would almost certainly have been predominantly royalist. The Convention therefore decreed that

---

[1] Paris did not recover its influence as an independent force until the Revolution of July in 1830, and there was no extensive popular rising there until 1848.

EPILOGUE: POWER PREVAILS

two-thirds of the members of the next legislature must be chosen from its own republican ranks. The Constitution itself was approved by a plebiscite which was in reality an overwhelming vote for the dissolution of the Convention. The two-thirds decree, however, won pathetically little support in a separate referendum, and well-founded suspicions that a favourable result had been secured by fraud led to a royalist and Right-wing rising in Paris on 5th October 1795 (the day of 13 Vendémiaire). Barras, again entrusted with the defence of the Convention, called the army into action, and for the first time since the Revolution began there was serious fighting in Paris. General Bonaparte, in charge of the artillery, used his guns against the crowd, which was eventually dispersed at the cost of some 300 casualties on each side.

After this the Convention gave way to its successors, the two new legislative councils and the five-man Directory. It bequeathed to them a rigid Constitution, which allowed no real control to either the executive or the legislative, and a distracted country, politically and economically close to chaos. Only abroad was France secure. In 1795 her earlier victories enabled her to impose a conqueror's peace upon Holland and to strike old-fashioned military and diplomatic bargains with Spain and Prussia. The fight against Austria (and, so far as was practical, Britain) nevertheless went on, for France was not now strong enough to dictate terms. Moreover, it was only by war that the Directory could hope to salve the economy by confiscations and to keep the soldiers from independent interference in politics. Even this could only endure as long as the war was moderately successful, for the reaction had coincided with the transference of real power to the army, in which indeed the revolutionary tradition was probably most truly preserved. That the new republican government should have survived for four more years is more surprising than that a succession of *coups d'état* should have led to the seizure of power by Bonaparte in 1799.

According to Bonaparte himself, it was this event which ended the Revolution. On 15th December 1799 a curt announcement of another Constitution concluded: 'Citizens, the Revolution is established upon its original principles. It is over.' Today, however, the years which preceded Napoleon's advent to power are usually regarded as a time of counter-revolution, remarkable chiefly for the emergence of a new ruling class of conservative property-owners and officials. The Revolution, it is now suggested, really ended in 1794, when Robespierre died, or in 1795, when the *sans-culottes* were defeated in the insurrection of Prairial.

The choice of one or other of these last two dates depends on an interpretation of the Revolution, for the importance that is attached to Prairial does not rest simply upon the evident fact that military force was then employed for the first time against the crowd. The selection of that date as decisive really implies that the Revolution should be regarded primarily as a

233

continuous class-conflict, in which the most popular and progressive social force was suppressed by those whose predominance was imperilled. The importance of class-conflict in the Revolution can however be exaggerated, as can the importance of the *sans-culottes* themselves. The militants of the sections of Paris in particular were, after all, only an influential minority group, and to say that their pressure on the Convention was constant is only to say that they could only act effectively through the Montagnards. The latter, who first represented and then ruled the educated townsmen of France, indeed depended on the *sans-culottes* to sustain the Revolution, but the two parties in the alliance had a good deal in common. Both believed in the ultimate authority of the people, even if they used the term differently, and both were concerned to establish a society in which this would prevail. The most advanced of the Montagnards also sympathised with the *sans-culottes* in their constant cry for cheaper food, and they shared their conviction that excessive wealth should be heavily taxed and some social services provided by the state. In practice, however, the autonomy of the sections had been yielded to the revolutionary government long before the power of the Committee of Public Safety was broken, and to Robespierre and his closest colleagues social legislation was but a means to an end, the moral improvement of mankind. Seen in this light, the insurrection of Prairial appears as no more than a forlorn attempt by the *sans-culottes* to obtain food and to recover a position which had been irretrievably lost in the previous spring. The establishment of the Republic of Virtue was the true objective of the most powerful and the most representative group in the Revolution, and it was when the champions of this died that the Revolution ended and reaction began.

This particular question of chronology is in itself an indication of the way in which contemporary attitudes affect interpretation of the Revolution. If the old disputes about royalism and republicanism, liberalism and anarchy, have now lost much of their sting, new controversies have developed about the nature of the democracy which the Revolution brought to birth. Some see this as a peculiarly 'totalitarian' type of authority, while others suggest that it was no more than one manifestation of a liberal and egalitarian movement which transformed the whole of the western world after the middle of the eighteenth century. In general, however, the Marxian view of history has had the greatest effect upon the recent study of the period. Few historians see much direct connection between modern communism and Baboeuf's 'Conspiracy of Equals' in 1796, but social and economic interpretations of the Revolution have become so important that the political significance of what happened has become somewhat obscured. To reassert this is not, of course, to deny the reality and significance of social and economic change. The methods by which men tried to regulate their lives were nevertheless of considerable

234

consequence at the time, and they have not failed to exercise a profound influence upon the world ever since.

Politically, the Revolution was most obviously a liberal movement. Liberty and Equality were its first two watchwords, and although the exigencies of war and the advent of popular democracy for a time gave Equality pride of place, the two were not initially separable. The men of 1789 were concerned to regenerate a state which had become politically and socially moribund under the rule of a benevolent but ineffectual monarchy and an entrenched and exclusive aristocracy of office-holders. This meant much more than the abolition of venality and the disappearance of medieval dues and seigneurial justice, important though these preliminaries were. The first revolutionaries strove to establish a society in which all men would enjoy civil liberty and equality of status and opportunity, as well as one in which constitutional parliamentary government would prevail. To do this was to substitute for an immensely complex static society one which was far more simple, unified and fluid. Where the fundamentally medieval *ançien régime* had rested upon established hierarchies and corporations, the regenerated France was to be a single nation in which each individual would be free to realise his full potentialities. If this too often implied the freedom of the monied classes to manipulate the economy to their own advantage, it also meant the end of innumerable vested interests and arbitrary and inequitable practices. If the goal was never wholly attained, it has nevertheless ever since encouraged the restricted and the oppressed to aspire to a greater degree of personal freedom.

As Edmund Burke remarked however, when men act in societies, liberty is power.[1] The Revolution always had a strong authoritarian tendency. This may have been derived in part from the writings of some of the *philosophes*, who were confronted by Divine Right and prescriptive authority and had to assert 'natural' human rights in equally uncompromising terms. More probably, however, the revolutionaries were compelled by circumstance to adopt the traditional theory of royal absolutism and to translate this into terms of popular sovereignty, developing it empirically in order to overcome the obstacles that perpetually loomed before them. The most notable single example of this process is that which began the Revolution of 1789. Faced by a completely intransigent element in each of the two senior orders, and finding no effective support in royal authority, the Third Estate simply assumed that the authority of the nation was absolute and omnicompetent. As Étienne Dumont wrote in his *Souvenirs sur Mirabeau*, 'The Commons should have acted in co-operation with the Clergy, the Nobility and the King. The Commons subjugated the Clergy, the King, the Nobility, and acted

---

[1] *Reflections on the Revolution in France* (Macmillan, 1930), p. 9.

without them and against them. That is what the revolution was'. Although some time elapsed before even the most hostile of the nobility were officially persecuted, their opposition had led the revolutionaries to accept the view which Sieyès had expressed in the pamphlet *Qu'est-ce que le tiers état ?*, by which 'the nobility does not belong to the social organisation at all; . . . its civil rights already render it a people apart in a great nation . . . it is foreign to the nation in principle'.

In fact, the nobility survived the Revolution to a far greater extent than is usually supposed, and it has remained for the twentieth century to realise the full implications of Sieyès's words, which can of course be applied to any dissident minority in a democratic state. Those who opposed the nation, however, certainly suffered sufficiently in the 1790's. Moreover, in repudiating aristocracy the revolutionaries also rejected all the political good that was latent in the aristocratic outlook. The idea that power should be dispersed amongst a variety of corporate bodies disappeared as the old institutions gave way to the administrative unity and concentrated authority of the nation. The belief that the rights of the state ought to be limited by ancient fundamental law, which the parlements had upheld against the crown, yielded before the new belief in the supremacy of the general will of the people.

Liberal democracy was thus sadly compromised in France even before it was officially established. In practice, the initial distinction between constitutional laws, which were derived from the sovereignty of the people, and the lesser legislation of a parliament acting in accordance with the Constitution, soon became blurred; for the greater part of the Revolution a single assembly sanctioned both without worrying too much about the particular capacity in which it was supposed to be acting. Consequently minor decisions were soon being invested with the sanctity of sovereignty, and an authoritarian attitude developed in parliament. This was hardened by the enormous problems involved in the attempt to reconstruct a country that was really in desperate need of competent government, and before long disunity and the necessities of war had driven France far towards a dictatorial system of administration and an exceedingly doctrinaire conception of democracy. At the same time the course of the Revolution had sharpened the definition of the nation, and as constitutional government was set aside in favour of the revolutionary use of sovereign right, so parliamentary authority was mastered by the exclusive Jacobin *élite* which claimed to represent the nation more directly. By 1794 the 'individuals', not merely the corporate bodies, were being damned as persons whose partial will was incompatible with the general will and whose existence jeopardised the political and moral salvation of the community. The terrible term 'enemy of the people' has ever since symbolised this state of affairs, which left France dreadfully divided between two

236

equally absolutist ideas, legitimate Divine Right monarchy and Jacobin republicanism.

Nevertheless, an interpretation of the Revolution which presented it only as a transition from liberal theory to tyrannical practice would be inadequate. The reforms that were effected in the early years made France a far freer state than it was before, and beyond both the local violence and the centralised Terror of later years there lay a finer and a more fundamental faith in the importance of public opinion. This essential quality of the Revolution, which was rather distorted than reflected by the use of the jargon of sovereignty, is apparent in the very real respect men of all kinds had for any law or institution which seemed to be based on general acceptance. When Louis XVI fled towards the frontier in 1791, almost everyone calmly assumed that the National Assembly could legitimately take charge of France. A year later, when the Constitution of 1791 was a dead weight upon a nation near defeat, men held to it as the sheet anchor of their security and only released their hold on it on the understanding that the people would again be consulted about the future. Later still Robespierre, who had long regarded himself as the 'Defender of the Constitution', held the new Rule of Law to be greater even than his own vision of virtue: since he believed that the authority of the Committee of Public Safety emanated from the Convention and was derived from the people, he constantly and indignantly repudiated all accusations of dictatorship, and when the Convention turned against him he was a man without confidence or purpose.

This same attitude is as much, if not more, apparent in the behaviour of ordinary people. On all the great *journées* of the Revolution, and most notably on 2nd June 1793, these assumed that the mere manifestation of what seemed obviously the general wish would suffice to win the respectful consent of all deputies and officials. The threat of force was therefore almost incidental, and when the Convention resisted the movement, as it did in Thermidor 1794 and in Prairial 1795, the insurgents in fact failed to fire the guns which were on both occasions trained against the Tuileries. Although the Convention was at intervals purged from within and subjected to very great pressure from without, it was not abused by the people, who indeed refused to act against it in support of either Hébert or Robespierre.

The Revolution was not, of course, a gentlemanly affair. The deputy Féraud, who tried to oppose the incursion of the crowd into the Convention in Prairial, was struck down and beheaded on the spot, and his head was borne into the building on the point of a pike. The true tragedy of the time, however, was that the revolutionaries respected popular authority sincerely but never managed to embody it in any free institutions which could command general support and obedience. The vision of free and equal brotherhood which had inspired and united France in 1790 remained a

237

lively democratic force in innumerable popular societies and in the general assemblies of the sections, but it could not be reconciled with the problems of governing a swelling national state. The revolutionaries perceived the possibility that all men might participate in the regulation of their own communal affairs, but they could not discover how this could be done. Where they failed, however, no other modern society has as yet succeeded.

Chronology

Italics are used here not only to indicate foreign terms but also (a) to emphasise the progress of reform in 1789–91 ; (b) to distinguish events related to the course of the war after 1792.

1. THE ENDING OF THE ANCIEN RÉGIME

1786	August	Calonne proposes the general taxation of land, assessment to be determined by Provincial Estates
1787	February	MEETING OF THE NOTABLES
	April	Fall of Calonne
	May	Appointment of Loménie de Brienne
		DISSOLUTION OF THE NOTABLES
		—Conflicts with the parlements renewed
1788	May	Lamoignon's MAY EDICTS: suspension of the parlements creation of new Courts of Appeal
	June/July	THE REVOLT OF THE NOBILITY
	August	Convocation of the States-General
		Resignation of Brienne, return of Necker to office
	September	Recall of the parlements
		The Parlement of Paris rules that the States-General should be formed as in 1614
	December	The Royal Council approves the doubling of the Third Estate
1789	February	Sieyès' *Qu'est-ce que le Tiers État?*
	April	The Réveillon riots at Paris
	May	MEETING OF THE STATES-GENERAL

2. THE REVOLUTION OF 1789

1789	May	5	OPENING OF THE STATES–GENERAL
	June	17	THE THIRD ESTATE ASSUMES THE TITLE OF 'THE NATIONAL ASSEMBLY'
		20	The Tennis Court Oath
		23	The Royal Session
		27	The king orders the clergy and the nobility to join the Commons
	July	11	Dismissal of Necker
		14	THE FALL OF THE BASTILLE
		16	Recall of Necker
		17	The king visits Paris
		22	Murder of Fouillon and Berthier
	July–August		The Great Fear in the countryside
	August	4–11	Decrees abolishing 'feudal' rights and privileges
		26	THE DECLARATION OF RIGHTS
	September	10	The Assembly rejects the proposed Second Chamber
		11	The Assembly accepts the Suspensive Veto for the king

October   5– 6   THE MARCH OF THE WOMEN TO VERSAILLES and the king's return to Paris

3. THE REGENERATION OF FRANCE, 1789–91

1789 October		19	National Assembly meets in the Archevêché in Paris
		21	Decree providing for the use of martial law
		29	Electoral regulations distinguishing 'active' and 'passive' citizens
		31	Decree providing for a uniform tariff throughout France
	November	2	Nationalisation of the property of the Church
		7	Exclusion of deputies from ministerial office
		9	National Assembly moves into the Manège
	December	14–22	*Decrees reorganising local government*
		12	First issue of *assignats*
1790 May		21	Paris reorganised into Sections
		22	Renunciation of wars of conquest
	June	19	Abolition of nobility
	July	12	*The Civil Constitution of the Clergy*
		14	FIRST FÊTE DE LA FÉDÉRATION
	August	16	*Decree reorganising the Judiciary*
			Debate on the mutiny at Nancy
	November	27	Decree to enforce the clerical oath
1791 April		2	Death of Mirabeau
		13	Papal Bull *Charitas* condemns the Civil Constitution
	May	16	The 'Self-denying Ordinance' excludes deputies from membership of the first Legislative Assembly
	June	14	The Loi Chapelier
		20	THE FLIGHT TO VARENNES
	July	14	Second Fête de la Fédération
		16	Decree providing for the reinstatement of the king on the completion of the Constitution
		17	THE MASSACRE ON THE CHAMP DE MARS
	August	27	The Declaration of Pilnitz
	September		Annexation of Avignon
		14	*The king accepts the Constitution*
		30	DISSOLUTION OF THE NATIONAL ASSEMBLY

4. THE COLLAPSE OF THE CONSTITUTION, 1791–92

1791 October		1	MEETING OF THE LEGISLATIVE ASSEMBLY
		20	Brissot calls for military action to disperse the *émigrés*
	November	9	Decree against the *émigrés* (vetoed 12th November)
		29	Decree against non-juring priests (vetoed 19th December)
	December	16	Brissot threatens the king with insurrection
		30	Robespierre opposes Brissot at the Jacobin Club
1792 March		10	Formation of Dumouriez's 'Patriot Ministry'
	April	20	DECLARATION OF WAR ON AUSTRIA
	May	27	Decree against non-juring priests (vetoed 19th June)

June	8	Decree providing for a military camp at Paris (vetoed 19th June)
	13	Dismissal of the 'patriot' ministers
	20	FIRST INVASION OF THE TUILERIES
	28	Brissot returns to the Jacobins
	29	LaFayette attempts to close the Jacobin Club
July	1	Petition of 20,000 against the events of 20th June
	11	Decree provides for the proclamation of *La Patrie en danger*
	14	Third Fête de la Fédération
	22	Proclamation of *La Patrie en danger*
	25	The permanence of the Sections is recognised
	28	The Brunswick Manifesto reaches Paris
	30	The Théâtre Français Section admits 'passive' citizens, and the Marseillais reach Paris
	31	The Mauconseil Section repudiates its allegiance to the throne
August	3	Petition of the Sections demanding that the king be deposed
	4	Vergniaud condemns the Mauconseil Section for its republicanism
	8	The Assembly exculpates LaFayette
	9	The Assembly postpones consideration of all republican petitions
	10	THE REVOLUTION OF 10TH AUGUST
		—Suspension of the king
		—Reinstatement of the 'patriot' ministers.

5. THE ELIMINATION OF THE KING, August 1792–January 1793

1792 August	10	THE REVOLUTION OF 10TH AUGUST
		—Suspension of the king
		—Reinstatement of the Roland Ministry
	17	The Commune forces the Assembly to create the Extraordinary Tribunal of 17th August
	19	Defection of LaFayette. *Prussian army crosses the frontier*
	20	*Fall of the fortress of Longwy*
	30	The Assembly attempts to dissolve the Commune
September	2	*Fall of the fortress of Verdun*
	2–6	THE SEPTEMBER MASSACRES
	18	The Assembly attempts to provide an armed guard for the Convention
	20	*BATTLE OF VALMY: Prussian retreat begins*
	21	FIRST SESSION OF THE CONVENTION
		The abolition of the monarchy. BEGINNING OF THE YEAR I
	24–25	The Brissotins lead an attack upon the power of Paris
October	10	Brissot is expelled from the Jacobin Club
	11	Formation of the Constitutional Committee
	19	The Sections protest against the attacks on Paris
	29	The Brissotins' second attack upon the power of Paris
November	5	Robespierre defends Paris and the Montagnards
	6	*BATTLE OF JEMAPPES: French conquest of Belgium*

241

6. THE PURGING OF PARLIAMENT, January–June 1793

7. THE EVOLUTION OF THE TERROR, June–December 1793

	28	*Fall of the fortress of Valenciennes.* Eighteen 'Brissotin' deputies outlawed
August	10	Festival of Unity in honour of the Constitution of 1793
	23	*Levée en masse* decreed
	27	*Surrender of Toulon to the British*
September	5	'HÉBERTIST' RISING IN PARIS: Terror 'the order of the day'
	8	*Battle of Hondschoote:* British forced to retire from Dunkirk
	11	*Fall of the fortress of Lequesnoy*
	17	The Law of Suspects decreed
	22	BEGINNING OF THE YEAR II
	25	The Committee of Public Safety survives attack in the Convention
	29	The General *Maximum* in restraint of prices and wages
October	3	Impeachment of Brissot and forty-four other deputies
	5	Revolutionary Calendar established (as from 22nd September)
	9	Recapture of Lyons by the forces of the Convention
	10	DECREE SANCTIONING REVOLUTIONARY GOVERNMENT FOR THE DURATION OF THE WAR
	(?)12	Fabre d'Eglantine denounces the 'Foreign Plot'
	16	*BATTLE OF WATTIGNIES* relieves Maubeuge; Execution of Marie-Antoinette
	17	Vendéans defeated at Cholet
	22	Creation of Central Food Commission
	24–30	Trial of Brissot and twenty other deputies
	31	Execution of the 'Brissotins'
November	10	Festival of Reason in Notre Dame
	21	Robespierre denounces atheism as aristocratic
	22	Closure of the churches in Paris
December	4	THE LAW OF REVOLUTIONARY GOVERNMENT (14 Frimaire)

8. THE REPUBLIC OF VIRTUE, December 1793–July 1794

1793 December	4	THE LAW OF REVOLUTIONARY GOVERNMENT (14 Frimaire): Massacres at Lyons
	5	First issue of the *Vieux Cordelier* initiates a campaign against the Hébertists
	15	Third issue of the *Vieux Cordelier* challenges the Terror
	19	*The British evacuate Toulon*
	23	Defeat of the Vendéans at Savenay
	25	ROBESPIERRE'S SPEECH ON THE PRINCIPLES OF REVOLUTIONARY GOVERNMENT
	26	*Recapture of Landau by the French*
	30	The Festival of Victory
1794 January	12	Arrest of Fabre d'Eglantine
February	5	ROBESPIERRE SPEAKS ON THE PRINCIPLES OF POLITICAL MORALITY
	21	Revision of the policy of price control
	26	The 'Laws of Ventôse'
March	3	

	4	Attempted insurrection at the Cordeliers Club
	14	Arrest of the Hébertists
	24	Execution of the Hébertists
	30	Arrest of Danton
April	5	Execution of the Dantonists
	27	The Police Law of 27 Germinal
May	7	ROBESPIERRE INTRODUCES THE WORSHIP OF THE SUPREME BEING
	18	*BATTLE OF TOURCOING : rout of the British in Belgium*
	23	Admiral affair⎫ presumed attempts to assassinate Robes-
	24	Renault affair⎰ pierre
June	1	*British naval victory, the 'Glorious First'*
	8	Festival of the Supreme Being
	10	Law of 22 Prairial expedites the work of the Revolutionary Tribunal
	26	*BATTLE OF FLEURUS : French reconquer Belgium*
July	23	Introduction of wage regulation in Paris
	26	Robespierre's last speech
	27	Proscription of the Robespierrists (9 Thermidor)
	28	EXECUTION OF ROBESPIERRE

9. 1794–1799: SOME SALIENT DATES

1794	July	30–31	Reorganisation of the Committee of Public Safety
	November	12	Closure of the Jacobin Club
	December	24	Abolition of the *maximum*
1795	April	1	Day of 12 Germinal
		5	*Peace of Basle with Prussia*
	May	16	*Peace with Holland*
		20	DAY OF 1ST PRAIRIAL
	June	8	Death of Louis XVII
	July	21	Hoche destroys the *émigré* forces at Quiberon
		22	*Peace with Spain*
	August	22	CONSTITUTION OF THE YEAR III and the two-thirds decree (30th)
	October	5	Revolt of 13 Vendémiaire
		26	DISSOLUTION OF THE CONVENTION, RULE OF THE DIRECTORY
1796	May		Conspiracy of Babœuf: *French victory at Lodi*
	November		*French victory at Arcola*
1797	January		*French victory at Rivoli*
	September	4	*Coup d'état of 18 Fructidor*
	October		*Treaty of Campo-Formio with Austria*
1798	July		*Napoleon's victory at the battle of the Pyramids*
	August		*Nelson destroys the French Fleet at Aboukir Bay*
1799	March		*War of the Second Coalition*
	November	9–10	*THE COUP D'ÉTAT OF BRUMAIRE*

THE REVOLUTIONARY CALENDAR

After the fall of the Bastille, the year 1789 was known as the 1st Year of Liberty. When royalty was abolished in France on 21st September 1792, the 4th Year of Liberty became the 1st Year of the Republic, the two terms sometimes being used concurrently. When the Revolutionary Calendar was adopted in October 1793, its effect was retrospective to the first anniversary of the abolition of royalty, so that the 22nd September 1793 became the 1st day of the month of Vendémiaire of the Year II of the Republic. Thereafter the months of the Year II ran as follows:

Vendémiaire	1–30	*the month of vintage*	= 22nd September	– 21st October
Brumaire	1–30	*the month of fog*	= 22nd October	– 20th November
Frimaire	1–30	*the month of frost*	= 21st November	– 20th December
Nivôse	1–30	*the month of snow*	= 21st December	– 19th January
Pluviôse	1–30	*the month of rain*	= 20th January	– 18th February
Ventôse	1–30	*the month of wind*	= 19th February	– 20th March
Germinal	1–30	*the month of budding*	= 21st March	– 19th April
Floréal	1–30	*the month of flowers*	= 20th April	– 19th May
Prairial	1–30	*the month of meadows*	= 20th May	– 18th June
Messidor	1–30	*the month of harvest*	= 19th June	– 18th July
Thermidor	1–30	*the month of heat*	= 19th July	– 17th August
Fructidor	1–30	*the month of fruit*	= 18th August	– 16th September

17th–21st September inclusive: *sans culottides*

Further Reading

Since the French Revolution has always been recognised as being of profound importance in the making of the modern world, an immense amount has been written about it. The titles listed here have been selected in order to help both the general reader and the student to find his way further into the subject, preference being given so far as possible to books which are available in English. Fuller information may be obtained in the first instance from the useful bibliographical essays contained in Crane Brinton, *A Decade of Revolution, 1789–1799* (New York, 1953 and Harper Torchback edn., 1963) and A. Cobban, *A History of Modern France, Vol. I: 1715–1799* (Penguin Books, revised edn., 1961, also Jonathan Cape, 1962); beyond these, students should consult *A Select List of Works on Europe and Europe Overseas, 1715–1815*, ed. J. S. Bromley and A. Goodwin, (Oxford, 1956); G. Walter, *Répertoire de l'Histoire de la Révolution Française* (2 vols., Paris, 1941, 1951); and A. Martin and G. Walter, *Catalogue de l'Histoire de la Révolution Française* (5 vols., Paris, 1936–55).

Fortunately the main lines of historical dispute about the Revolution are readily discernible, and an able summary of the course of the controversy appears in G. Rudé, *Interpretations of the French Revolution* (Historical Association pamphlet G.47, 1961). P. Geyl's chapter on Michelet in his *Debates with Historians* (Collins, London, 1955, and Fontana Books, 1962) will also be found stimulating. Moreover, some recent paperback editions provide valuable brief introductions to the Revolution. The best of these is still Professor Lefebvre's *Quatre-vingt-neuf*, available in the translation by R. R. Palmer as G. Lefebvre, *The Coming of the French Revolution* (Vintage Books, Princeton U.P., 1957). Others are: A. Cobban, *A History of Modern France, Vol. I: 1715–1799* (Penguin Books, revised edn., 1961); A. Goodwin, *The French Revolution* (Hutchinson, 1953 and Grey Arrow Books, 1959); L. Gershoy, *The Era of the French Revolution 1789–1799: Ten Years That Shook the World* (Anvil Books, Princeton, 1957); and G. Rudé, *Revolutionary Europe, 1783–1815* (Collins' Fontana Books, 1964).

More detailed general histories of the Revolution in English are understandably few in number. Crane Brinton, *A Decade of Revolution, 1789–1799* (*Rise of Modern Europe Series*, ed. Wm. L. Langer, Harvard Univ., New York, 1963) reviews developments in both France and Europe, often challenging orthodox belief in the spontaneity of the Revolution, and a readable conservative account of the events which led to the fall of the French monarchy in 1792 is given by G. Salvemini, *The French Revolution* (trans. from the Italian by I. M. Rawson, London, 1954). J. M. Thompson, *The French Revolution* (Oxford, 1943, 2nd edn., 1944, reissued 1959) is still the standard English authority for the period ending with the fall of Robespierre. Student and general reader alike, however, should also be familiar with the recent work of N. Hampson: *A Social History of the French Revolution* (London, 1963), an indispensable book.

Works such as these may lead to the longer standard works of the principal French historians. These will at once involve the reader in a continuing controversy. The classical interpretation of the Revolution in terms of republican democracy is F. V. A. Aulard, *Histoire politique de la Révolution française* (4 vols., Paris, 1901), translated by B. Miall as *The French Revolution, A Political History, 1789–1804* (4 vols., London, 1910). This view, and Aulard's admiration for Danton, was sharply challenged by A. Mathiez, whose *La Révolution Française*, (Paris, 1922, reprinted 1959) is translated by C. A. Phillips as *The French Revolution* (London, 1928). Mathiez, who was much influenced by Jean Jaurès, secretary of the French Socialist Party and author of the *Histoire socialiste de la Révolution française* (4 vols., Paris, 1901–04), was more aware than Aulard of economic and social factors; he saw the Revolution as the advent of social democracy, which he believed to be both championed by, and defeated with, Robespierre. A remarkable synthesis of these views, and one which places the Revolution firmly in its European setting as 'an episode in the bourgeois revolution', is that of G. Lefebvre: *La Révolution française* (*Peuples et Civilisations* series, ed. L. Halphen and Ph. Sagnac, 2nd revised edn., Paris, 1951 or 3rd edn., revised by A. Soboul, 1963). This remains an essential book for all advanced study; although it has not proved easy to translate, it is now available in two volumes as *The French Revolution: From its Origins to 1793* (trans. E. Moss Evanson) and *The French Revolution: From 1793 to 1799* (trans. J. H. Stewart and J. Friguglietti) (London and N. York, 1962 and 1964). Still more recent is A. Soboul, *La Révolution française, Vol. I: De la Bastille à la Gironde; Vol. II; De la Montagne à Brumaire* (Paris, 1964). Although even the same author's briefer *Précis d'histoire de la Révolution française* (Paris, 1962) is not yet available in translation, it is clearly and concisely written. Soboul, who follows Mathiez closely in places, nevertheless rejects his view of the importance of Robespierre and asserts instead that the *sans-culottes* were the driving force behind the Revolutionary movement during its most critical years.

Despite the very considerable differences between them, Mathiez and his successors have been alike in interpreting the Revolution as a class-conflict and in Marxist terms. The most recent work of Professor A. Cobban, *The Social Interpretation of the French Revolution* (C.U.P., 1964), provides a stimulating challenge to this view: indicating in his usual lively fashion the dangers implicit in the use of preconceived terminology, Professor Cobban calls for more thorough and more detached examination of the realities of the social structure of France at the time of the Revolution.

The **origins of the Revolution** are of course a major subject of study in themselves, and opinion has always differed sharply about the relative importance of the social, economic, political and intellectual antecedents of 1789. Much of this controversy is conveniently summarised in A. Cobban, *The Causes of the French Revolution* (Historical Association pamphlet G.2, 1946) and in Stanley J. Idzera, *The Background of the French Revolution* (American Historical Association, Service Center publication No. 21, Macmillan, 1959). Two publications in the *Problems in European Civilisation series* (D. C. Heath of Boston, and Harrap) also give useful extracts from the principal secondary authorities: these are R. W. Greenlaw, *The Economic Origins of the French Revolution: Poverty or Prosperity?* (1958) and P. Amann, *The Eighteenth-Century Revolution: French or Western?* (1963). Other useful introductions to the subject are A. Cobban, *A History of Modern France, Vol. I* (as above); Max Beloff, *The Age of Absolutism* (Grey Arrow edn., 1963); Harold Nicholson, *The Age of Reason* (London, 1960); and J. Lough, *An Introduction to Eighteenth-Century France* (London, 1960).

This debate may be studied more fully in such works as A. Cobban, *In Search of Humanity: the Role of the Enlightenment in Modern History* (London, 1960), which emphasised the concern of the majority of the *philosophes* for individual morality and liberal institutions; Jean Egret, *La Pré-Révolution française, 1787–1788* (Paris, 1962); C. A. Labrousse, *La Crise de l'Économie française à la fin de l'Ancien Régime et au début de la Révolution* (Paris, 1944); Kingsley Martin, *French Liberal Thought in the Eighteenth-Century* (2nd edn., London, 1954); R. R. Palmer, *The Age of the Democratic Revolution: A Political History of Europe and America 1760–1800, Vol. I, The Challenge*, and its succeeding *Vol. II, The Struggle* (Princeton and Oxford, 1959 and 1964); Ph. Sagnac, *La formation de la Société française moderne, Vol. II: 1715–1789* (Paris, 1946); H. Sée, *La France économique et sociale au XVIIIᵉ siècle* (Paris 1925), trans. as *Economic and Social*

FURTHER READING

Conditions in France during the Eighteenth-Century (1927); J. L. Talmon, *The Origins of Totalitarian Democracy* (London 1952, Mercury Books 1961), which asserts the essential authoritarianism of some at least of the *philosophes* and of the Jacobinism of the Revolution; and the classic work of A. de Tocqueville, *L'Ancien Régime et la Révolution* (Paris, 1856), available in several translations, including S. Gilbert, *The Old Regime and the Revolution* (Anchor Books, New York, 1955). Serious study of the origins and nature of the Revolution should also include at least the major political texts: John Locke, *Two Treatises on Civil Government* (1690, Everyman No. 751); J. J. Rousseau, *The Social Contract* (1762, Everyman No. 660); and Edmund Burke, *Reflections upon the Revolution in France* (1790, Everyman No. 460).

Among other important general authorities are:

Collins, I. *The Age of Progress: A Survey of European History between 1789 and 1870* (London, 1964)

Godechot, J. *Histoire des institutions de la France sous la Révolution et l'Empire* (Paris, 1951)
La Grande Nation: L'expansion révolutionnaire de la France dans le monde, 1789–1799 (2 vols., Paris, 1956)

Goodwin, A. (ed.) *The New Cambridge Modern History, vol. VIII* (C.U.P. 1965)

Hobsbaum, E. J. *The Age of Revolution, Europe 1789–1848* (London, 2nd edn., 1964)

Lindsay, J. O. (ed.) *The New Cambridge Modern History Vol. VII: The Old Régime* (Cambridge, 1957)

Pariset, G. *La Révolution française, 1792–1799* (Vol. II of *Histoire de la France contemporaine*, ed. Lavisse) (Paris, 1920)

Sagnac, Ph. *La Révolution française, 1789–1792* (Vol. I of *Histoire de la France contemporaine*, ed. Lavisse) (Paris, 1920)
La Législation civile de la Révolution française, 1789–1804 (Paris, 1898)

Sorel, A. *L'Europe et la Révolution française* (8 vols., Paris, 1885–1904, 23rd edn., 1942)

More original material on the Revolution is gradually becoming available to the English reader. C. Maxwell, *The English Traveller in France* (London, 1932) and J. M. Thompson, *English Witnesses of the French Revolution* (Oxford, Blackwell, 1938) are unfortunately hard to obtain, but Arthur Young, *Travels in France and Italy, 1787–1790* (ed. C. Maxwell, Cambridge, 1929) remains an invaluable book, though Young's impressions of French social and economic conditions must be related to the results of later scholarship. Moreover, Sieyès's *What is the Third Estate?* is at last available in a translation by M. Blondel (Pall Mall Press, London, 1964). S. Flessier and G. Pernoud, *The French Revolution* (London, 1960) provide a selection of extracts, some more reliable than others, while L. Gershoy, *The Era of the French Revolution, 1789–1799* (Anvil Books, 1957) includes a substantial section of relevant documents. More systematic study may be developed from: J. M. Thompson, *French Revolution Documents, 1789–1794* (Oxford, 1948); J. H. Stewart, *A Documentary Survey of the French Revolution* (New York, 1951); L. G. W. Legg, *Select Documents Illustrative of the French Revolution* (2 vols. to 1791, Oxford, 1905); P. Mautouchet, *Le Gouvernement révolutionnaire* (Paris, 1912); H. Morse Stephens, *The Principal Speeches of the Statesmen and Orators of the French Revolution, 1789–1795* (2 vols., Oxford, 1892); and W. Markov and A. Soboul, *Die Sansculotten von Paris* (Berlin, 1957, printed in French and German). There are also many volumes of memoirs and correspondence, amongst the more important of which are E. Dumont, *Souvenirs sur*

248

Mirabeau (ed. J. Bénétruy, 1950) and G. Michon, *Correspondance de Maximilien et Augustin Robespierre* (Paris, 1926). The publication of the works of Robespierre, too, now includes his speeches from 1789–93 (*Œuvres complètes de Maximilien Robespierre*, Vols. VI–IX, Paris 1950.) Accounts of the proceedings of the Assemblies and the Jacobins are to be found in the *Archives Parlementaires* (Paris, 1868–1912, 1962); in *L'Ancien Moniteur* (31 vols., Paris, 1850–54); in the *Journal des Débats des Amis de la Constitution séante aux Jacobins* (Paris, 1791–24 Frimaire An II); and in F. A. Aulard, *La Société des Jacobins, Recueil des Documents* (6 vols., Paris, 1889–97). Other valuable sources are P. J. B. Buchez and P. C. Roux, *Histoire Parlementaire de la Révolution française* (43 vols., 1834–38); F. A. Aulard, *Recueil des actes du comité de salut public* (28 vols., Paris 1889 ff.); and the *Croker Collections* of pamphlets in the British Museum.

For **special aspects** of the Revolution, books in **English** are:

Brinton, C.	*The Jacobins* (New York, reprinted 1961)
Clapham, J. H.	*The Causes of the War of 1792* (Cambridge, 1899)
Greer, D. M.	*The Incidence of the Terror during the French Revolution* (Cambridge, Mass., 1935)
	The Incidence of the Emigration during the French Revolution (Cambridge, Mass., 1951)
Hales, E. E. Y.	*The Revolution and the Papacy* (London, 1960)
Harris, S. E.	*The Assignats* (Cambridge, Mass., 1930)
Herbert, S.	*The Fall of Feudalism in France* (London, 1921)
Kaplow, J.	*Elbeuf during the Revolutionary Period : History and Social Structure* (Baltimore, 1964: a recent study in detail of a small town in Normandy)
Mathiez, A.	*The Fall of Robespierre and other essays* (trans. London, 1927)
Palmer, R. R.	*Twelve Who Ruled* (Princeton, 1941)
Phipps, R. W.	*The Armies of the First French Republic* (4 vols, Oxford 1926–39)
Robiquet, J.	*Daily Life in the French Revolution* (trans. London, 1964)
Rudé, G.	*The Crowd in the French Revolution* (Oxford, 1959)
Sirich, J. B.	*The Revolutionary Committees in the Departments of France* (Cambridge, Mass., 1943)
Soboul, A.	*The Parisian Sans-Culottes in the French Revolution 1793–1794* (Oxford, 1964: translation by G. Lewis of the central section of the original, cited below)
Sydenham, M. J.	*The Girondins* (London, 1960)
Thomson, D.	*The Baboeuf Plot* (London, 1947)
Thompson, E.	*Popular Sovereignty and the French Constituent Assembly, 1789–1791* (Manchester, 1952)
Thompson, J. M.	*Robespierre and the French Revolution* (London, 1952)
	Leaders of the French Revolution (Oxford, 1929)
Wilkinson, S.	*The French Army before Napoleon* (Oxford, 1915)

Books in **French** include:-

Braesch, F.	*1789 L'année cruciale* (Paris, 1950)
	La Commune du dix août (Paris, 1911)
Cobb, R.	*Les armées révolutionnaires, instrument de la Terreur dans les départements, Avril, 1793–Floréal An II* (2 vols., The Hague, 1961–1963)
Caron, P.	*Les Massacres de septembre* (Paris, 1935)

Deville, P.   *La Commune de l'an II* (Paris, 1946)
St. Claire
Égret, J.   *La Révolution des notables: Mounier et les monarchiens* (Paris, 1950)
Godechot, J.   *La contre- révolution: doctrine et action, 1789–1804* (Paris, 1961)
Guérin, D.   *La lutte des classes sous la Première République: Bourgeois et 'bras nus'* (2 vols., Paris, 1946: controversial)
Jacob, L.   *Les suspects pendant la Révolution, 1789–1794* (Paris, 1952)
Latreille, A.   *L'Église Catholique et la Révolution française, Vol. I* (Paris, 1946)
Lefebvre, G.   *La Grande Peur de 1789* (Paris, 1922)
                     Études sur la Révolution française (Paris, 2nd edn., revised 1963)
                     Les Thermidoriennes (Paris, revised edn. 1960)
                     Le Directoire (Paris, 1946 and 1950)
Mathiez, A.   *Le Dix Août* (Paris, 1931)
                     La vie chère et le mouvement social sous la Terreur (Paris, 1927)
                     Girondins et Montagnards (Paris, 1930)
                     La Réaction Thermidorienne (Paris, 1929)
Michon, G.   *Robespierre et la guerre révolutionnaire, 1791–1792* (Paris, 1937)
Schmidt, A.   *Tableaux de la Révolution francaise* (3 vols., Leipzig, 1867)
Soboul, A.   *Les Sans-culottes parisiens en l'an II* (Paris, 1958)
Tarle, E.   *Germinal et Prairial* (Moscow, 1959)
Tønneson, K. D.   *La Défaite des Sans-culottes* (Paris, 1959)
Vandal, A.   *L'avènement de Bonaparte, Vol. 1* (Paris, 1903)
Walter, G.   *Histoire des Jacobins* (Paris, 1946)
                     La Guerre de Vendée (Paris, 1953)

Amongst many **biographies**, there are the following (the language being indicated by the place of publication):

Barthou, L.   *Danton* (Paris, 1932)
Bradby, E. D.   *Barnave* (2 vols., Oxford, 1915)
Clapham, J. H.   *The Abbé Sieyès* (London, 1912)
Cooper, Duff   *Talleyrand* (London, 1947)
Curtis, E. N.   *Saint Just, Colleague of Robespierre* (New York, 1935)
Ellery, E.   *Brissot de Warville* (New York, 1915)
Gershoy, L.   *Bertrand Barère, A Reluctant Terrorist* (Princeton, 1962)
Gottschalk, L.   *Jean Paul Marat* (London, 1927)
Jacob, L.   *Hébert, le Père Duchesne* (Paris, 1960)
Lintilhac, E.   *Vergniaud: le drame des Girondins* (Paris, 1920)
Reinhard, M.   *Carnot* (2 vols., Paris, 1950–52)
Thompson, J. M.   *Robespierre* (2 vols., Oxford, 1935)
Walter, G.   *Robespierre* (Paris, 1946)
Welch, O. J. G.   *Mirabeau: A Study of a Democratic Monarchist* (London, 1951)

The journals *The English Historical Review*, *Economic History Review*, *History* (the journal of the Historical Association) and *Past and Present* often contain valuable articles and reviews of current writing on the Revolution. *French Historical Studies*, published by the Society for French Historical Studies, N. Carolina, is a useful newcomer, while the *Annales Historiques de la Révolution Française* remains indispensable for research.

Index

Note: The various assemblies appear here under *National*, as National Legislative Assembly; the sections of Paris appear under *Paris*; and such major laws as the Law of Suspects appear under *Law*. The names of persons appear in capitals.